The 90th Anniversary Publications are available in digital form for free through First Fruits Press. They can be found by visiting First Fruits' Website, under the Heritage Collection: place.asburyseminary.edu/firstfruits

Asbury Theological Seminary 90th Anniversary Publications

Henry Clay Morrison
"Crusader Saint"
by Percival A. Wesche

A Short History of Asbury Theological Seminary
by Howard Fenimore Shipps

The Distinctive Emphases of Asbury Theological Seminary
by Harold B. Kuhn

Theological Foundations
Fiftieth Anniversary Scholarly Essays

All Things Are Ours...
Photographic Record of Asbury's Fiftieth Year

Asbury Theological Seminary 90th Anniversary Publications

Audio Recordings from the 50th Anniversary Celebration
and Special Lecture Series
March 11-15, 1974

50th Anniversary Banquet Speeches
*by Franklin D. Morrison, Frank Bateman Stanger, and
J. C. McPheeters*

**"Salvation Today," "Ingredients of the Gospel,"
"The Mind of Christ," and "Keep the Hope of Heaven"**
by Bishop Roy C. Nichols

"Whither Wesleyan Theology?" in four parts
by Dr. Albert C. Outler

"Whiter Christology?" in four parts
by Dr. C.F.D. Moule

"Whither Mission?" in four parts
by Bishop Stephen Neill

Theological Foundations

Fiftieth Anniversary

Scholarly Essays

First Fruits Press
Wilmore, Kentucky
c2013

ISBN: 9781621711056
Theological Foundations: Fiftieth Anniversary Scholarly Essays by members of the Seminary Faculty.
First Fruits Press, © 2013

Digital version at http://place.asburyseminary.edu/firstfruitsheritagematerial/30/

First Fruits Press is a digital imprint of the Asbury Theological Seminary, B.L. Fisher Library. Asbury Theological Seminary is the legal owner of the material previously published by the Pentecostal Publishing Co. and reserves the right to release new editions of this material as well as new material produced by Asbury Theological Seminary. Its publications are available for noncommercial and educational uses, such as research, teaching and private study. First Fruits Press has licensed the digital version of this work under the Creative Commons Attribution Noncommercial 3.0 United States License. To view a copy of this license, visit http://creativecommons.org/licenses/by-nc/3.0/us/.

For all other uses, contact:

First Fruits Press
B.L. Fisher Library
Asbury Theological Seminary
204 N. Lexington Ave.
Wilmore, KY 40390
http://place.asburyseminary.edu/firstfruits

Theological Foundations: fiftieth anniversary scholarly essays / by members of the Seminary Faculty.
    v, 259 p. ; 21 cm.
    1st ed. / revised by Robert Danielson and Faith E. Parry
    Wilmore, Ky. : First Fruits Press, c2013.
    Asbury Theological Seminary 90th Anniversary Publications ; no. 4
    Includes bibliographical references.
    Contents: Preface / Robert Danielson – Biblical authority / G. Herbert Livingston – Man and sin in the perspective of Biblical theology / Fred D. Layman – The person and work of Jesus Christ / Robert W. Lyon – The person and ministry of the Holy Spirit / Kenneth Kinghorn – Justification / Robert E. Coleman – Entire sanctification / Frank Paul Morris – The church / Howard F. Shipps – Apologetics / Harold B. Kuhn – The use and abuse of power / Gilbert James – Eschatology / Delbert R. Rose.
    ISBN: 9781621711056 (pbk.)
    1. Theology, Doctrinal.
BT10 .A82 2013   230.08

Cover design by Kelli Dierdorf

asburyseminary.edu
800.2ASBURY
204 North Lexington Avenue
Wilmore, Kentucky 40390

Preface

Robert Danielson
Editor, *The Asbury Journal*

As part of Asbury Theological Seminary's 90th Anniversary, First Fruits Press decided the timing was right to republish some of the past works created by the Seminary during the celebrations of its 40th and 50th Anniversaries. During the academic year of 1973-1974, the Seminary's 50th Anniversary, President Frank B. Stanger encouraged the celebration through two different series of lectures. The first was to assign various faculty members key theological topics and have them present scholarly papers at Estes Chapel throughout the year. These papers were separately published in The Asbury Seminarian at the time, but never together as a collection, until now.

These papers are presented here in the order in which they were given. Some unnamed librarian in the B.L. Fisher Library collected the typed papers and had them bound together with a flyer about the 50th Anniversary celebration. Finding this volume was the event that encouraged us to publish this collection as a new edition. Many of the names in this volume are illustrious names from Asbury's past that will be familiar to many alumni. I have the fortunate pleasure to know two of these men who are still present at Asbury Theological Seminary in this our 90th year. Both Dr. Kenneth C. Kinghorn and Dr. Robert E. Coleman are retired, but still active on campus and occasionally teaching. Their passion for the Kingdom of God is still evident in their lives today as a testimony of the power of the Holy Spirit to transform lives through the teaching ministry of Asbury Theological Seminary.

The second special series of lectures encouraged by Dr. Stanger occurred during the week of March 11-15, 1974. Although no written papers or sermons are available for publication, these lecture were recorded and are now available electronically on First fruits Press under the Heritage Material (place.asburyseminary.edu/firstfruitsheritagematerial). Four important names in the history of the Church of the 20th Century were present on campus at the same time. Anglican theologian and scholar of the New Testament, C.F.D. Moule (1908-2007) from Cambridge University came and spoke on the topic "Whither Christology?" The Anglican missionary, bishop, and scholar of Church History, Stephen Neill (1900-1984) gave a presentation on "Whither Mission?" One of the greatest American Methodist theologians, Dr. Albert C. Outler (1908-1989), known for his scholarship of Wesley, spoke on the topic, "Wither Wesleyan Theology?" Bishop Roy C. Nichols (1918-2002), the first African-American bishop of the United Methodist Church, conducted preaching during the week. It must have been an inspiring week for students, faculty, staff, and alumni to hear these four influential voices of the Church.

As we enter our 90th year as a Seminary, we face a world with many new challenges, but still impacted by the same problems of sin. Asbury Theological Seminary has always held fast to the idea that our hope lies in Jesus Christ and the Good News preached through scripture. These essays are a reminder, that even in this new millennium, some truths never change. As we look to the future, let us also remember the heritage from which we come as we read these timely messages from forty year ago.

Table of Contents

Preface i
   Robert Danielson

Biblical Authority 1
   G. Herbert Livingston

Man and Sin in the Perspective of Biblical Theology 23
   Fred D. Layman

The Person and Work of Jesus Christ.. 55
   Robert W. Lyon

The Person and Ministry of the Holy Spirit 85
   Kenneth C. Kinghorn

Justification.. 103
   Robert E. Coleman

Entire Sanctification... 127
   William M. Arnett

The Church... 161
   Howard F. Shipps

Apologetics 183
   Harold B. Kuhn

The Use and Abuse of Power 211
   Gilbert M. James

Eschatology.. 233
   Delbert R. Rose

Biblical Authority
G. Herbert Livingston
September 12, 1973

The basic purpose of this lecture is to probe the phenomenon of authority, which pervades both the Old and the New Testaments. The authority of the Scriptures has been at the center of debate and commitment within the believing community through the ages. Authority remains as one of the most crucial elements of the acceptance of Christianity in the modern world.

Briefly, the discussion will touch upon the following conceptual categories of biblical authority: (a) the biblical means of portrayal of the God of authority, (b) the credentials of selected persons through whom authority was channeled, (c) the authenticating marks of God's messages as authoritative, (d) the alternatives facing those who receive the authoritative message, whether in oral and/or written form, and (e) the burden resting on ministers today to proclaim an authoritative word.

In regard to the first three and the fifth of these categories, three elements will be discussed, (a) the right to exercise authority, (b) the power to carry out authority, and (c) the integrity which undergirds authority. In the fourth category, those factors which account for variations in the response of the audience to which God's word and action is directed will be examined.

Due to limitations of time, the observations presented here must be general in nature; affirmations must be compressed and concise. The temptation to supply careful exegetical support for each statement and to draw upon many biblical stories and speeches for illustrations is great. This temptation has been resisted. The appeal to supply a philosophical and/or a theological rationale for biblical authority is alluring, but also has been rejected. Since the writer specializes in Old Testament studies, there has been a tendency to draw heavily from that portion of the Scriptures, but the New Testament has, by no means, been neglected.

Dominating the Scriptures from beginning to end is the vision of the majestic sovereign God Who leaves no doubt by word or action that ultimate authority is His possession and His alone. The second Person of the Godhead, the incarnated, resurrected Christ shares that same authority.

To convey an overview of God's authority, the Bible makes affirmations about God's identity and power, utilizes the ancient frameworks of covenant and communication constructs, and insists on the integrity of God.

The Old Testament does not discuss abstractly God's authority on the basis of His right to have such authority, but it does affirm repeatedly that God is powerful, is mighty, and is without peer. The Old Testament is replete with descriptions of God acting powerfully as the Creator and Preserver of nature, as the One Who works miracles in the natural realm and in the affairs of men, as the One Who creates anew the individual and the nation. The devout Hebrew believed that the manifest power of God was adequate basis for recognizing the Living God to be the supreme authority figure of the universe.[1]

For the New Testament, the situation is much the same. Instead of an academic analysis of the authority of God, there are affirmations that God is powerful and testimonies of a divine display of His miraculous acts. All other possessions of authority ultimately have their source in the Almighty Himself.[2]

The supreme power of God is communicated in ways other than through more or less impersonal demonstrations in nature and human history. In the Scriptures, there are frameworks of personal relationships which function to reveal to man the person-to-person dimensions of divine authority.

A primary structure by which God chose to reveal His sovereignty is the covenant. Students of the Bible have long been aware of the theological significance of the covenant in God's relationship to man. They have clearly seen in the covenant God's superior status. However, archaeological discoveries in recent decades have opened to us new vistas, which have broadened the horizon of our understanding of the covenant relationship. Much of this new knowledge has deepened and reinforced the long-held conviction that God, from the beginning, revealed Himself as the ultimate source of all power and authority.

A significant number of inscriptions found in ancient Asia Minor and throughout the Mesopotamian Valley record covenant agreements. These covenants were political in nature and represent treaties between an emperor and lesser kings in his empire. Many are dated in the Late Bronze Age, approximately from 1500-1300 B.C.[3]

These new discoveries suggest that God took up from the overall Semitic civilization a basically political construct of person-to-person relationship, transformed it into a vehicle for revealing His will to man, and filled it with profound theological truth. All evidences of polytheism were stripped from the covenant structure. Old Testament scholars have called this a suzerainty covenant, because in it the covenant-maker is supreme over all other participants in the covenant. This characteristic fits well the sovereignty of God over all mankind. Basically, this kind of covenant has three foci: the supreme covenant maker, the selected human mediator of the covenant, and the covenant community. All are regarded as persons in dynamic relationship to each other. A better framework, current in ancient Near East cultures, could scarcely be found and adapted to the revelations of the Living God to mankind.

The key elements of the ancient covenant model which bear upon ultimate authority are, (a) only the covenant-maker initiated and established the covenants described in the Old and the New Testaments; (b) the covenant-maker set up the regulations which governed the covenant relationship; (c) the covenant-maker set up the sanctions in the form of curses should the covenant be broken; and (d) the covenant-maker had the exclusive right to reconstitute a broken covenant.

Many biblical passages show how the supremacy of God was communicated in ancient times through the covenant. In the light of the above-mentioned features of the covenant-maker's status, one can examine with profit the import of the prohibition given Adam, and the promises and/or commands in the accounts of God's covenants with Noah, with Abraham, Isaac and Jacob, with Israel at Sinai and at Shechem, and with David. The book of Hebrews can also be instructive.

In biblical accounts of miracle authorization, God's commands are cast in the imperative mood. Moses was the first to be authorized to perform miracles, and the rod became the symbol of the announcement and the performance of God's wonders during the Exodus and the wilderness wanderings. Explicit instructions were given to Joshua, Gideon, Samuel, and a host of prophets in relation to the preparation for and the performance of God's marvelous miracles.

Another related framework, well known in ancient times, is the messenger construct, in which there were the messenger-sender, the messenger, the message, and the individuals or groups addressed.

According to the Scriptures, God began to relate to man in this manner with Moses, and it became a common pattern in the God-prophet relationship. In addition to God's identification of Himself, there are certain verbs, which stress God's supreme position. One verb is *salah*, normally translated "send." This is a commissioning verb and is found with God as the subject in regard to Moses (Exodus 3:12-16), Samuel (1 Samuel 15:1), Isaiah (Isaiah 6:8,9), Jeremiah (Jeremiah 19:14), Ezekiel (Ezekiel 3:6+), and Zechariah (Zechariah 2:12). The other basic verb used is *natan*, which is, in the messenger context, translated as "put," "ordained," "appointed," or by other synonyms. The call of Jeremiah is a prime example (Jeremiah 1:5,9; cf. Deuteronomy 18:18). The verbs "go" and "speak" with their synonyms, in the imperative mood, highlight the Lordship of God over the messenger. These verbs are often followed by a designation of the addressee and coupled with the well-known statement: "Thus saith the Lord," in its various formulations. This statement is a prime signature of authority in the Old Testament message-sending situation. Hannaniah misused this authority formula with fatal consequences (Jeremiah 28).

Correlative to the right of authority and the power to back up authority is the integrity of the authority figure. We have seen in our present national crisis, called the Watergate affair, the intimate relationship of integrity to the authority of the top governmental leaders. In the Scriptures, integrity of being and action is fundamental to the viability of divine authority.

Integrity has to do with a state of being whole, of being unimpaired in basic qualities, and/or of being organically entire. Integrity has to do with soundness of moral character in which honesty, sincerity, dependability, and consistency are untainted by deception, artificiality, or guile. In the Old Testament, this concept is primarily carried by the verb *tāmām*, and its derivatives,[4] which depict man's relationship to God and to each other. It also designates the quality of a sacrificial animal. Twice the verb refers to God's work, way, knowledge, and law (Deuteronomy 32:4; 2 Samuel 22:31; Job. 37:16; Psalms 19:7). In the New Testament, the equivalent word is *teleios*, which twice designates the perfection of God (Matt. 5:48; Romans 12:2).

In a variety of ways, the integrity of God is affirmed in both the Old and the New Testaments. These affirmations generally draw upon words which are equivalent to the English words "oneness," or "simplicity," because there is a strong emphasis on the self-existence, the self-consciousness, and self-decision of God. He is distinct from all aspects of nature. In contrast with the deities in polytheism, He is not confused with natural objects, or with man. He cannot be manipulated. The integrity of God is implicit in declarations on the holiness, fullness, righteousness, justice, omnipresence, omniscience, faithfulness, truth, and eternity of God.

Both the Old and the New Testaments present men and women of faith as grounding their lives and their messages upon the reality of a God of authority, power, and integrity. This conviction was no less intense in regard to Jesus Christ. A minister of Christ must be just as convinced that the ground of biblical authority is also the Living Lord. From this foundation we may now examine the human side of biblical authority.

The Mediator-Messenger's Authority

According to the Scriptures, Moses was the first man to serve authoritatively as God's surrogate. In him was combined the functions of both the covenant-mediator and the covenant-messenger. As covenant-mediator, Moses led the Israelites out of Egypt to Sinai where the covenant was forged. Then he organized them and led them through the wilderness to the east side of the Jordan River. As covenant-messenger, Moses received from God a series of messages to be delivered to the Pharaoh and others, with Aaron as his helper.

The credentials of the mediator-messenger rested upon the commission he received from God, the power with which God endued him, and the integrity of his character.

Moses' authority was rooted in his commissioning to these tasks by God at the burning bush (Exodus 3:1-4:23), and later in Egypt (5:22-6:13; see also 6:28-7:7). In reference to basic Hebrew words of commissioning, mention has been made of God's authoritative status, which is reflected in them. These verbs, particularly "send," also portray the conferral of authority on Moses to act for God (3:10) as deliverer. Throughout Moses' meetings with Pharaoh, God's commands authorized Moses to perform miracles for Him. In the call experience, the rod was given to symbolize this God-given power, which was displayed in a series of miracles after the Exodus till the end of Moses' ministry. The power of the mediator was also evident in Moses' shining face when he descended from Mount Sinai with the second set of law tablets (34:29-35). On one occasion, Moses sought to take personal credit for the power vouchsafed to him with drastic consequences. God forbade him to enter Canaan (Numbers 20:10-13).

Moses' authority as mediator was evidenced with special force by his access to the presence of God on Mount Sinai during the covenant-making event (Exodus 19-24). Only

Moses could receive the divine instructions, the law, and the right to officiate as leader of the covenant ceremonies. To a lesser extent, Joshua was promised authority and power to lead Israel into the land of promise (Joshua 1:1-9). Joshua realized that power at the Jordan River, at Jericho, and at the battle of Beth-Horon. Joshua demonstrated his authority at the covenant renewals at Shechem (Joshua 8:30-35; 24:1-28)

At a higher level, Jesus Christ possessed authority and power as mediator of the New Covenant; for He, the Son of God, was sent into the world to establish it. New Testament passages in support of this assertion are widespread, but the Gospel of John and the book of Hebrews are especially rich sources.

In regard to Moses' function as messenger, similar observations can be made. Against Moses' protest, God commissioned him to transmit messages and finally gave him Aaron as an assistant. Moses was commissioned to speak repeatedly in the name of Yahweh; the three books, Exodus, Leviticus, and Numbers, are replete with: "The Lord spoke to Moses," and the repetition of the divine message to the designated audience.

The same divine commission to speak is found in the opening chapters of Joshua and in relationship to a host of prophets during the Kingdom Period. Their credentials lay in their commissioning by God and the varied formulae based on: "Thus saith the Lord."

The inner experience of being commissioned was matched by an inner enablement to speak. Several of God's men protested their own inadequacy to do the task but God touched them, changed them, and filled them with courage and power to face the most awesome audiences. The stories of these encounters show that these people performed miracles, and endured suffering, and death without fear. An important aspect of their power lay in the fulfillment of their predictions, often dramatically.

The personal integrity of the servants of God were credentials of authority and evidence of power; they were able to come through periods of crisis as more mature persons. A basic aspect of their crisis was a dilemma, which arose from their relationship to both God and man. The clearest statement of this dilemma is found in Jeremiah 1:17-19. A paraphrase may put it thus: "Go out and speak; if you crumble under the opposition, God will punish; if you continue to speak faithfully, everyone will fight against you." During forty years of prophesying, Jeremiah was gored by the sharp horns of that dilemma, but the display of poise and fearlessness in trial and in prison made clear to all the quality of his integrity. The same was true of Moses and many another Old Testament worthy.

And what shall we say of the dilemmas of Christ who spoke with authority and healed with power? What of the quality of His life of love as well as His steel-like opposition to sin and cruelty? He died with forgiveness on His lips and rose from the grave with power. What of the apostles who were authorized by Christ to proclaim the gospel? From Pentecost on, they were flames of fire and power, willing to take up the cross without flinching and suffer joyfully for Christ 's sake. They knew the compulsion of the commission and the: "Woe is unto me, if I preach not the gospel!" (1 Corinthians 9:16). They held true and died gloriously.

The foregoing comments have tried to demonstrate the biblical ground of authority in the one true God and His delegation of authority to the covenant-mediators and the covenant-messengers in both the Old and the New Testaments. This authority will now be examined in terms of the ancient means of conveying it via oral and/or written messages, the sanctions, which backed them up, the basis for canonicity, and the evidences of biblical authenticity.

The Word of God was not proclaimed to Israel in a cultural vacuum; "earthen vessels" were utilized to bear it and to preserve it. Reference has already been made to the ancient treaties as structural models by which God was portrayed as

Sovereign with Moses and Christ as covenant-mediators. These same treaties provided a model for messages, which were intended to be authoritative. Many treaties had clauses, which ordered that their texts should be written, that copies be made for the vassals, and that a written text be deposited in the national temple. Strictures were declared against unilateral changes in the written text, and curses were pronounced as sanctions against all illegal acts. These features were adapted to the needs of establishing a covenant with Israel.

Most of the reference in the Pentateuch to materials put into writing have to do with covenant law, covenant curses, and covenant commitment (Exodus 24:3; 31:18; 34:1,27-28; Deuteronomy 6:9; 27:3,8; 31:9-13,19-22,24-26; cf. Deuteronomy 4:13; 5:22; 10:2,4; also Joshua 1:8; 8:32-25). But the greater portion of God's word is depicted in the Pentateuch as transmitted orally to the people through God's messenger, Moses. No less authority is ascribed to these oral proclamations, which provided instructions in time of crisis, laws for community organization, blueprints for tabernacle construction, and regulations for worship procedures. There were moments of rebellion against the message delivered, but the exhibition of divine power soon put a stop to them. The oral messages also effectually declared God's victory over all enemies, and the achievement of deliverance of His people from bondage. The word of power constituted Israel as His own: "I take you to me for a people..." (Exodus 3:7; Deuteronomy 4:20). God's presence coincided with the declaration of the word: "...that the people may hear when I speak with thee, and believe thee forever" (Exodus 19:9).

Whether in oral or written form, the word of God was backed by sanctions of curses and threats of punishment should His words be rejected. These were not idle words, for God repeatedly carried out His word in acts of retribution.

Meredith Kline has maintained that all the literature of the Old Testament bears the canonical authority of the constituting event of the covenant making at Sinai. Genesis and

Exodus 1-18 make up the historical prologue, which records the acts of God leading to Sinai. Numbers recounts the acts of God throughout the wanderings. Deuteronomy is the retelling of the covenant event, and is structured according to the key components of the ancient suzerainty treaty. The historical books highlight events of covenant-breaking and covenant renewal. They provide the framework for the prophets, who served as God's persecutors against a people, which had forsaken the covenant. The prophets were also evangelists who called Israel back to a covenant renewal, who pointed to the future plans of God to fulfill His covenant, and to forge a new covenant.

The Psalms are expressions of commitment, or recital of God's deeds, and of participation in covenant fellowship before God within a structure of worship. The wisdom literature is the transformation of law into maxims and teachings of how an upright man walks before God, and the wicked man pollutes the covenant community and experiences the covenant sanctions.

On the basis of covenant renewal and the changes evident in covenants with Adam, Noah, Abraham, Moses, Joshua, and David, Kline holds that the New Testament is also a body of literature grounded in the salient features of the ancient covenant, yet with differences. Through His death, Jesus Christ put the new covenant into effect. He called into being a new community, the church, rooted the law in the inner being and proclaimed a new commandment, love. Jesus Christ gathered to Himself the functions of prophet, priest, and king and all that pertained to them. In the combined events of Resurrection and Pentecost, spiritual life and power became realized as never before, in the new community, which now broke all barriers as it spread out into the world.

The oral words of Christ and the written words of the gospels bear the authoritative impress of this new covenant; so also do the oral words of the apostles and the written account of their acts, which provide the historical framework of the epistles. The epistles draw heavily on the prophets, the Psalter, and the wisdom literature of the Old Testament, and tie them to the new covenant. New obligations are set forth and sanctions are proclaimed and enforced against those who turn their back on the Lord of the new covenant. The book of Revelation consummates the new covenant in the triumphal word of the victorious, returning Christ; it goes full circle to the Garden of Eden with its Tree of Life. The New Testament literature has authority as canon because it revolves around and explicates the new covenant.[5]

In neither the Old Testament or the New Testament is there an indication that authority was conferred upon their literature by act of human decision, whether done in assembly or in one's inner being. Rather, the context of personal encounters with God and covenant-making assemblies is interlaced with recognition of the intrinsic authority of the oral messages and written materials declared as the Word of God.

The integrity of biblical literature is grounded in the legitimacy of its source in the one true God who revealed His will to man. The Bible is His vehicle in written form to convey His message. It is the sole record and the authentic interpretation of the events of history in which God acted as Judge and Savior. From only the Bible do we have information of the birth, life, death, resurrection, and Second Coming of Jesus Christ and the significance of that information to us.

The integrity of the Scriptures is rooted in the validity and authentic quality of the mediator-messenger relationship with God, and in the responsible leadership of the persons who experienced this relationship as they functioned in the establishment of the covenant with the covenant community. The Scriptures record the messenger's responsible transmission of God's message to His people and contains a trustworthy transcript written either by those select servants or their close associates.

The integrity of the biblical literature extends to those who wrote the Scriptures. If these servants of God had been involved in recording events that never happened, guilty of falsifying the past by distorting it with unwarranted religious interpretation, or participants in pious fraud, then their integrity would have been dealt a fatal blow. A credibility gap at this portion of the chain of authority would invalidate whatever supposed genuineness the other foci of authority may possess. If the intention and conduct of the biblical writers were not pure, our ability to reach through to the hearts and minds of the apostles, to the Person of Jesus Christ, to the reality of God's dealings with the ancient Hebrews is incapacitated. We are at a loss to make an authentic contact with more than a present subjective experience.

The integrity of biblical literature bears upon its relationship to succeeding generations, to differing cultures, and to men in every variety of lostness. To be effectual in bringing a message of judgment and salvation, the Bible must continue to be universally, infallibly authoritative for faith and practice. It was not a simple operation to maintain the viability of the covenant theology in the presence of the stifling, oppressive polytheism of the ancient Near East. The Old Testament was a daring challenge to paganism and its temptations. Most remarkable is the persistence of the Old Testament in our Bibles in the face of centuries of Marcionism and allegorizing tendencies within Christianity. Both attitudes have been detrimental to the validity of the Old Testament's theological witness. And the New Testament literature has had its battles with Gnostic and mystic emphases in the church, but has stood its ground and maintained its authenticity.

The Audience's Response's Response to Biblical Authority

There is still a vital segment of the chain of authority, which must be discussed; it is the response of the listening audience. The factors, which account for variations in the response of the audience are freedom of choice, a fundamental dilemma, a conceptual construct of faith statements, and a practical application to lifestyle.

A most significant aspect of the covenant at Sinai was the voluntary, whole-hearted affirmation: "All the Lord has spoken we will do" (Exodus 19:8; cf. 24:7b). Similar commitments were made in the presence of Joshua (Joshua 24:16-22); in the presence of Josiah (2 Kings 23:3); and in the presence of Ezra (Neh. 8:6).

The Israelites were not always positive in their responses to the messages delivered by God's messengers. The Old Testament is replete with accounts of Israel's rebellions and apostasies. There is nothing in the Old Testament, which indicates that positive responses conferred authority on the messages, or that negative responses withheld authority from them. It is no different in the Gospels or in the Acts of the Apostles. Decisions made by individuals or groups affected their lives profoundly, but did not affect the reality of God's authority, the authority of the messenger, or the authority of the message.

Positive commitments did recognize the identity and authority of the Message-Sender. Since the messenger was physically present, people could examine and recognize his authority and if they reject it, they could abuse him; but God was beyond their grasp, and could not be manhandled by them. People could hear or read the messages and accept or reject their authority, but even a king—Jehoiakim—could not burn a prophet's scroll without bringing upon himself divine sanctions. Though God is invisible, He must be taken seriously.

After receiving a message, the audience often found decision-making difficult. The Message-Sender was not a physical object, the messenger was often a lowly, unknown person, and the message was frequently very critical. A painful dilemma normally accompanied the message. If the sinful Israelites responded positively they would have to repudiate the pagan practices they had come to enjoy. If the Israelites responded negatively, they would have to face the covenant sanctions.

Those who listened to Jesus faced the same dilemma, and many decided to crucify Him. The congregations who listened to the apostles were no different. Some said yes, some said no. Those who listen to the Word of God or read it today must too make decisions in the presence of the same dilemma so bluntly put by Jesus: "If any man will come after me, let him deny himself, and take up his cross, and follow me" (Matt. 16:24).

It is not the privilege of an audience to confer authority on all or parts of the Bible, or to withhold authority; it is their responsibility to yield to the Lord of the Scriptures and to feed on the written Word, illuminated and guided by the Holy Spirit and the fellowship of the saints.

In ancient times, the chain of authority was the sovereign revealer, the commissioned messenger, the message transmitted in oral and/or written form, and the listening audience. Today, the chain of authority is the Living Word, Jesus Christ; the written Word, i.e., the Scriptures, the preacher, and the congregation.

Within recent times, philosophical idealism, positivism, and existentialism, separately or in combination, have been inclined to reject this chain of authority, to question the theological formulations of the Scriptures, and to recast its concepts and terminology into more acceptable thought patterns.

The Scriptures remain a challenge to all attempts to subvert or transform their basic theological proclamations. The living, triune God is not dead; He is still the creator and sustainer of all nature. Jesus Christ, the Son of God, is the contemporary Christ, redeeming sinners. The Holy Spirit is working in the hearts of a multitude of believers. Sin and judgment are still realities; conversion and sanctification are still experienced by those who turn to God by faith.[6] Suffice it to say, the authority of the Scriptures remains viable. It is effective in leading sinners to God, in illuminating the depths of sin and the possibilities of grace, which is the representation of the power of biblical authority. The Bible is indispensable for maturing saints as persons, which is illustrative of its integrity. The written Word places on each believer the responsibility to witness in an evil age, which is an extension of the right of biblical authority.

The Bible remains authoritative in the area of practice, but here the problem of applying its authority is not easily solved. The simplistic approach is to regard all divine commands touching on practice in isolation from historical, cultural contexts, and therefore to bind believers for all time regardless of differences of culture.

It is instructive to note that those divine commands which the prophets, Jesus Christ, and the apostles regarded as permanently valid were the Ten Commandments and, with Christ, the two supreme laws stated in Deuteronomy 6:5 and Leviticus 19:18. These commandments were each directed to the individual. Many of the other laws, mostly case law, had to do with the lifestyle of the community, and these changed to some extent at each covenant renewal. In the covenant renewal called the New Testament, radical changes were made in regulations related to the community way of life, mostly by rooting motivation deeply in the inner life.

Nevertheless, at the very beginning of Israel's national life, the laws governing many phases of her lifestyle represented a radical change from the cultures, which surrounded her on every hand. Perhaps these changes can be labeled as cultural adaptations. A century and a half ago knowledge of the cultural environment of the ancient Near East was exceedingly limited and students of the Bible did-not recognize this element of adaptation, for there was little with which the Old Testament could be contrasted. Now the contrast is quite clear in the areas of theological concepts of God, man, sin, and salvation. The differences are striking in terms of the manner in which God, nature, individual, and group were related. A gulf existed between the pagan's understanding and practice of divination, magic, kingship, law, and cultic worship on the one hand, and the Hebrew understanding of prophecy, miracle, leadership, law, and worship practice on the other hand.

By counterbalancing the similarities between the Hebrew and the pagan with the differences between them, one can grasp some of the guidelines governing changes of community lifestyle. A key guideline was the clear prohibition of any practice contrary to the nature and will of a God of holy love and contrary to healthy, moral living among men. Another guideline was the lifting up of neutral terms and practices from common Semitic culture, the cleansing of these terms of pagan connotations and the attaching to them of new meanings and overtones consonant with the covenant theology. Much of the case law, dealing with domestic, economic, and governmental matters found in the Old Testament, was constructed according to this guideline, and many of the changes of cultic practice in the Old Testament seem to follow this procedure. The radical changes proposed by Jesus, illustrated in the Council of Jerusalem, and provided by the epistles seem to be motivated in much the same way. Each covenant in a new culture needed new expressions.

In a similar fashion festivals common to the Semites were replaced with celebrations rooted in events of supreme importance to the Hebrews. The feasts of Passover, of Pentecost, and of Tabernacles are illustrations. In turn, these Hebrew feasts were replaced in the church by the Lord's Supper, by Easter, and by Christmas, for these festivals were grounded in events in Christ's life. Event and feast were closely tied together.

Another guideline was a reorientation of vocations in the new communities. As Hebrew priest was different from pagan priest, so the Christian minister was different from either one, because the covenant was different; hence, leadership developed along different lines than in either paganism or in Israel. So also the structure of the individual church was adapted to each new culture, which it penetrated.

Cultural practices, which were adapted to Israelite or church life, were transient elements and for that reason posed dangers. When spiritual life was at a low ebb, the customs, institutions, laws, and rites, which were adapted from surrounding culture, and thus similar to the pagan lifestyle, could be polluted by pagan attitudes and emphases. On the other hand, when adapted practices became obsolete due to cultural changes, the very: "Thus saith the Lord" formula, which initiated them, would seem to prohibit further change. So obsolete regulations would become a burden on future generations.

The Christian church has faced problems of cultural adaptation as it has evangelized people of differing ways of living. This problem is crucial today as Christians face rapid cultural changes at home and engage in missionary activities in all areas of the world.

It may be that an in-depth study of how God revealed Himself to the Hebrew people, how He led them to build a new community with new ways of practice, how Jesus fulfilled the law of the Old Testament, and how He and the apostles built the church would provide guidelines for living in today's world. The precepts must be sifted for principles so the Scriptures will truly serve us authoritatively in our practices.

Since this is a seminary-training preachers for future service, a word about preaching and biblical authority may be in order as a conclusion. A preacher without an authoritative message is an anomaly; he is a living contradiction. Several factors must combine to transform him into a transmitter of the authority of· God.

Like the messenger of old, a true preacher must experience a call to preach; he/she must receive a commission from the Holy Spirit to perform the preacher's task. This divine call should be augmented by the church's commissioning of the preacher, who in response must have a deep conviction that the Bible is the authoritative Word of God. The preacher should study the whole Bible with diligence, care, and honesty.

The preacher must know the reality of the regenerating and sanctifying power of the Holy Spirit. Authority and power go together and they must be joined in the preacher's life if he/she is to deliver Scriptural messages effectively. Followers of John Wesley often refer to the unction of the Holy Spirit, which may be-defined as God's present support and help during the preaching of the Word.

The preacher must be a real person. He/she must be open before God and man, and be willing to pay the price of faithful proclamation of the Word of God. The preacher must be a person of integrity, honest, pure in motive, permeated with love, and outgoing in concern for others. Priorities must be fixed on service to God and man rather than on such peripheral matters as salary or status.

The exhortation of Paul to Timothy still rings out across the years: "Preach the Word; be instant in season, out of season; reprove, rebuke, exhort with all longsuffering and doctrine" (2 Timothy 4:2).

Notes

[1] A study of Hebrew or English words for power in standard lexicons and concordances will provide many passages to support these assertions.

[2] Consult standard Greek lexicons and concordances for the usage of ἐξουσία and δύναμις, or English concordances for equivalents, such as "authority" and "power."

[3] D. R. Hillers, Covenant: The History of Biblical Idea (Baltimore: The Johns Hopkins Press, 1969), pp. 25-45. Also, D. J. McCarthy, Treaty and Covenant: A Study in the Ancient Oriental Documents and in the Old Testament

(Rome: Pontifical Biblical Institute, 1963), pp. 28-106.

[4] The derivatives are *tōm*, *tummāh*, and *tāmîm*.

[5] Meredith Kline, *The Structure of Biblical Authority* (Grand Rapids: Wm. B. Eerdmans Publishing Company, 1972), pp. 27-110.

[6] Donald G. Miller, *The Authority of the Bible* (Grand Rapids: Wm. B. Eerdmans Publishing Company, 1972), pp. 70-91.

Works Cited

Abba, Raymond, *The Nature and Authority of the Bible*. Philadelphia: Muhlenberg Press, 1958.

Bright, John, *The Authority of the Old Testament*. Nashville: Abingdon Press, 1967.

Bryant, Robert H., *The Bible's Authority Today*. Minneapolis: Augsburg Publishing House, 1968.

Cunliffe-Jones, Hubert, *The Authority of the Biblical Revelation*. Boston: Pilgrim Press, 1948.

Dodd, C. H., *The Authority of the Bible*. New York: Harper and Row, 1958.

Hillers, Delbert R., *Covenant: The History of a Biblical Idea*. Baltimore: The Johns Hopkins Press, 1969.

Kline, Meredith G., *The Structure of Biblical Authority*. Grand Rapids: Wm. B. Eerdmans Publishing Company, 1972.

McCarthy, Dennis J., *Treaty and Covenant*. Rome: Pontifical Biblical Institute, 1963.

Miller, Donald G., *The Authority of the Bible*. Grand Rapids: Wm. B. Eerdmans Publishing Company, 1972.

Ramm, Bernard, *The Pattern of Religious Authority*. Grand Rapids: Wm. B. Eerdmans , Publishing Company, 1965.

Richardson, Allan, and Schweitzer, W. (eds.), *Biblical Authority for Today*. London: SCM Press, 1951.

Ridderbos, H. N., *The Authority of the New Testament Scriptures*. Philadelphia: Presbyterian and Reformed Publishing Company, 1963.

Snaith, N. H., *The Inspiration and Authority of the Bible*. London: The Epworth Press, 1956.

Shroyer, M. J., *The Authority of the Bible in Christian Belief*. Nashville: Tidings, 1961.

Tenney, Merrill C., *The Bible: The Living Word of Revelation*. Grand Rapids: Zondervan Publishing House, 1968.

Williams R. R., *Authority in the Apostolic Age*. London: SCM Press, 1950.

Man and Sin in the Perspective of Biblical Theology

Fred D. Layman
October 3, 1973

The limits of this study are suggested by the title. Consideration will be given to the theme of "Man and Sin" from the perspective of contemporary Biblical Theology. The restrictions of space suggested for these essays, however, require further limitations in the number of matters, which can be treated profitably. The temptation to do an analysis of the various psychical and physical terms found in biblical anthropology—as important as that would be for the theme—had to be resisted.[1] A word study on the numerous designations for sin in the Old and New Testaments could deepen our understanding of that theme,[2] but the present study attempts only to approach the subject generally and then to consider in some depth the matter of original sin in the biblical perspective.

Within these limits then, the theme "Man and Sin" will be under three main headings: Man As the Image of God, The Holistic Man, and Original Sin in the Biblical Perspective.

One remaining preliminary observation: A common weakness of studies on the theme of man and sin is that they are highly individualistic and attempt to consider man in isolation from the community. The present essay does not escape that criticism. As originally planned, this study was to include an additional section titled Man in His Relatedness. Biblical man is viewed in the context of human history, and particularly within the communities of Israel and Church. He is involved in society and cannot be isolated from it. Even more significant is the fact that man is understood in relation to God in the Bible, apart from whom his existence disintegrates into absurdity and meaninglessness. This relatedness to God and to the community is a basic premise underlying all of the anthropological statements of Scripture.[3]

This line of thought has not been developed in the present study, however, because later essays in this series will treat various dimensions of Christian social ethics.

Fred D. Layman | 25

Man As The Image Of God

The Old Testament references to man as the image and likeness of God are few and brief. Genesis 1:26 reads in part, "Then God said, Let us make man in our image, after our likeness..." There is a further reference to the creation of man "...in the likeness of God" in Genesis 5:1, and a final statement in Genesis 9:6 that "...God made man in his own image." This is the extent of the image motif in the Old Testament. The scarcity and brevity of the Old Testament passages however, stand in contrast to the abundant and often lengthy interpretations of the theme in the history of theology. Karl Barth has surveyed the treatment of the doctrine and has shown that the general tendency has been to divorce the concept from its biblical framework and to fill in its meaning in terms of the view of man which has prevailed at given points in history.[4]

Speaking broadly, the various interpretations of the image of God in the history of theology may be classified as "substantive" or as "relational" interpretations.[5] The substantive view regards the image of God to be some entity structured into man's being by the Creator; it then proceeds to attempt to identify that entity. Both physical and rational faculties have been designated as the *locus* of the image in man.[6] In contrast to most other creatures, it has been noted by some interpreters that man was created to stand and to walk in an upright physical posture. This symbolized his place in the creation, both as having a special relationship to the Creator and as commissioned with a ruling vocation in relation to the other creatures.[7]

More often, however, the image of God has been identified with the rational side of man's nature. From at least the second century A.D. onward, a progressive synthesizing of biblical and Greek thought was carried out by Christian theologians, with the result, in this instance that the biblical view of man came to be interpreted in categories supplied by the Greek idealistic tradition.[8] When this view of man was carried over into Christian theology, the image of God was identified with the human soul, which, in turn, was then invested with the attributes of the Greek soul, that is, with spirituality, rationality, and immortality.

Since Karl Barth, Western theology has been engaged in restating Christian thought in interpersonal and relational language, rather than in abstract language, which is divorced from man's life situation. In this approach, the vertical I-Thou relation between God and man became determinative for explicating the various themes of theology. Under this influence, recent theologians have generally abandoned the attempt to identify the image of God as some element in man's nature, finding it rather in the unique relationship which man is given with God in his creation. For Barth, the image of God is not a quality or attribute of man which corresponds to a like entity in God (*analogia entis*), but is a relationship established by God into which man is called (*analogia relationis*).[9] For Brunner, the image refers to a being-in-relation in which man has been called into existence by the Creator to answer God in believing and responsive love, and to exist in obedience and responsibility for all that that relationship involves.[10]

Twentieth century Old Testament Biblical Theology has not produced any more unanimity on the meaning of the image of God than has Dogmatic Theology. D. J. A. Clines has delineated the same tendencies toward spiritual and physical interpretations of the term among the Old Testament theologians, which have been found among the systematicians.[11] Until 1940, Biblical theologians generally understood the image of God to have spiritual, or vocational, or relational meanings.[12] After 1940, largely due to the influence of Herman Gunkel, the interpretation of the image as a correspondence between the external forms of God and man came to dominate Old Testament scholarship. From the History of Religions perspective it was pointed out that in Babylonian religion, man's outward form is a copy of God's form so that man bears a structural similarity to God.[13] Thus H. Wheeler

Robinson concluded that the most obvious meaning of Genesis 1:26 was that "the bodily form of man was made after the pattern of the bodily form of God (the substance being different…)."[14]

The discussion to this point has attempted to set the boundaries and to suggest the major issues in the interpretation of the image of God concept. A more detailed analysis of the relevant passages is now in order.

The two Hebrew words for "image" and "likeness" are *ṣelem* and *demuth* respectively.[15] In the Old Testament the word *ṣelem* most commonly refers to two or three dimensional representations of gods, of men, or of other creatures (2 Kings 11:18; 2 Chronicles 23:17; Numbers 33:52; Amos 5:26; Ezekiel 7:20; 16:17; 23:14f; 1 Samuel 6:5,11). Twice the word is used in a metaphorical sense and means "shadow" (Psalm 39:6), "dream" or "phantom" (Psalm 73:20). The word is used once to speak of the image conveyed from Adam to his son Seth (Genesis 5:3). Finally, the word is used three times to refer to man as the image of God (Genesis 1:26f., 9:6). Man is thereby understood to be created after the pattern of God. He is thus a representation, which corresponds to a model, a copy of an original.[16] Though such language was understood literally and physically most everywhere else in the Ancient Near East, this is probably[17] not the case in the Old Testament. The anthropomorphisms and anthropopathisms, whereby human bodily parts and psychical functions are ascribed to God, function to depict God as a Person rather than to describe His physical form.[18]

The second word, "likeness," is commonly understood to have a limiting effect on the word "image." Since the Hebrew word *ṣelem* was more commonly applied to idols, the intent of the second word, *demuth*, is to define the first term more closely within the context of the Hebrew belief in the "otherness" and uniqueness of God. Von Rad points out that the Old Testament reservations in this connection are related to the larger view of the transcendence of God in Hebrew faith.

The central emphasis in Old Testament anthropology is on the dust-character and frailty of man who cannot stand before the presence of the divine holiness. The image idea, though highly significant, is nonetheless secondary to the thought of man's creatureliness.[19]

It is significant to note here that man himself, in his totality, is created in the image of God. The Hebrew view of man emphasizes the unity and wholeness of man, in contrast to later Greek dualistic views, which made qualitative distinctions between man's rational and physical natures.[20] Thus the image of God is limited neither to man's soul nor to his body, but is a statement about man as a whole.[21]

Further, it is to be noted that all men are created in the image of God. The significance of this fact becomes apparent when it is observed that in all the Ancient Near East the term "image of God" is limited almost exclusively to the king, only rarely is it ascribed to the priest, and is almost never a designation applying to common men.[22] In Israel the image of God was characteristic of all mankind without distinction, including king and commoner, Israelite and non-Israelite, man and woman.[23] This understanding is reflected, among other things, in the relatively higher dignity given to women, in the democratic equality of all Hebrews, in the humane treatment of foreigners and slaves, and in the restraining laws imposed to limit inhumanity in warfare.[24]

The designation "image of God" means in the first instance that man has a special relation to God unique to the rest of the creation. He is in some way like God to a degree not true of any other creature. He is understood fundamentally from above rather than from below. He is more than the most highly developed of animals. His significance goes beyond that of an infinitesimal speck of dust within the enormous expanse of the universe. As the image of God he has been made a "...little less than God" (Psalm 8:5), subject only to the lordship of his Creator. He has been called into communion with God and to responsibility before God.[25]

Genesis does not go further to define explicitly the content of the image of God nor to state what was given to man to make him capable of such communion with God above all other creatures. There are no descriptions of the special qualities of the human soul nor definitions of the Subjective nature of original righteousness. The author is concerned only to state the special place and responsibility of man in the creation and he does not answer the metaphysical questions of a later time. His outlook is fundamentally existential rather than ontological.[26]

However, the image of God would seem to involve more than a mere relationship because it continues in some manner even after the relationship between man and God is interrupted by sin (Genesis 9:2). For this reason, several recent writers have refused to regard the relational and substantial interpretations of the image of God as mutually exclusive, but rather as complementary to each other.[27] But definitions of the nature of man's superior endowment as a result of being created in God's image proceed more on the basis of logical implications from, rather than on the basis of, explicit pronouncements in the Genesis passage. Such attempts always run the risk of reading modern anthropological values into the biblical record. Precise definition seems to be eliminated due to the brevity of the image passages.

The term "image of God," in the second instance, involves a vocational dimension, that is, man is to rule over the creation as God's steward and vice-regent. Man is thus equipped by the Creator to carry out this function in the earth. In the Genesis passage, the vocation of rulership and development of the creation follows closely upon the statement of man's creation in God's image (Genesis 1:26-30). There is general agreement among Old Testament scholars that the eighth Psalm is closely related to the image motif, though the words *ṣelem* and *demuth* are not found in the passage. There mention is first made of man's creation whereby he was endowed with "glory" (*kābōd*) and "honor" (*hādār*). Horst comments, "This crowning with glory and honor, that is to say, with outward 'majesty' and with inward 'gravity' and 'power,' authorizes and legitimizes him in the exercise of the *dominium terrae*."[28] This is as close as the Old Testament comes to defining the content of the divine image. Further, it is to be noted that the image of God is never discussed in abstraction—as an entity in and of itself—in the Old Testament, but always in the context of its function in the divinely appointed vocation of rulership (Genesis 1:26-30; 9:1-7; Psalm 8:3-8). Clines thus concludes that "...though man's rulership over the animals is not itself the image of God, no definition of the image is complete which does not refer to this function of rulership."[29]

Finally, the image of God in the Old Testament carries a representational meaning—man is to be the representative of God in the earth. In the ancient world an image functioned as the representative of a personage who was spiritually present but physically absent. Kings placed their statues in conquered lands to signify their real presence there, even though they were physically absent. When the king was referred to as the "image of God," he was understood as the representative of the god to other men and the ruler of the creation at the appointment of the god. Idols were set up in the temples to signify the real presence of the god, even though it was known that the god was physically present in the heavens or at some other location. The image was thought to be united with the god by the presence of the divine fluid or spirit, which gave life to the dead matter making up the idol. The idol was very often fashioned in the supposed likeness of the deity, which it represented.[30]

This is the background out of which the biblical idea of man as the image of God developed. Clines has made a convincing case that the preposition in the Hebrew of Genesis 1:26f and 9:6 should properly be translated "*as* the image of God," rather than "*in* the image of God."[31] Man is places in the earth as the representative of the transcendent God. Until verse 26 of the first chapter of Genesis, the only connection between God and His creation was His word. After verse 26 the connection is established in man. Thus the context of the doctrine of man as the image of God is the larger tension of the Old Testament view of the transcendence and immanence of God. God stands outside the world order as its Creator and Lord and is not identified with, nor subject to, the creation. But he is immanently present within the creation in the person of the man whom he has brought into existence, called into fellowship, and established as his representative in the earth. As such, man is to serve the Creator faithfully, worship Him supremely, and glorify Him in the creation by portraying the character of the God whose image he is.[32]

The image and likeness motif is expressed in the New Testament by the words *eikōn, homoiōsis, morphēe,* and *charaktēr*. 1 Corinthians 11:7 and James 3:7 make it clear that the New Testament regards all en as yet being the image of God in some sense, in spite of sin. As in the Old Testament, the image theme is most usually stated in the context of the creation motif, particularly in the old creation—new creation dialectic. But the theme is especially connected with Christology and soteriology in the New Testament. The old creation, descended from the original man, is enslaved by sin and death. The image of God, though not effaced, has become enshrouded in darkness. Man has lost his way. As his worst, he suppresses the knowledge of God and his glory, substituting images of his own making (Romans 1:18-31). At his best, he gives only a partial and distorted answer to the call of God. He has lost the knowledge of what it means to be the image of God.[33] Christ was sent forth as God's image and representative to restore the knowledge of God and to manifest what man was meant to be. After declaring that Christ is the "image of God " in 2 Corinthians 4:4, Paul goes on to enlarge on the meaning of that term by saying:

> For it is the God who said, 'Let light shine out of darkness,' who has shone in our hearts to give

> the light of the knowledge of the glory of God in the face of Christ (2 Corinthians 4:6)

The author of Hebrews declares concerning the Son:

> He reflects the glory of God and bears the very stamp (*charaktēr*) of his nature, upholding the universe by the word of his power (Hebrews 1:3).

As such, Christ is creator and ruler in the new creation, as man was called to be in the old creation (Colossians 1:15-18; Hebrews 1:3-2:10; cf. Philippians 2:6-11). Just as Adam bequeathed his image to members of the old creation (cf. Genesis 5:3), so also Christ shares his image with members of the new creation (1 Corinthians 15:45-49). God has ordained that the new man will be conformed to the image of Christ who is the firstborn of the new order (Romans 8:29). The Christian, as new creation (2 Corinthians 5:17), is to put off the corrupted image of the old creation and is to "put on the new man which is renewed in knowledge after the image of him that created him" (Colossians 3:5-25, especially verse 10; cf. Ephesians 4:17-32). But the full implications of the image of God are realized in the Christian only progressively (2 Corinthians 3:18) and will be consummated only at the resurrection (1 John 3:2)[34] Clines' summary is a fitting conclusion to this' part of the discussion on the image of God in the New Testament. He writes,

> In Christ man sees what manhood was meant to be. In the Old Testament, all men are the image of God; in the New, where Christ is the one true image, men are image of God in so far as they are like Christ. The image is fully realized only through obedience to Christ; this is how man, the image of God, who is already man, already the image of God, can become fully man, fully the image of God.[35]

The Holistic View of Man

Much of recent study on biblical anthropology has sought to delineate the distinguishing features of the Greek and Judeo-Christian conceptions of man. Such distinctions are important because Western views of man generally have their roots in the Greek tradition. Christian theology has a long history since the early church fathers of appropriating biblical statements about man and filling them with Greek meanings.[36]

The Greek view of man from the sixth century B.C. onward may be designated as dualistic in nature.[37] Following Orphism Greek religion and philosophy were generally characterized by a body-soul dualism in which the highest state of man is achieved when the soul is finally liberated from matter to take up a purely spiritual existence or be merged into the prime substance of the universe. In this life the two components of man's nature are in necessary tension and conflict with each other. According to the Pythagoreans, the soul never established interdependent relations with the body, and lost nothing when it left the body. For Plato, the soul is immortal, indestructible and pre-existent I to the body. Its destiny, after many reincarnations, is re-absorption into the transcendental world of Ideas. In the Stoic view, the human soul is a spark of the divine soul with which it will merge again at death.

The Hebrew conception of man, by contrast, may be designated as an unitary view.[38] Man is a psychophysical unity who is less than man when this unity is dissolved by death. The various parts of man are not antithetical to each other—as in dualism—but are regarded as aspects of one personality. It is characteristic of Hebrew thought that it conceptualizes things in their totality. It is thus synthetic and existential rather than analytical and speculative. The Hebrew mind was generally unable to imagine physical and metaphysical functions in isolation. The whole man was regarded as involved in each function and there were no sharp distinctions between the emotional, the spiritual, the rational and the physical.[39]

Therefore, careful delineations and definitions of the components of human nature are lacking in the Old Testament because the Hebrews did not view man in this manner. For this reason, most discussions on the trichotomous versus the dichotomous natures of man are out of order because they are attempts to address questions arising out of a Greek conception of man to a view of man, which is essentially different.[40]

The unitary view of man is seen particularly in the fact that both the physical and psychological components of man's nature are identified with psychical functions. As W. D. Stacey has indicated:

> The Hebrew regarded the soul as almost physical and the physical parts as having psychical functions, so that, whatever activity a man was engaged in, the predominant aspect, be it soul, heart, face or hand, represented the whole person and included the other aspects.[41]

This interrelatedness can be illustrated by a study of the words "soul" and "spirit" in the Bible. The soul is designated as the vital principle of life in Genesis 2:7. This same function, however, is attributed to the spirit in Genesis 7:22, Job 27:3, Isaiah 42:5 and James 2:26. The emotions of anguish, distress, sorrow, anger and grief are ascribed both to the soul (Genesis 42:21, 1 Samuel 1:10, Psalm 6:3f., Jeremiah 18:25) and to the spirit (Genesis 26:35, 41:8, Judges 8:3, Job 7:11, Proverbs 16:32, Matthew 26:38, John 11:33). Rational functions are associated both with the soul (Psalm 139:14, Proverbs 19:2, 23:7, 24:14) and with the spirit (Exodus 28:3, Deuteronomy 34:9). The same is true of volitional functions in Deuteronomy 21:14, Exodus 35:21 and Matthew 26:41. Death can be described either as a departure of the soul (Genesis 35:18, Numbers 23:10, Luke 12:20, Acts 20:10) or of the spirit (Psalm 78:39, 104:29, Matthew 27:50, Luke 23:46, John 19:30, Acts 7:59, 1 Peter 3:19). The soul and spirit are paralleled in their experience of anguish and bitterness in Job 8:11 and yearning for God in Isaiah 26:9.

The integrative nature of biblical anthropology is seen even more clearly in instances when psychical functions are ascribed to the body. The bones may stand for the entire person (Isaiah 66:14) and may experience fear (Jeremiah 23:9), anguish (Psalm 6:2f.), impatience (Jeremiah 20:9), and envy (Proverbs 14:30). They are mentioned in parallelism with the soul in giving thanks to God (Psalm 35:9f.). The heart manifests joy (Judges 18:20), grief (1 Samuel 1:8), anger (Deuteronomy 19:6), hatred (Leviticus 19:17), envy (Proverbs 23:17), and courage (Psalm 27:3). The heart is connected with the will (1 Samuel 2:35, 2 Kings 12:5, Jeremiah 7:31), and with ethical judgments (Isaiah 6:10, Psalm 24:4). The bowels and inward parts are related to various emotional and rational activities (Isaiah 16:11, 63:15, Jeremiah 31:20, Proverbs 14:33, 22:18, Psalm 103:1, Job 20:20,23).[42]

The New Testament view of man is deeply rooted in the Old Testament rather than in Hellenism, and reflects this same unitary view of man.[43] New Testament authors, and particularly Paul, elaborate and expand the Old Testament anthropological terms,[44] but their thought remains in essential continuity with Old Testament anthropology.

Any study of the nature of man in the Bible must therefore first recognize the fundamental unity of that nature and the holistic character of Hebrew anthropology. Descriptions of the qualities and characteristics of the various aspects of man are functional descriptions rather than analytical definitions. Even here there is a wide overlapping of functions so that we can observe only major tendencies to identify a given psychical function with a particular aspect of man's nature, knowing all the while that this same function is commonly elsewhere associated with another side of man's nature.

Original Sin In The Biblical Perspective

The Christian doctrine of original sin involves three elements: 1) the recognition that sin is more than an act but that it is also a matter of the heart and inner life of man; 2) an apprehension of sin as a universal condition affecting all mankind; 3) the positing of a causal connection between the sin of Adam and the sinful condition of the race.

The Old Testament is already aware, of the distortion in human nature caused by sin. The connection between sinful acts and the condition of the heart is stated in the divine judgment pronounced on human nature in Genesis 6:5:

> The Lord saw that the wickedness of man was great in the earth, and that every imagination of the thoughts of his heart was only evil continually.

Lest we conclude that this description fitted only Noah's generation, it is reiterated again in Genesis 8:21 as a general statement about mankind. According to Eichrodt, these verses point to an "...inner proclivity toward evil as deep-rooted condition of man...," to "...the evil character of human nature...", and to "...the sinful quality attaching to human nature in general as confirmed by the word of God himself."[45]

Jeremiah concludes that, "the heart is deceitful above all things, and desperately corrupt; who can understand it?" (Jeremiah 17:9). This condition of human nature is traced back to man's youth in Genesis 8:21, to his birth in Psalm 58:3, to the prenatal state and to the moment of conception in Psalm 51:5 where the Psalmist exclaims, "Behold I was brought forth in iniquity, and in sin did my mother conceive me." Again, Eichrodt comments:

> This sin is not a matter of occasional deviation from the right way, but of the consistent outcome of the natural tendency of his being, which is already planted in him by the inheritance passed on to him at his birth.[46]

For the prophets, the hearts of the people were so corrupted and enslaved by sin the only remedy was the creation of a new heart in the eschatological age (Ezekiel 11:19, 36:26; cf. Jeremiah 24:7; cf. Psalm 51:10).

Another line of Old Testament thought speaks of the universality of sin in human experience. The Psalmist said,

> The Lord looks down from heaven upon the children of men, to see if there are any that act wisely, that seek after God. They have all gone astray, they are all alike corrupt; there is none that does good, no, not one (Psalm 14:2-3).

This passage was later quoted by Paul (Romans 3:10-12) as the scriptural proof for the universal extent of sin. The author of I Kings 8:46 observed parenthetically, "...there is no man who does not sin..." According to Proverbs 20:9 and Ecclesiastes 7:20, no man can claim that he is without sin. The guilt of all men before God is further affirmed by Psalms 130:3 and 143:2. F. R. Tennant concluded that:

> Such passages supply abundant evidence that, before the later Old Testament books were written, there was a deep sense among the Hebrews of sin as both absolutely universal in the race and all pervading in the individual's human nature.[47]

The causal connection between the sin of Adam and the sinful condition of mankind is more difficult to establish on the basis of the Old Testament alone. Authorities who approach the Old Testament on a purely History of Religions basis are generally skeptical about such a connection. These scholars point out that though the narrative of Genesis 2-3 is alluded to at several later points,[48] the rest of the Old Testament makes no explicit attempt to connect the sinful situation of the race with the sin of Adam as the primal cause. Adam is mentioned only as a bad example in Job 31:33[49] but is not understood as the originating cause of human sin.[50] On the other hand, Old Testament scholars who, in addition to carrying out a History of Religions analysis, also contend for the revelational character of the Old Testament, often insist that the causal connection is the intent of the Genesis narrative and that this is implicit in much of the subsequent discussion of sin in the Old Testament. Thus

Eichrodt, for instance, is of the opinion that the narrative in Genesis 2-3 was intended by the author to be more than an account of the historical beginnings of sin in human history, but that Adam is there primarily understood as the cause of sin in his descendants. This is borne out by the close connection between Genesis 2-3, 6:5 and 8:21. Furthermore, later discussions of sin are said to "echo" and "have spiritual affinity" with Genesis 3 "...whether the worshipper himself was conscious of this at the time or not."[51] It is probably best, however, with Th. C. Vriezen, to regard the Old Testament doctrine of original sin as developing gradually across Old Testament religious history, a development brought to full expression in the New Testament, particularly in Paul.[52] A proper understanding of progressive revelation does not demand that the full form of a New Testament doctrine be completely expressed in each part of the Old Testament. The understanding of original sin in the Jewish inter-testamental writings represents reflection based on the Old Testament scriptures.[53] A causal connection between the sinful predicament of the race and the primal sin of the first parents developed gradually from the book of Ecclesiasticus (ca. 180 B.C.) and attained its fullest statement in the last quarter of the first century A.D. in the books of 4 Ezra and Syriac Baruch. In Ecclesiasticus 25:34, it is said, "From a woman was the beginning of sin, and because of her we all die." The causal connection becomes more obvious in Slavonic Enoch, Chapter 40 (ca. first quarter of the first century A.D.), the apocalyptist had a vision of hell and remarked, "I saw our forefathers from the beginning with Adam and Eve, and I sighed and wept and spake of the ruin *caused* by their wickedness."

In 4 Ezra 7:119 (ca. the last quarter of the first century A.D.), the author laments,

> O thou Adam, what hast thou done! For though it was thou that sinned, the fall was not thine alone, but ours also who are thy descendants!

According to 4 Ezra 3:21, it was not only Adam who transgressed and was overcome by sin, but also all who were born from him. It is added in 4:30-32 that present human evil is the outgrowth of an evil seed, which was first planted in the heart of Adam. It is clear from 4 Ezra that Adam involved the race in sin and that his descendants have been overcome by sin and an evil heart because of his deed.

Both 4 Ezra and Syriac Baruch wrestle with the problem of determinism in connection with the doctrine of original sin. Syriac Baruch 54:15-19, states initially, "...Adam first sinned and brought untimely death upon all "...But the author wants to avoid determinism and to make a place for individual freedom and responsibility. He thus adds immediately,

> Yet those who were born from him, each one of them, has prepared for his own soul torment to come; and again each one of them has chosen for himself glories to come. Adam is, therefore, not the cause save only of his own soul, but each of us has been the Adam of his own soul.

Fourth Ezra 7:127-129 and 8:56 follows the same course. Human freedom and individual responsibility are asserted over against the doctrine of original sin with little attempt to resolve the tension. Adam is viewed as the originating cause of sin in human experience, but each man is made responsible for his own sin.

A second Jewish tradition dealing with the origin and nature of sin—especially significant for Pauline theology—is the rabbinic doctrine of the *yetzer hara*, or "evil inclination." The doctrine has its biblical basis in the Hebrew of Genesis 6:5 and 8:21 where the word for "imagination" of the heart of man is *yetzer*. The earliest inter-testamental reference to the *yetzer hara* is in Ecclesiasticus 15:11-14 (ca. 180 B.C.) where man's sin is traced to his *yetzer*. The later rabbinic doctrine elaborates this earlier passage.

W. D. Davies[54] has summarized the rabbinic teaching under six points, the essentials of which include the following emphases:

1) The locale of the *yetzer* is the heart, by which is understood the intellectual and volitional elements in man.
2) The evil *yetzer* motivates man to all kinds of sins but particularly to unchastity and idolatry.
3) God is said to be the origin of the *yetzer* but not of its evil. It was originally the divinely given impulse in human life toward self-preservation and propagation, which was subverted and enslaved by the fall.
4) The evil *yetzer* was always with man and could be held under control by reading of the Torah or by uttering an oath in the name of the Lord, but man could never be freed from it in this life.
5) But in the eschatological Age to Come, the evil *yetzer* would be slain and man would be freed from its power forever.
6) Most of the rabbis held that the evil *yetzer* entered man at birth, or before birth, but it was not until the age of thirteen, when a young man became a son of the covenant, that the struggle with the *yetzer* began.

The New Testament writers take for granted the Old Testament teaching on the corrupting effect an universal extent of sin.[55] But it is the Apostle Paul who develops the idea of original sin most fully in the New Testament. The *locus classicus* for the doctrine is found in Romans 5:12-21. It must be kept in mind, however, in approaching the passage that it is part of a larger context extending from Romans 5 through 8 and is related to the larger themes of justification and sanctification, which are treated there. Paul does not here attempt to develop an exhaustive and systematic treatment of original sin. He is content merely to affirm that the present experiences of sin and death have their historical origin and cause in the sin of the first man. Throughout, his larger concern is to magnify the comprehensiveness of the work of Christ, over against whom Adam is placed in antithesis.

The limits of this study exclude any treatment or evaluation of the various interpretations of the Romans 5 passage, which have been advanced in the history of the church.[56] The tendency has been to raise more questions than Paul answered here and to answer questions, which Paul probably never had in mind when he wrote the passage. The Apostle does not make clear in what sense Adam acted for his descendants, or, vice-versa, how his posterity was involved in his original act of sin. Nor does he specify clearly how sin and death are transmitted to each generation from the original parents.

Our concern at this point must be limited to the more obvious content of the passage. The causal connection[57] between the sin of Adam and the sin of mankind is stated by Paul in 5:12 as an axiom, which needs no further proof. The sin of the first man had three results for his descendants: the race became enslaved to sin (5:12,19), it was made subject to death (5:12,14, 15, 17, 21), and it passed under divine judgment and condemnation (5:16, 18). As such, the family headed by Adam became the old creation, which is characterized by sin and death, and stands in contrast to the new family headed by Christ, which is characterized by righteousness and life (Ephesians 4:22-24; Colossians 3:9f.; Galatians 6:15; 2 Corinthians 5:17).[58]

In Romans 5, Paul discusses the problems of sin and death as a matter of history and in their collective aspects with reference to the race as a whole. In Romans 7, he discusses what it means to the individual to be under the powers of sin and death. Romans 5 thus treats original sin from the historical and racial perspectives, while Romans 7 approaches the same theme in terms of the personal and psychological aspects of original sin.[59]

It should be stated at the outset that Paul does not suggest that the sin of Adam injected some substantive virus into each of his descendants, which was absent before the fall, but was added afterward as a biological impulse to sin. This is not what it means to be "carnal" (*sarkinos*, v. 14). Such a view would involve a metaphysical dualism whereby the body is regarded as inherently evil, an unacceptable idea to a Hebrew who believed that God was the Creator of all material being.[60] The "principle of sin" (v. 25)[61] at work in the flesh is not understood by Paul in such a crassly materialistic fashion.

But neither is the language of deprivation adequate to understand Romans 7. Paul has in mind more than a loss of fellowship with God and the disintegration of a relationship. The rabbinic doctrine of the *yetzer hara* is here appropriated and adapted by Paul to speak of the power of sin in human life.[62] He understands that a dynamic force of sin has taken up residence in fallen human personality and operates to bring the total man under its control. Throughout the passage, sin is regarded as an immanent power, sharply distinguished from the individual in whom it dwells, but nonetheless subjectively present, dominating the life and holding it in bondage.[63] Notice in Paul's language how the dynamic force of sin is carefully distinguished from the self at the same time that it wages a successful battle against and within the self:

> But sin...wrought in me all kinds of covetousness (7:8). For sin...deceived me and...killed me (7:11). It was sin working death in me...(7:13). So then it is no longer I that do it, but sin, which dwells within me (7:17, 20).

But I see in my members another law at war with the law of my mind and making me captive to the law of sin, which dwells in my members (7:23) immediate sphere of this "principle of sin" is the flesh, or, synonymously, the "members" of the body. Besides its reference to the physical substance of which man is made, the word "flesh" is also used in both Testaments to denote man in his creaturely weakness.[64] Paul uses the word "flesh" both in a morally neutral and in a morally bad sense. In the latter instance, there is an almost automatic association of flesh with sin. Sin for him is a "quasi-personal power"[65] which sets up its base of operation in the weakest part of man's nature and from that base it spreads its control to all parts of man's being. W. D. Stacey's description of this process is worth noting:

> In it [Romans 7] sin is the active power, the flesh is passive. Sin aims at subduing the entire man and the flesh is the element most easily corrupted. Sin and the flesh are thus differentiated, the former being dynamic and corrupting, the latter being passive and corrupted...Sin, residing in the flesh, sets up a war against man's better nature (Romans 7:23). Man's natural desires are no longer the morally indifferent expressions of the will to live, they become sinful and rebellious, and they alienate the man from God and envelop him in spiritual death.[66]

The principle of sin then is not fundamentally some impulse, biological or psychological, which belongs essentially to fallen human nature, but rather is a spiritual dynamic, alien and distinct from human nature at the same time that it is immanently present within human nature. The operation and function of this spiritual dynamic is to enslave and condition the biological and psychological drives of human life in the service of sin.

Just as Christ and Adam are paralleled in Romans 5, two spiritual dynamics are juxtaposed in Romans 7 and 8 and set in antithesis to each other. To be in Adam is to be indwelt by the power of sin and bound by death; to be in Christ is to be indwelt by the power of the Holy Spirit and set free for life. This indicative becomes the basis for the imperative to holy, spirit-filled living. The rabbinic expectation that the *yetzer hara* would be destroyed in the Messianic Age has become a reality for Paul, because to him the Christ-event signaled the turn of the ages and the dawning of the new creation.[67] This in turn accounts for the radical death and liberation language which he uses with reference to original sin and all that belongs to the old creation (Romans 6:1-11, especially verse 6; 8:2, 10. 12, 13, 15, etc.)

But that is the subject for a later essay in this series, so this discussion must be terminated at this point.

Conclusion

Reinhold Niebuhr has observed that "the Christian view of human nature is involved in the paradox of claiming a higher stature for man and of taking a more serious view of evil than other anthropology. "[68] The assertion that man bears the image of God is to affirm his uniqueness with reference to the sphere of nature. Man does not find his destiny by total identification with nature as the most intelligent of animals. There is that within him, which seeks to transcend, his world and which orients him toward his Creator.[69] Man's destiny in the world is only realized as he responds to the call of God in loving obedience and responsibility.

But the Scriptures tell us that this is precisely what man has failed to do. He refuses to acknowledge his creatureliness and attempts to set himself in the place of God. He wants to look to himself as the source of his life and personal security. But he is constantly brought under bondage to the very sphere of nature, which he has attempted to control from himself, and loses his true identity and selfhood in the process.[70] This is the meaning of sin, and it is to this paradoxical situation that the biblical message of salvation is addressed.

Notes

[1] Helpful studies in this connection include: A. R. Johnson, *The Vitality of the Individual in the Thought of Ancient Israel* (Cardiff: University of Wales Press, 1949); H. Wheeler Robinson, *The Christian Doctrine of Man* (Edinburgh: T. and T. Clark, 1947 reprint); C. Ryder Smith, *The Bible Doctrine of Man* (London: Epworth Press, 1951); W. D. Stacey, *The Pauline View of Man* (London: Macmillan and Co., 1956); Robert Jewett, *Paul's Anthropological Terms* (Leiden: E. J. Brill, 1971); W. G. Kűmmel, *Man in the New Testament* (London: Epworth Press, 1963).

[2] See Stefan Porubcan, *Sin in the Old Testament* (Rome: Herder, 1963); C. Ryder Smith, *The Bible Doctrine of Sin* (London: Epworth Press, 1953). Most of the standard Old and New Testament theologies also have sections on the theme.

[3] Jean R. Zurcher, "The Christian View of Man: I," *Andrews Seminary Studies*, 2 (1964), 157; Choan-Seng Song, "Man and the Redemption of the World," *Southeast Asia Journal of Theology*, 2 (4, 1961), 64f.; W. R. Nelson, "Pauline Anthropology: Its Relation to Christ and His Church," *Interpretation*, 14 (1960), 14ff; Otto A. Piper, "The Biblical Understanding of Man," *Theology Today*, 1 (1944), 191.

[4] Karl Barth, *Church Dogmatics* (Edinburgh: T. and T. Clark, 1958), III/I, 192f.; cf. also K. L. Schmidt, "'Homo Imago Dei' im alten und neuen Testament," *Eranos-Jahrbuch*, 15 (1947/48), 158-162.

[5] R. G. Crawford, "The Image of God," *Expository Times*, 77 (1966), 233f.

[6] James Barr, "The Image of God in the Book of Genesis," *Bulletin of the John Rylands Library*, 51 (1968), 12.

[7] D. J. A. Clines, "The Image of God in Man," *Tyndale Bulletin*, 19 (1968), 57f.

[8] Reinhold Niebuhr, *The Nature and Destiny of Man* (New York: Charles/ Scribner's Sons, 1943), 49, 152-161. This tendency is already observable, however, in the inter-testamental Hellenistic-Jewish book of Wisdom 2:23.

[9] Barth, ibid., 184f., 195f., 199.

[10] Emil Brunner, *Man in Revolt* (Philadelphia: Westminster Press, 1947), 102-105.

[11] Clines, ibid., 54-61. Clines' presentation is a summary of a survey by J. J. Stamm, "Die Imago-Lehre von Karl Barth und die altestamentliche Wissenschsft," in *Antwert. Festschrift für Karl Barth*, ed. by E. Wolf *et. al.* (Zelliken-Zurich: Evangelischer Verlag, 1956), 84-98.

[12] Clines, ibid., 55f.

[13] Walther Eichrodt, *Theology of the Old Testament* (London: SCM Press, 1967). II, 122.

[14] H. Wheeler Robinson, "Hebrew Psychology," in *The People and the Book*, ed. by A. S. Peake (Oxford: Clarendon Press, 1925), 369.

[15] Of the several Hebrew words which could have been used to convey the idea intended in the Genesis 1:26f passage, Barr, "Image of God," 15-24, has shown that ṣelem and deuth had less provocative associations with idolatry and were least offensive to the belief in the uniqueness of God.

[16] On this basis, Friedrich Horst has suggested that the references to man as "image" and "likeness" of God implies in turn that God is the "prototype" and "original." See his "Face to Face. The Biblical Doctrine of the Image of God," *Interpretation* 4 (1950), 259-277.

[17] Those who interpret the image of God to have reference to man's upright posture or physical form generally see some connection between the Old Testament and the larger Ancient Near Eastern view. Cf. Clines, "Image of God," 56-59, 70-73, and the bibliography there.

[18] Clines, ibid., 70f.; cf. Th. C. Vriezen, *An Outline of Old Testament Theology* (Newton, Massachusetts: Charles T. Bradford Co., 1970), 319-323.

[19] See von Rad's essay in the *Theological Dictionary of the New Testament*, ed. by Gerhard Kittel (Grand Rapids: Wm. B. Eerdmans Publishing Co., 1964), II, 390. Cf. Horst, op. cit., 261, and Barr, "Image of God," 24. The disclaimer by Clines, op. cit., 91f., in this connection, however, suggests some caution along this line of interpretation.

[20] Cf. pp. 11 below.

[21] Clines, op. cit., 57, 79, 87, 101; cf. von Rad, *TDNT*, II, 391.

[22] Clines, op. cit., 83ff., 92-95.

[23] On Barth's view that the image of God is found fundamentally in the man-woman relationship, see his *Church Dogmatics*, III/1, 184f., 195f., 199.

[24] Clines, op. cit., 60, 94f.; Vriezen, *Old Testament Theology*, 170f., 387-390, 398f.; Eichrodt, Theology of the Old Testament, I, 140, II, 318f.

[25] Clines, ibid., 53f.; Horst, "Face to Face," 266f.

[26] Eichrodt, *Theology of the Old Testament*, II, l29f.; Barr, "Image of God," 25f.; Clines, ibid., 101.

[27] Crawford, "Image of God," cites J. K. S. Reid's *Our Life in Christ* (London: SCM Press, 1963), in this connection.

[28] Horst, "Face to Face," 262.

[29] Clines, "Image of God," 97; cf. P. C. Craigie, "Hebrew Thought About God and Nature and Its Contemporary Significance," *Canadian Journal of Theology*, 16 (1970), 6.

[30] Clines, "Image of God," 83f., 87-92; cf. Jean R. Zurcher, "The Christian View of Man: II," *Andrews Seminary Studies*, 3 (1,965), 71f.; Kleinknecht, *TDNT*, II, 389f.

[31] Clines, "Image of God," 70-80. It is the difference between the *beth essentiae* and the normative *beth* in Hebrew. It should be pointed out, however, that most Old Testament interpreters opt for the narrative *beth* excluded under either interpretation, but it is strengthened if the preposition is regarded as a *beth essentiae*.

[32] Clines, "Image of God," 88, 92.

[33] This accounts for the common occurrence of the themes of darkness, old creation, light, glory, knowledge, understanding and seeing in close proximity to the image theme in the New Testament, cf. 2 Corinthians 4:4, Colossians 1:9-15, 3:5-11, Hebrews 1:3.

[34] Horst, "Face to Face," 269f.; Clines, "Image of God," 101f.

[35] Clines, "Image of God," 103; cf. Kittel, *TDNT*, 395f.

[36] Samuel Laeuchli, "Monism and Dualism in the Pauline Anthropology," *Biblical Research* 3 (1958), 15f.; Piper, "Biblical Understanding of Man," 190; Niebuhr, *Nature and Destiny of Man*, 4-12.

[37] A convenient survey of the Greek understanding of man has been written by W. D. Stacey, "The Greek View of Man," in his *Pauline View of Man*, 59-81.

[38] The adjective "unitary" is preferable to the term "monistic" which has been used by several recent authors who seem to think that the proper alternative to dualism is monism when describing the biblical view of man. The word "unitary" signifies that man is composed of more than one entity but that these separate entities intercohere in the one reality of man. The term "monistic" more properly fits the modern empirical view of man in which man is regarded as composed of only one substance, matter, and in which such words as "spirit," "soul," "mind," and "conscience" are poetic word-symbols describing brain and nerve cell activities or glandular functions.

[39] A. R. Johnson, *Vitality of the Individual*, 7f.; cf. Stacey, *Pauline View of Man*, 85, 87.

[40] Eichrodt, Theology of the Old Testament, I, 148f.; Vriezen, Old Testament Theology, 407f.

[41] Stacey, *Pauline View of Man*, 85, cf. 88-95.

[42] H. Wheeler Robinson, "Hebrew Psychology," 353; Stacey, op. cit., 91-95.

[43] W. G. Kűmmel, *Man in the New Testament*, 83; cf. D. E. H. Whiteley. *The Theology of St. Paul* (Philadelphia: Fortress Press, 1964), 37f.

[44] E.g., Paul's use of the word *nous* to denote functions of the heart (*leb*) in the Old Testament, cf. Stacey, *Pauline View of Man*, 196f., 198-205.

[45] Eichrodt, Theology of the Old Testament, II, 389, 407, 396.

[46] Eichrodt, ib.d., 410.

[47] F. R. Tennant, *The Sources of the Doctrines of the Fall and Original Sin* (New York: Schecken Books, 1968 reprint of 1903 ed.), 104.

[48] Gen. 5:29, Isaiah 65:25, Job 10:9, 34:14f., Psalms 104:29f., 146:4, Ecc. 12:7, Proverbs 3:18, 11:20, 13:12,14; Gen. 13:10, Isaiah 51:3, Ezekiel 28: 13-15, 31:7-9, 16-18, 36:25.

[49] Possibly also in Hosea 6:6, depending on the translation of *adam* as a proper name or as a generic reference to mankind.

[50] Cf. H. Wheeler Robinson, The Christian Doctrine of Man, 58-60; F. R. Tennant, Sources, 89-94, 100, 104; N. P Williams, The Ideas of the Fall and of Original Sin (London: Longmans, Green and Co., 1927), 12-20. It is interesting in the connection that although there is a highly developed conception of social solidarity in the Old Testament whereby guilt and punishment for the sins of kings, clan heads, and fathers are visited on their nations, clans, and families, there is no explicit attempt in the Old Testament to connect the sin of Adam with the guilt and punishment of the race. Cf. Stefan Porubcan, Sin in the Old Testament, 383-399.

[51] Eichrodt, *Theology of the Old Testament*, II, 406f., 409, 411.

[52] Vriezen, *Old Testament Theology*, 415f.; cf. W. B. Neenan, "The Doctrine of Original Sin in the Scripture," *Irish Theological Quarterly*, 28 (1961), 55.

[53] For surveys on the Jewish doctrine of original sin from 200 B.C. to 100 A.D., see Tennant, *Sources*, 106-247, Williams, *Fall*, 15-91, Smith, *Doctrine of Sin*, 59-113.

[54] W. D. Davies, *Paul and Rabbinic Judaism* (New York: Harper and Row, 1948), 21-23.

[55] Tennant, *Sources*, 248; Smith, *Doctrine of Sin*, 159-169; Kűmmel, *Man in the New Testament*, 18-34.

[56] A survey of the various interpretations may be found in J. P. Lange, *The Epistle of Paul to the Romans* (New York: Charles Scribner's Sons, 1869), 191-197

[57] Davies, Paul and Rabbinic Judaism, 31f., n. 3.

[58] Alan Richardson, *The Theology of the New Testament* (New York: Harper and Row, 1958), 242-249.

[59] Tennant, *Sources*, 252.

[60] Whiteley, Theology of St. Paul, 37.

[61] There is general agreement that *nomos* here has no reference to the law of Moses, but means "principle," "norm," or "constraint." Cf. Rudolf Bultmann, *Theology of the New Testament* (New York: Charles Scribner's Sons, 1951), I, 259; W. F. Arndt and F. W. Gingrich, *A Greek-English Lexicon of the New Testament* (Cambridge: University Press, 1957), 554, col. 1.

[62] Davies, Paul and Rabbinic Judaism, 23-27

[63] Tennant, *Sources*, 268.

[64] Stacey, *Pauline View of Man*, 93, 157f.

[65] H. H. A. Kennedy, *The Theology of the Epistles* (New York: Charles Scribner's Sons, 1920), 33.

[66] Stacey, op. cit., 162f.

[67] Davies, Paul and Rabbinic Judaism, 30f.

[68] Niebuhr, Nature and Destiny of Man, 18.

[69] Wolfhart Pannenberg, *What is Man?* (Philadelphia: Fortress Press, 1970), 1-13; Niebuhr, op. cit., 14f.

[70] Niebuhr, op. cit., 16f,; Pannenberg, op. cit., 28-40.

Works Cited

Arndt, W. F. and Gingrich, F. W. *A Greek-English Lexicon of the New Testament* (Cambridge: University Press, 1957).

Barth, Karl. *Church Dogmatics* (Edinburgh: T. and T. Clark, 1958).

Barr, James. "The Image of God in the Book of Genesis," Bulletin of the John Rylands Library, 51 (1968).

Brunner, Emil. *Man in Revolt* (Philadelphia: Westminster Press, 1947).

Bultmann, Rudolf. *Theology of the New Testament* (New York: Charles Scribner's Sons, 1951).

Clines, D. J. A. "The Image of God in Man," Tyndale Bulletin, 19 (1968).

Craigie, P. C. "Hebrew Thought About God and Nature and Its Contemporary Significance," Canadian Journal of Theology, 16 (1970).

Crawford, R. G. "The Image of God," Expository Times, 77 (1966).

Davies, W. D. *Paul and Rabbinic Judaism* (New York: Harper and Row, 1948).

Eichrodt, Walther. *Theology of the Old Testament* (London: SCM Press, 1967).

Horst, Friedrich. "Face to Face. The Biblical Doctrine of the Image of God," Interpretation 4 (1950).

Jewett, Robert. *Paul's Anthropological Terms* (Leiden: E. J. Brill, 1971).

Johnson, A. R. *The Vitality of the Individual in the Thought of Ancient Israel* (Cardiff: University of Wales Press, 1949).

Kennedy, H. H. A. *The Theology of the Epistles* (New York: Charles Scribner's Sons, 1920).

Kűmmel, W. G. *Man in the New Testament* (London: Epworth Press, 1963).

Laeuchli, Samuel. "Monism and Dualism in the Pauline Anthropology," Biblical Research 3 (1958).

Lange, J. P. *The Epistle of Paul to the Romans* (New York: Charles Scribner's Sons, 1869).

Neenan, W. B. "The Doctrine of Original Sin in the Scripture," Irish Theological Quarterly, 28 (1961).

Nelson, W. R. "Pauline Anthropology: Its Relation to Christ and His Church," Interpretation, 14 (1960).

Pannenberg, Wolfhart. *What is Man?* (Philadelphia: Fortress Press, 1970).

Piper, Otto A. "The Biblical Understanding of Man," Theology Today, 1 (1944).

Porubcan, Stefan. *Sin in the Old Testament* (Rome: Herder, 1963).

Reid, J. K. S. *Our Life in Christ* (London: SCM Press, 1963).

Richardson, Alan. *The Theology of the New Testament* (New York: Harper and Row, 1958).

Robinson, H. Wheeler. *The Christian Doctrine of Man* (Edinburgh: T. and T. Clark, 1947 reprint).

_____. "Hebrew Psychology," in The People and the Book, ed. by A. S. Peake (Oxford: Clarendon Press, 1925).

Schmidt, K. L. "'Homo Imago Dei' im alten und neuen Testament," Eranos-Jahrbuch, 15 (1947/48).

Smith, C. Ryder. *The Bible Doctrine of Man* (London: Epworth Press, 1951).

_____. *The Bible Doctrine of Sin* (London: Epworth Press, 1953).

Song, Choan-Seng. "Man and the Redemption of the World," Southeast Asia Journal of Theology, 2 (4, 1961).

Stacey, W. D. *The Pauline View of Man* (London: Macmillan and Co., 1956)

Tennant, F. R. *The Sources of the Doctrines of the Fall and Original Sin* (New York: Schecken Books, 1968 reprint of 1903 ed.).

Vriezen, Th. C. *An Outline of Old Testament Theology* (Newton, Massachusetts: Charles T. Bradford Co., 1970).

Whiteley, D. E. H. *The Theology of St. Paul* (Philadelphia: Fortress Press, 1964).

Williams, N. P. *The Ideas of the Fall and of Original Sin* (London: Longmans, Green and Co., 1927.

Zurcher, Jean R. "The Christian View of Man: I," Andrews Seminary Studies, 2 (1964).

_____. "The Christian View of Man: II," Andrews Seminary Studies, 3 (1,965).

The Person and Work of Jesus Christ

Robert W. Lyon
October 24, 1973

Introduction

An essay about Jesus Christ is an essay on Christology and so must begin with a definition: does Christology consider only the person of Christ and leave the work of Christ to be treated under Soteriology, as R. H. Fuller suggests?[1] Or does Christology involve both the person and work of Christ, as Cullmann assumes?[2] Because it is virtually impossible to discuss the person of Christ without discussing his work, and because the early Church for the most part approaches the person of Christ through and in terms of his work, we find the approach of Cullmann much to be preferred—indeed inescapable. But the definition of Christology is not so easily solved, for in a theologically significant sense Christology should include not only what he has done, but what he is doing *now* in the Church through the Spirit and what he *will do* when he comes again. Any full statement of the "work of Christ" ought, therefore, to include the past (i.e., the "historical" Jesus), the present, and the future.

As to sources we may confine ourselves to the New Testament canon since extra-biblical sources add almost nothing to our knowledge, are almost all later than the New Testament documents, and, whether orthodox or otherwise, theologically tendentious.[3]

As sources the New Testament documents give us the primitive account of the ministry of Jesus and the apostolic response. They contain both *description* of the Word become flesh and *interpretation* of the meaning and significance of the event. This twofold reference to the New Testament documents as description and interpretation brings us to the heart of our understanding of the New Testament as an inter weaving of event and response. It is the New Testament of Jesus Christ in that from beginning to end it is the result of his ministry and word. We find not only the story of Jesus but also how the significance of that story was shared with varied audiences and how it addressed various issues. Any essay must preserve and relate this richness and diversity of the biblical witness.

At this point it is necessary to set forth very briefly some concerns and convictions, which determine the character of the rest of this essay. We need to assert at once the primacy of the ministry and message of Jesus in all theological reflection. Apostolic doctrine is not only subsequent to, but also subservient to, derived from, and dependent upon that ministry and message. Jesus as the Son and the Word of God (Hebrews 1:1ff; John 1:1) is he by whom all former Scripture and all subsequent apostolic doctrine are measured. His word and being determine how we shall approach all the biblical tradition. What we have in the New Testament are two events— the ministry of Jesus and the ministry of the primitive Church. The former is immediate, the latter mediate: that is, the latter grows out of the former and obtains its significance through the former. A survey of New Testament Christology must necessarily, therefore, give major emphasis to that first event. Otherwise we face the danger that the ministry of Jesus is viewed as only the originating impulse and so give the impression that the nature of Christianity was determined by the early theologians such as Paul, John, or Luke. Major epochs of church history have not avoided this pitfall.

We need to recognize at the same time that all the New Testament documents are post-Easter literature and grew out of the life and work of the Church. The gospels are not objective history, that is, written without bias. On the contrary they are evangelistic-apologetic-didactic. They give the story of an event told by those committed to it, who believe their own lives have been transformed by it, and told for the purpose of drawing others to faith in Christ. The gospels were written out of a passionate desire to make Jesus Christ known and to create a community, which fulfills his commission to it. In all four gospels the story is set forth not only to show how eye-witnesses recalled the events, but also in such a way and in such terms as to portray their own faith. They contain the faith of the community as well as the story of Jesus, a fact that needs to be kept in mind if the gospels are to be understood rightly and if we are to avoid falling for some modern false alternatives. The selection of material, its arrangement and, in part, its vocabulary belongs to the evangelists and to the early Church to meet its needs and serve its purpose.

At the same time the material is historical and, within limits, biographical in that it records what was said and what happened. The basic reliability of the material, the variations within it notwithstanding, is established by the fact that the early Church defined the nature of its faith on the basis of what happened. The historical basis of its message was Jesus and his word. The early Church knew that the historical roots of its *kerygma* were a basic asset in comparison with all contemporary religious propaganda. Even Judaism had become largely a-historical in its treatment of its traditions. But Christian faith was faith in Jesus Christ about whom they had reliable traditions. New congregations were formed and rooted in those traditions.

I. The Word Become Flesh

It is necessary at the outset to point out that a summary of the ministry and word of Jesus is not due to biographical interests, but is rooted in the fact that the story of Jesus is the proclamation of the early Church, that it informs us of the nature of biblical faith and thereby becomes the precipitant of faith. The story begets faith and *for this reason* it is set out again. We have little interest in a life of Jesus as such, but in what the early Church proclaimed, that is, the story of Jesus.

A capsule presentation of the ministry and word of Jesus is required also by the fact that Jesus is seen in Scripture as the subject of all Christian experience. He is Actor. He is not only the object of faith but also its subject. The Spirit is the Spirit of Jesus Christ whom Jesus sends and who mediates the work of Christ. Jesus is Lord, sovereign subject, and by virtue of his atonement all men stand before him. For this reason we are able to speak of "normative" Christian experience and question those so-called "movements of the Spirit" which appear to move independently of the Jesus tradition. This tradition is the primary means of telling us what faith and obedience involve. This tradition gives substance to Christian freedom.[4]

The Proclaimer. Two of the four evangelists begin their story with the birth of Jesus. Although the accounts differ considerably, both include features, which underscore their primitive and Semitic character. Both tell, for example, of the birth largely in terms of Jewish thought and forms. The narratives are unadorned, straightforward and restrained—with due allowance for the Lucan hymns. In neither account do we find any exaggeration or elaboration of the miraculous birth: in due course Mary, the virgin, gave birth to a child to whom the name Jesus was given. Both accounts relate the virgin birth to the work of Christ (Matthew 1:21; Luke 1:32) in redemption and it is this, which gives the virgin birth its significance. The circumstances of his birth point to his unique ministry as Messiah and Savior of the world. This is the consummate act of God (Hebrews 1:1ff). In that the transcendent God enters into human history to initiate that final work which will eventually bring about the redemption of all things. The virgin birth serves to underscore the decisive character of the work of Christ; that Is, it is a sign in that it directs proper attention to the One coming into the world. Though in the primitive Church the virgin birth did not bear the same importance as the resurrection, the evidence suggests that it was told as serious history, that it was known and received in Semitic and Hellenistic communities as the opening into the Christian Gospel. The church that ignores the virgin birth will sooner or later fail to recognize the ultimately decisive ministry of Jesus and find itself struggling to comprehend what is the substance of Christian proclamation and faith.[5]

The Beginning of Ministry. Little is said about the life of Jesus prior to his baptism by John when he was about thirty years old. And it is not for the Church to speculate (or preach) on these "hidden years." The goal of gospel research is not primarily biography, but a recalling and hearing again of that ministry and word to the end that men may believe. This is εὐαγγέλιον.

All four gospels agree that his ministry began at his baptism, which served as a sign of his solidarity with humanity and his commitment to the human predicament. We find no evidence to believe that Jesus came like others seeking repentance and forgiveness and that in the baptism "sensed" his call. His baptism at the hand of John creates a correspondence with the message and eschatological focus of John. At his baptism the Spirit comes "upon" or "into" him (cf. Mark 1:10, parr.); this too signifies what is taking place. The pouring out of the Spirit was to indicate the inauguration of the new age, which was to be the age of the Spirit. The reading of Isaiah 61 in the synagogue in Nazareth is seen by Jesus as an opportunity to define the character of his ministry. He is the eschatological messenger who is to fulfill the promise to the fathers (Luke 4:16ff). He casts out demons by the Spirit of God (Luke: finger of God) and this is ground for recognizing that the Kingdom has in fact come (Matthew 12:28). Thus equipped Jesus becomes the proclaimer of the new age for the people of God.

The ministry of Jesus is a combination of success and apparent failure, gladness and hostility. It takes place within the religious community, but also outside it. His disciples are never far away. In order to gain an adequate perspective we shall attempt to describe the word and ministry of Jesus as it related to the religious establishment, to the masses and finally to the disciples.

<u>Ministry to the Devout</u>. Our sources agree that Jesus taught in the synagogues,[6] that he raised questions of the Law and that people were often taken back by his authority and wisdom. In contrast to the Baptist, Jesus attempted to work within the establishment. Yet his ministry has a special thrust. Our gospels portray the leadership of synagogue and temple as

moribund, bound by its own traditions, in bondage to a repressive view of Scripture and lacking in any type of spontaneity by which care and love might be expressed. The harsh words of Jesus are always directed toward the religious leadership, not because they were a threat to him, but because they were leading the people into, rather than out of, bondage. By their traditions they had cancelled out the commandments of God (Mark 7:11), which even when held were given a rigid and narrow, rather than expansive, reference (Matthew 5:21-48). They were preoccupied with minutiae and neglected the weighty matters (Matthew 23.23). The *reductio ad absurdum* is to be found in the debates over the Sabbath, especially those involving healing miracles. The debates that followed these events reveal a distorted sense of values, which gave preference to the cult over against the Word of God and human compassion.

But we must note another issue raised by Jesus *vis a vis* the establishment. Not only was it largely oppressive and without compassion: it was also guilty of violation of the Old Testament revelation in terms of their view of God, the covenant and righteousness. The moments of pathos in his ministry are when he sees their resistance hardening. It is tragic when, as with the prophets, the Word of God is not heeded, but it is infinitely more painful when the elect miss the moment of fulfillment, because afterward all is darkness (Matthew 23:37ff; Luke 13:34ff; 19:41ff). In the end it is Jesus' independence of human tradition and his binding himself to the Father's will that brings about the concluding events. A caveat may not be out of order. When Jesus set himself against authorities, it was because they had set themselves against the purpose of God. His was no arbitrary independence. He stood by the common expressions of faith in his regular habits of prayer and attendance at the synagogue. He bore the burden of his people's sins from within the community. His was an identification with the nation, including its leaders. He did not think in terms of classes of men, but in terms of men before God.

Ministry to the Masses. The hostility toward Jesus on the part of the religious leadership was due in no small part to his willingness to relate to the outcasts of society. Perhaps the most distinctive feature of his ministry was his contact with the masses both outside and inside the religious institutions. His beatitudes are directed to the dispossessed. He gives time and support to the friendless. He refuses to discriminate when it comes to dispensing the Word of God and the offer of forgiveness. He is found in the home of tax collectors and sinners. He allows a prostitute to wash his feet. He alone hears the cries of the people and offers a blanket invitation.[7] His ministry is one of "release to captives" in the broadest sense.

Numerous parables reflect this aspect of his ministry— as e.g., the parable of the Pharisee and the Tax Collector, the rich man and Lazarus, the sheep and the goats, the prodigal son and the great banquet. Here we see his positive message: in the climactic Day of the Lord all men are encouraged to come and taste of the water of life freely. The great central fact is the free grace of God to all men. The banquet is ready and the call has gone out. The pious are not allowed to stand in the way or to preempt the best seats. The last are first; Lazarus has his place; the prostitute is set free. Zacchaeus is allowed to host the Son of Man. All traditional patterns of a stratified society are shattered in the presence of the Word. All prerogatives are overturned. The Word of God is a Word for all men, and no man regardless of office may impede its outward flow. Jesus marches on— creating hope, offering liberty, restoring sight, and preparing a people for the Father.

Ministry to the Disciples. There can be no doubt that a core of followers participated in Jesus' ministry. Luke refers to the sending out of seventy-two to proclaim the same message and to take part in the same healing ministry (10:1ff). But for the most part the traditions have in mind a group of twelve, who clearly play a special role. The synoptic tradition is not always clear in defining their relationship to Jesus— and even gives different names when listing them. Yet at the same time it is quite clear that Jesus gave himself to them in a special way. They accompanied him by special invitation; they "imitated" his ministry when they were sent out (Mark 6:7; Luke 9:1). They were given special instruction, undoubtedly for the time when he would not be with them. Some of the parables are interpreted privately to them— in spite of much recent criticism that regards this material as later and redactional.

They are disciples because he has called them, a clear distinction from the disciples of contemporary rabbis who attached themselves at their own initiative to the rabbi of their choice. Furthermore, the twelve were disciples by virtue of their participation with him in his ministry. They were an extension of his ministry at the same time they were learning from him.

In these three aspects of his ministry to the established religious community, to the masses and dispossessed and to the disciples we see the unfolding of the nature of the three traditional "offices" of prophet, priest and king.

The Consummation of Ministry. Though Jesus knows the nature of the consummation of his ministry, events begin to rush on with ever increasing speed. He is conscious that he must end his ministry in Jerusalem, and it is his decision to go to the sacred city that is the real beginning of his passion. There can be little doubt that the event, which precipitated his death, was the cleansing of the temple, an act that must have been especially appalling in view of the festive atmosphere. The die is now cast.

In recent times scholars have debated the nature of the final accusations against Jesus as well as the question of who was finally responsible for the execution. The variations in the narratives do not help. Some have argued that the charges against Jesus were political in view of his claims of kingship and authority; therefore he was removed by Roman authorities, though not without support from Jewish leaders. The argument from this view is that only Roman officials could carry out the death penalty. Some, on the other hand, have argued that Jesus was only a threat to the religious establishment and that the events leading to his death were staged by the Jewish hierarchy.[8] This latter view seems much to be preferred. His ministry was to the lost sheep of the house of Israel and it was this house that did him in. "He came to his own and his own people did not receive him." We have no clear evidence that Jesus was regarded as a menace to Roman authorities. Recent attempts to link him with zealot-type movements have failed to demonstrate their thesis.[9] Every stratum of the early tradition (Mark, M, Q, L, John, Paul, the early sources in Acts) associate the crucifixion with the conniving of Jewish, not Roman, officials. The supposed desire of the early Church to minimize the role of Roman authorities cannot account for the widespread tradition that Jewish leadership, with a legal assist from Rome, put him to death.

But he was raised from the grave and his work entered a new phase. The resurrection narratives are extremely difficult and probably impossible to harmonize. All are extremely selective and their authors have telescoped the accounts so that we simply have no way of piecing together all the separate items. In addition the unique character of the resurrection leaves us without criteria for a thoroughgoing historical study. One thing, however, can be said for certain: attempts by scholars such as Bultmann, John Knox and Don Cupitt[10] to define the resurrection in terms of the faith or memory of the primitive Christian community have not stood the test of scholarly scrutiny. They are derived not from the available texts but from a philosophical base. While these men manifest a deep concern to understand the resurrection, at the same time they fail to show evidence of a subordination either to the New Testament itself or to historical method. The resurrection is the resurrection of Jesus whom God raised to his own right hand (Acts 2:33); so then the risen Jesus is now Lord of the Church and the bestower of the Spirit.

During the period of the appearances Scripture informs us that Jesus sought to show the disciples why all has taken place κατὰ γραδάς. In so doing he established the connection between his ministry, death and resurrection and their faith; this was a resurrection faith given substance and direction through their reflection on his prior ministry. Their faith was not in the risen Jesus but in Jesus who had been raised. Thus everything they knew about him was constitutive for their faith and part of the proclamation, which sought to bring about faith.

The Proclamation. Having taken a brief overview of his ministry we must now consider his Word. The most common term by which he is addressed is "teacher." We read repeatedly that he was found in the synagogues teaching. Scholars remind us that Matthew and Luke differ from Mark in that they record more of the teaching material, yet at the same time it should be noted that Mark makes more references to the fact that Jesus taught than either Matthew or Luke. That the Old Testament played a large part in his teaching is to be seen in the fact that much of his teaching took place within the synagogues of the villages and cities. Yet his teaching was much more than a rabbinic-type discussion of fine points of the Law.

The best-known feature of his teaching ministry was the use of the parable, whose function is more closely related to the Old Testament *mashal* than to the rabbinic. Its basic purpose is not so much to inform or instruct in a formal way, as it is to challenge to decision and action.[11] They are essentially *kerygmatic* in that they relate to the good news of judgment and grace. They call attention to what Jesus is doing and the crucial significance of his being with them. The parables underscore the nature of the moment and the opportunity opened up by his presence. They are both frightening in terms of impending disaster (The Ten Maidens, Matthew 25:1ff) and enthralling in the character of grace that is portrayed (The Lost Son, Luke 15:11ff). The important point is that they relate to the ministry of Jesus— that is, they represent what may be called a "homiletical commentary" on Jesus' ministry.

As a part of his preaching and teaching ministry the gospels give great prominence to his healing ministry, which is regarded by Jesus as a ministry of compassion. But we associate it with his teaching ministry because we have clear evidence that he also intended it to be indicative of the new situation created by his coming. We note how frequently preaching and healing are associated together (Matthew 4:23; 9:35; 10:7f; 11:2ff; Mark 1:38f; 3:14f; 6:12f; Luke 7:18ff; 8:1f; 9:1f). When challenged by certain Pharisees about a miracle, Jesus declared that it was a substantiation of his message of the arrival of the Kingdom (Matthew 12:22-28; Luke 11:14-20). These miracles of Jesus represent the power of the new age, which has power over Satan, and so signal the imminent end of Satan's dominion. The fourth gospel by referring to the miracles as signs (e.g., 2:11) underscores this aspect. Though Jesus is portrayed as refusing to give a sign "on demand" (Mark 8:11f), at the same time he does indicate that these mighty deeds are a pointer toward an adequate assessment and response to his Word.

<u>The Kingdom of God</u>. "After the arrest of John, Jesus came into Galilee preaching the Good News from God, saying, 'Time is fulfilled and the Kingdom of God has come; repent and believe in his Good News,'" (Mark 1:14f). Anyone who is familiar with the synoptic tradition cannot doubt that at the heart of his ministry was this proclamation of the Kingdom of God. (Matthew's "Kingdom of Heaven" is merely a Jewish circumlocution and has no separate or special meaning.) But the question is: what did Jesus proclaim when he proclaimed the Kingdom? The answer is to be found by reference to the Old Testament and the intertestamental literature. In the prophetic literature God rules alone over all the world. He is King. But it is also painfully obvious that in some very real sense He does not yet rule, as He will some day. So there is frequent reference to a future day of the Lord when He shall truly rule. The hope of the people of God is focused on a day when he will act to fulfill all the promises to His people. This comes to

apocalyptic expression in Daniel 7. Thus, when Jesus came proclaiming the Kingdom; he aroused the eschatological aspirations of the people and created a climate of fulfillment. His language is "fulfillment language." In Nazareth he reads from Isaiah of the acceptable year of the Lord and speaks of its present fulfillment (Luke 4:18). His casting out of demons is a similar pointer. The first point, then, to note about the proclamation of Jesus is its eschatological character— a point caught in the *Nunc Dimittis* of Simeon: "Now, Lord, let your servant depart in peace according to your word; for my eyes have seen your salvation…," (Luke 2:29f). With the ministry of Jesus a sense of finality enters history and a new stage is set.

A second major point focuses on the tension between the present and future, between fulfillment and "not yet." On the one hand a number of texts seem to speak unmistakably of the arrival of the eschatological moment. But just as clearly there is a "not yet" aspect which cannot be denied. We err when we attempt to explain one aspect in terms of the other, or to choose one at the expense of the other. The whole tenor of the ministry and message of Jesus is that now men may participate in and enjoy what generations have longed to see. Yet it is equally true that the Kingdom is still future in an ultimate sense. Men may now enter the Kingdom and experience God's saving work, but it is a work still to be consummated. Paul expressed the same tension by speaking of the ἀρραβών (Ephesians 1:14), the "down payment" until such time as the whole is possessed. The present aspect of the Kingdom does, however, underscore the definitive character of Christ's offer of forgiveness, freedom, and joy, while the future aspect makes all labor in the Kingdom anticipatory. "He who loses for my sake shall receive a hundredfold."

A third point that is to be stressed relative to the Kingdom is its close relationship to the person of Jesus himself. In Luke 18:29 we read of those who leave their homes and families "for the sake of the Kingdom of God," while the parallel passages in Matthew and Mark read respectively, "for the sake of my name" and "for my sake and for the sake of the Gospel." In Mark 9:1 Jesus speaks of those who will not taste death before they see the Kingdom having come in power, while the Matthaean parallel refers to seeing the Son of Man coming in his Kingdom. When we move outside the synoptic tradition the language and references of identification are more varied. Both Jesus and the Kingdom are proclaimed as the Gospel.[12] Christians pray both for the coming of the Kingdom and for the coming of the Lord.[13] Men are said to receive the Kingdom and Christ.[14] Both the Kingdom and Christ are at the same time present and yet future.[15] Both are spoken of in terms of absolute commitment and sacrifice.[16]

What does all this mean? Can we summarize what the Kingdom of God is? It is the announcement by Jesus that in his own coming, his ministry and Word, the final Word of God is being spoken in incipient form. This word is so identified with himself that he draws men to himself and becomes both the precipitant and the object of their faith. The proclaimer becomes the proclaimed in a natural and necessary way in that the event that inaugurates the Kingdom (viz., the work of Christ) is spoken of in the same way as the Kingdom. Thus some of the parables of the Kingdom, such as the parables of growth, the fish net, the sower and the wheat and the weeds, are really attempts to explain the ministry of Jesus. All these relate to the power of the Word and to ultimate success, though in the present ministry of Jesus one sees very little of what is supposedly to characterize the eschatological Kingdom. But to receive his word is to be transferred into a new age, to enter into life, to enjoy the freedom of true deliverance, and to anticipate ultimate fulfillment of the whole purpose of God.

<u>The Son of Man</u>. Much scholarly effort has been directed toward an understanding of titles, especially titles Jesus may have used or accepted. By what titles did he refer to himself? And what was his attitude toward other titles? Negatively, it seems quite clear that he avoided the title "Christ" or "Messiah," though that is not to say it was an inappropriate

title. After Peter's confession at Caesarea Philippi the disciples are directed not to use the term. At the trial the High Priest asks if he is the Christ. The answer of Jesus differs in the three accounts. What we appear to have is a refusal to deny the title and at the same time an unwillingness to use it. Richard Longenecker, following a suggestion by David Flusser, has suggested that the reason for Jesus' reticence to use the title is due to the contemporary concept that the Messiah is not to claim the title until *after* his work is accomplished.[17] On this question, however, we have no certain answer.

But perhaps the best way to consider the messiahship of Jesus is by way of the one title, which the tradition indicates was his chosen self-designation, and that is the Son of Man. An enormous amount of literature has sought to identify the origin and significance of the term.[18] Clearly the problems are not simple. Outside the gospels the title appears only twice in Revelation and once in Hebrews (all quoting the LXX) as well as on the lips of Stephen at his stoning (Acts 7:56) Within the gospels it is always used by Jesus. At times he appears to be referring to someone other than himself, as in Mark 8:38, and this has lead some, e.g., Bultmann[19] to conclude that Jesus did not regard himself as the Son of Man, but as the one who was to precede the arrival of that Son of Man. But this position creates more— and more difficult— problems than it solves. Without attempting to pass over very difficult problems it seems that in the synoptic tradition and in the fourth gospel the use of the Son of Man as a self designation correlates well with the other data to portray the obliqueness or hiddenness of Jesus' earthly ministry, while at the same time indicating the basis for his personal authority and power. As the Son of Man he is Head of the new man, yet he comes as one who serves. It is an excellent example of the ability of Jesus to draw into his own ministry various and divergent themes to portray the character of his work. As Eduard Schweizer has said, he fits no formula.[20] His ministry is not determined by set formulas, traditions, texts, or popular expectations. Rather formulas and traditions develop on the basis of that ministry.

With this in mind it seems impossible to believe he regarded his ministry as anything other than messianic. It is eschatological in substance; it is a ministry of direct and immediate authority and power. It is an inclusive ministry, which sets history on the threshold of a new age. By every measure he himself was messianic in perspective, scope, and purpose. Nothing was left for another to do after him.[21]

II. The Word in the World

The New Testament defines and describes the work of Christ through various themes and motifs, and it is important for the Church not to reduce this variety for the sake of uniformity. No doubt the origin of much of this diversity lies with Jesus himself, but in part it arose due to the issues, which confronted the early Church. It is impossible in the brief compass of this essay to set forth fully all that the New Testament says about the work of Christ; therefore only basic themes will be treated.

<u>The Death of Christ</u>. The crucifixion represented for early Christianity both a stumbling block and its crowning glory. Its centrality for the primitive *kerygma* is seen not only in the explicit statements in the epistles but also in the fact that the passion narrative takes up a large part of all the gospels and in the fact that a significant part of the New Testament vocabulary (e.g., blood, cross, baptism, Eucharist) derives from the death of Jesus. We have every reason to believe that meaning and significance began with Jesus himself. Despite attempts to regard the passion predictions of Jesus (Mark 8:33; 9:33; 10:31 and parr.) as *vaticinia ex eventu* of the early Church,[22] there is good reason for Jesus, if he attached any meaning to his impending death, to have spoken about it beforehand. J. Jeremias, for example, has pointed out that in the contemporary Jewish tradition a martyr's death may have atoning significance attached to it, but only if that atoning

significance is stated beforehand.[23] It may be noted, further, that reference to the death of Jesus is found throughout the tradition, and not least in the parables. How does it come through?

N. Snaith has suggested that Jesus deliberately modeled his whole ministry on the concept of the suffering-triumphant Servant of Isaiah.[24] It would probably be better to say that it was one of the models, since his ministry really fits no single model. The servant consciousness of the early Church is derived from its Lord whose purpose was to do the Father's will. The idea is expressed in Jesus' comments on greatness (Mark 10:43ff), in the Johannine account of the foot washing (13:1ff, especially verse 14) and more generally in what is often called the "hidden" character of his ministry. The cross is seen as the culmination of that servant posture and as embracing all that the ministry itself meant. For him to be servant ($\delta o\tilde{u}\lambda o\varsigma$) means even to give his life as a means of redemption for many (Mark 10:45) He is the one who by ministry and death has set men free (John 8:36; chapter 17). The life and death of Jesus are seen together and cannot be separated. Thus Paul, when he proclaims Jesus Christ and him crucified, is not expressing indifference to the material of the synoptic tradition as though he had no interest in or knowledge of the earthly Jesus. For the early Church the "cross" meant the whole ministry culminating in crucifixion. In this sense, the gospels are as a whole to be seen as passion narratives. This may be seen in the Acts, which recognizes the gospel as beginning with the baptism of John (1:21f, 10:37) and yet still embodies a *theologia crucis*. By his total obedience (John 17:4) Jesus gives access to the Father.

But the Church also recognized the priestly character of the work of Jesus by drawing upon the sacrificial motifs. He is seen as the one whom God set forth to be the means of atonement for the sins of the world (Romans 3:25). It is by his blood that we have redemption (1 Peter 1:19). He is seen as the sacrificial lamb (Revelation 7:14; 1 Peter 1:19; John 7:29, 36).[25] Such references are to be taken seriously when working through the meaning of the death of Christ, and at the same time related to other categories with which they are often bound. Thus the sacrificial focus stands with the idea of deliverance because sin is personified as a power by which man is enslaved and from which he must be freed. Romans 3:24f is a good example of this comingling of categories as Paul attempts to portray the all-encompassing achievement of Christ.

Closely related to these themes is the idea of substitution, the removal of which from the New Testament cannot honestly be achieved. Though ἀντί is found only infrequently in the New Testament, ὑπέρ is clearly to be seen as its equivalent in a number of passages. F. C. Baur himself recognized the clearly substitutionary character of 2 Corinthians 5:14.[26] And more recently G. Delling has made the same point for Romans 5:6-8.[27] We can see also the same perspective in the Eucharistic words of Jesus as well as in the ransom saying. At the same time it must be said that not all attempts to develop a substitutionary theory have been successful; indeed some have been little more than a new legalism.

The general term by which the meaning of the death of Christ is defined is "atonement," a word found in the New Testament only in Romans 5:11 in the AV and not at all in the RSV. But it seems to express what takes place by virtue of the work of Christ in that man by faith comes to a knowledge of God. Various theories of atonement only approximate biblical realism; all have their limitations and problems. It is not possible for a single "theory of atonement" to encompass all that Scripture expresses, since Scripture is so fully orbed and multi-faceted. The term redemption relates to the idea of slavery and deliverance from it; reconciliation speaks of the removal of barriers and the establishment of fellowship; propitiation relates to wrath; expiation to sin; forgiveness to guilt; justification to judgment. At the center is the conviction that Christ by his obedience (Romans 5:15ff) and death has made available to mankind the new and living way and has become the pioneer and perfector of our faith.

The Resurrection. That Jesus had been raised from the dead and was alive was the basic conviction of the early Church, the character of whose worship, ministry, and message was shaped by it. Two additional points were equally clear: (1) that he was raised by God; and (2) that his resurrection was at the same time a transformation unbound by that which characterized his incarnate ministry. That is, it was an "eschatological" resurrection (Paul's "spiritual body" 1 Corinthians 15:35ff) of the type all believers shall have at a future time.

Knowing, then, that the resurrection was not after the manner of other restorations of life (such as Lazarus), the Church had to understand and interpret its *meaning* which needed to be as all-encompassing as the event was unique. In the first place the resurrection was seen as the vindication of Jesus, his whole ministry and his word. The Church repeated the story because it had been confirmed by the resurrection. The preaching of the early chapters of Acts expresses this point clearly: you crucified him, but God raised him from the dead! Though the precise meaning of passages like Romans 1:4 and Acts 2:36 are difficult to determine, it is at least clear that by the resurrection Jesus is established as effective Son of God and takes his place at the Father's right hand (cf. Acts 2:33; Colossians 3:1; Romans 8:34).

Secondly, the resurrection is viewed not only as a vindication of Jesus but as a triumph over sin, death, and the forces of evil. He was raised with a view to our justification (Romans 4:25).[28] If it is not true that Christ has been raised, then we are foolish to believe; and moreover we are still sinners (1 Corinthians 15:17). The latter part of this chapter rings of the triumph over the grave: death has lost its sting. He is the firstborn from the dead (Colossians 1:18) and so the first among many (Romans 8:29). He is the first fruit of those who sleep (1 Corinthians 15:20). His resurrection is the antecedent to Christian life, the character of which is defined by the resurrection of Jesus. As Christ was raised from the dead through the glory of the Father, thus we walk in new life (Romans 6:4). Our hope is grounded in the resurrection of Jesus (1 Peter 1:3).

It is no exaggeration to say that all the theology— and of course all Christology— has the resurrection as its focal point. It opens up the full meaning of the Old Testament (Luke 24:45). The narrative of our Lord's ministry is stamped by it. The gospels are indeed post-Easter narratives; one cannot conceive of any early Christian writing or liturgy that did not reflect the Easter-faith of the Church, for there can be no other starting point. From the resurrection on, God is not the "God of Abraham, Isaac and Jacob" but the God who raised Jesus from the dead (Acts 2:32; 3:15; 5:30; Romans 4:24; 8:11; Galatians 1:1). God is spoken of in terms of His primal act and all else that God has said and done is to be fitted into a structure built on that act of power. All ethics are rooted in the resurrection, since New Testament ethics are predicated on the fact of new life. Christians are described as having passed through a death and having been made alive (Romans 6:1ff; Galatians 2:20; Colossians 3:1). The Christian life is characterized by power, but it is the power of his resurrection, which is presupposed, e.g., in Paul's pressing toward maturity in Christ (Philippians 3:9-16).

The Lordship of Christ. Jesus as Lord is the basic confession of the early Church and the most common ascription to him in the New Testament. The Lordship of Jesus is tied to the resurrection in Ephesians 1:20-23: by His own might God raised Jesus and seated him at His right hand in heaven; God has put all things under his feet and made him Head of the Church. Christ as Head of the Church is the risen Lord. Something of this is expressed in the Pauline expression ἐν χριστῷ in that Christ now holds the dominion over the Church that Adam has held since the fall (cf. Romans 5:12ff; 1 Corinthians 15:20). He exercises this Lordship over the Church through his Spirit, his gift to the Church. The Spirit is not Lord but makes the Lordship of Christ present. It is to the Church's advantage that Jesus departs, for then the Spirit may come and continue his (Jesus') ministry in an ever-expansive way. The Spirit is the Spirit of Power, but it is the power of God and of the risen Lord. Being led by the Spirit (Romans 8:14) means to be subservient to the Lordship of Christ. That is the reason why the early Christians did not rely solely on private or personal inspiration in daily life but made themselves dependent on the Jesus-tradition and the Old Testament. The gift of the Spirit was no invitation to individualism, but a means by which all former words of God (Hebrews 1:1) were interpreted and related to the one Word given in the last days.

Another point to be noted is that the early Church looked upon itself as the continuation of the ministry of the incarnate Jesus. Note, for example, the correlative expressions in the latter chapters of the fourth gospel: as I have washed your feet…(13:15); as I have loved you…(13:34); as I have kept my Father's commandments and abide in His love…(15:10); as You have sent me into the world…(17:18); just as we are one…(17:22); as the Father has sent me (20:21). Theologically, the description of Acts as the "Acts of the Risen Lord" is accurate, in that it reports what Jesus continued to do in and through the apostles and prophets. The signs that accompany their ministry parallel his earthly ministry.

The origin of the title is thought by many to be derived from the Aramaic *maran* which, when translated in Greek communities as *kyrios*, was understood in terms of a savior God. Though it sounds plausible, in terms of linguistic history, the theory overlooks the fact that in all strata of the tradition (however these are finally defined) Jesus is portrayed as one who exercises divine prerogatives— such as forgiving sin, and being a "Son" in a way no other man has ever been a son of God. That type of immediate authority needs to be reckoned with alongside the linguistic data in any explanation of the title "Lord."

Scripture also speaks of the Lordship of Christ over all creation. In the grand Christological hymn included in Colossians 1:12-20, Paul speaks of Christ's relationship to the created order in terms that are parallel to his relationship to the Church, and thereby indicating that the rule of Christ is universal, that all of creation will ultimately come under his redemptive work. As the Church recognized the peculiar relationship of Jesus to the Father it was inevitable that it would come to define his work in terms that would involve all creation. This "cosmic Christology" is widely attested in the early Church. Not only do we find it in this possibly pre-Pauline hymn,[29] but it is expressed by Paul himself in 1 Corinthians 8:6 in a way that suggests the readers were familiar with the theme. The writer of the epistle to the Hebrews begins his writing by referring to the creative work of Christ. Paul in Romans 8:19ff speaks of the ultimate deliverance from bondage of the whole created order. Finally, there is the Johannine prologue. In these passages Christ is seen as the one through whom all things were created; he sustains all things, that is, holds it all together to prevent a real disintegration of creation.[30] Here we see an echo of the eschatological hope expressed, e.g., in Isaiah 2:4 when the harmony and unity of the created order is realized perfectly. It is an affirmation of God's creative activity, which is not to be undone or done away with, but is to find fulfillment through the redemptive work of the Son. Bo Reiche, in noting the very frequent use of ($πας$ $πὰ$ $πάντα$) in the New Testament, refers to the concept of totality in the primitive Church.[31] Piper considers it natural and unavoidable that the Church would regard its Lord as being involved not only in personal salvation but also in the ultimate purpose of God.[32] All this comes to grand expression in Ephesians 1:10 where Christ is described as the one in whom ($ἐν$ $τῷ$ $χριστῷ$) all things find their consummation— are brought to purposive fruition. The Lordship of Christ and his redemptive work are seen to be co-extensive with Creation, for nothing lies beyond the concern of God. This is to be seen as an affirmation of this world and a commitment to it. At the same time all this means that without and apart from the work of the Son this present age is darkness— a void— and men labor in vain to find meaningful freedom. Apart from the Son all liberty is license, all hope is despair, and all love is vanity.

The final work of Jesus as Lord is to take place at his coming again when the work begun in his earthly ministry will be completed. He will come as Judge (Matthew 25:31ff) of all peoples. We find this theme primarily in apocalyptic form (Mark 13; Revelation; Matthew 25) but it is by no means limited to this literature, as we note from Acts 1:11; John 16:16, etc. This coming again is, indeed, the hope of the Church whose own witness will then be confirmed. It is that forward moment, that distant star, which provides for a steady course through treacherous history.

The descriptions of that moment and that event are varied and the Church will be cautious not to press for details (Acts 1:7). The nature of apocalyptic literature is to inform and impress, and its descriptive features serve only those ends. We are to know that he will come again, that we are to anticipate that coming, but to leave all details to the Father. In the meantime ours is to be the holy life and witness of power.

In closing an all too inadequate study of the person and work of Jesus I shall refer you to what is undoubtedly the one all-encompassing ascription of the early Church as to who and what Jesus is. John calls him the Word of God, by which of course he intended to bestow on Jesus all that is known by the Word. The Word is powerful; it goes forth only to inform and redeem. By the Word the Father comes to, and is known by, the world. Redemption and judgment— grace and truth— are by the Word of God. The Word is the extension of the Father in the world; by it the world is sustained (Hebrews 1:3). There is no knowledge apart from the Word, and so whoever believes not stands in judgment because he will not hear the only true Word. And so he— Jesus— is the fullness of God in that he fulfills the Father's redemptive purpose. He is Alpha and Omega.

Notes

[1] *Foundations of New Testament Christology* (New York: Scribners, 1965), p. 15.

[2] *The Christology of the New Testament.* ET (Philadelphia: Westminster, 1957), p. 1. For P. Althaus it is the person and history of Jesus Christ; see his *The So-Called Kerygma and the Historical Jesus* (Edinburgh: Oliver & Boyd, 1959), p. 13.

[3] A survey of extra-biblical references to Jesus in F. C. Grant, "Jesus Christ," *Interpreter's Dictionary of the Bible* (Nashville and New York: Abingdon, 1962), Vol. II, p. 875f; cf. also H. Conzelmann in *Religion der Geschichte and Gegenwart*; 3. Auflage, III, 622.

[4] Cf. Adolf Schlatter, *Der Glaube im Neuen Testament.* 5. (Stuttgart: Calwer, 1963)

[5] Cf. Otto A. Piper, "The Virgin Birth: The Meaning of the Gospel Accounts," *Interpretation*, 18.2 (1964), 132-148.

[6] E.g., Mark 1:21, 39; 3:1; Matthew 4:32; 9:35; Luke 4:15f; 13:10f; John 6:59; 18:20.

[7] Luke 19:1ff; 7:35ff; Matthew 11:28.

[8] A very helpful study of this issue may be found in David Catchpole, *The Trial of Jesus* (Leiden: Brill, 1971).

[9] E.g., S. G. F. Brandon, *Jesus and the Zealots* (Manchester: The University Press, 1967)

[10] John Knox, *Christ the Lord* (New York, 1945). R. Bultmann, *Theology of the New Testament*. I, p. 45 *et passim*; also "The Primitive Christian Kerygma and the Historical Jesus" in *The Historical Jesus and the Kerygmatic Christ*, eds. Braaten and Harrisville (1964), p. 42; Don Cupitt and C. F D. Moule, "The Resurrection: A Disagreement" in *Theology*, 75 (1972), 507-519; cf. also W. Marxsen, "The Resurrection of Jesus As a Historical and Theological Problem" in *The Significance of the Message of the Resurrection for Faith in Jesus Christ*, SBT, II. 8 (London: SCM, 1968), pp. 15-50.

[11] Isaiah 5 and 1 Samuel 12 with the parables of Mark 4 (parr.) Cf. C. H. Dodd, *Parables of the Kingdom* (London: Nisbet, second ed. 1961).

[12] Compare Mark 1:14; Matthew 9:35; 24:14; Luke 4:43; 8:1; 9:2; Acts 20:25; 28:31 with Acts 5:42; 8:35; 19:13; 1 Corinthians 1:23; 2 Corinthians 1:19; 11:4; Galatians 1:16.

[13] Mark 9:1; Matthew 6:10; 1 Corinthians 16:22.

[14] Mark 10:15; Matthew 25:34; Luke 8:40; John 1:12; 2 Corinthians 7:15.

[15] Mark 1:14; Matthew 12:28; Mark 9:1; Matthew 6:10; 18:20; 28:20; 1 Corinthians 16:22.

[16] Mark 9:47; Matthew 19:12; Luke 18:29; cf. Mark 10:29; Matthew 19:29; Romans12:1f; 2 Thessalonians 1:5.

[17] Richard Longenecker, *The Christology of Early Jewish Christianity*, SBT, 2:17 (London: SCM, 1970), p. 71ff. cf. D. Flusser, *Israel Exploration Journal*, 9 (1959), 107ff.

[18] The following is only a small selection of what could be listed: M. Bluck, "The Son of Man Problem in Recent Research and Debate," *BJRL*, 45 (1963), 305-318; A. J. B. Higgins, "Son of Man-Forschung Since 'The Teaching of Jesus.'" *New Testament Essays*, ed. Higgins (Manchester, 1959), pp. 119-135; J. Y. Campbell, "The Origin and Meaning of the Term 'Son of Man,'" *JTS* 48 (1947), 145ff; M. P. Hooker, *The Son of Man in Mark* (London: SPCK, 1967). A. J. B. Higgins, *Jesus and the Son of Man* (Philadelphia: Fortress, 1964) H. E.

Tödt, *The Son of Man in the Synoptic Tradition*, ET (London: SCM, 1965) F. H. Borsch, *The Son of Man in Myth and History* (Philadelphia: Westminster, 1967) I. H. Marshall, "The Son of Man in Contemporary Debate," *Evang. Qu.*, 42.2 (1970), 67ff; Ragnar Leivestad, "Exit the Apocalyptic Son of Man," *NTS*, 18.3 (1972). 243-267.

[19] *Theology of the New Testament*, Vol. I, pp. 26ff.

[20] In his book on Jesus, Schweizer titles one of his chapters, "The Man Who Fits No Formula"; see *Jesus* (Richmond: John Knox, 1971).

[21] Cf. E. Käsemann: "The only category which does justice to his claim (quite independently of whether he used it himself and required it of others) is that in which his disciples themselves placed him—namely, that of the Messiah." See, *Essays on New Testament Themes*, SBT, I. 41. (London: SCM, 1964), p. 38.

[22] E.g., H. Conzelmann, RGG^3, III, 630.

[23] *New Testament Theology*: Vol. 1, *The Proclamation of Jesus* (New York: Scribners, 1971), p. 287.

[24] Isaiah 40-66. *A Study of the Teaching of Second Isaiah and Its Consequences*. Vet. Test. Supplement XIV, 1967 Chapter six.

[25] C. H. Dodd, however has argued for another interpretation of the "Lamb" in *The Interpretation of the Fourth Gospel* (Cambridge, 1953), pp. 230ff.

[26] *Vorlesungen über neutestamentliche Theologie* (Leipzig, 1864), p. 158f. quoted from R. W. Dale, *The Atonement*, 18th edition (London, 1896), p. 477f.

[27] *Gesammelte Aufsätze*, 1970, p. 180.

[28] Cf. C. F. D. Moule, *An Idiom Book of New Testament Greek* (Cambridge, 1953), p. 194.

[29] See R. P. Martin, *Carmen Christi* (Cambridge, 1967).

[30] Hebrews 1:3; Colossians 1:16; cf. B. F. Westcott on ἄθεοι of Ephesians 2:12: "They were of necessity face to face with all the problems of nature and life, but without Him in Whose wisdom and righteousness and love they could find rest and hope. The vast, yet transitory, order of the physical universe was for them without its Interpreter, an unsolved enigma."

[31] *TDNT*, V, 893.

[32] *Interpretation*, III. 3 (1949), 286-298.

Works Cited

Bluck, M. "The Son of Man Problem in Recent Research and Debate," *BJRL*, 45 (1963).

Borsch, F. H. *The Son of Man in Myth and History* (Philadelphia: Westminster, 1967).

Bultmann, R. *Theology of the New Testament*.

_____. "The Primitive Christian Kerygma and the Historical Jesus" in *The Historical Jesus and the Kerygmatic Christ*, eds. Braaten and Harrisville (1964).

Campbell, J. Y. "The Origin and Meaning of the Term 'Son of Man,'" *JTS* 48 (1947).

Cupitt, Don and Moule, C. F D. "The Resurrection: A Disagreement" in *Theology*, 75 (1972).

Dale, R. W. *The Atonement*, 18th edition (London, 1896).

Dodd, C. H. *Parables of the Kingdom* (London: Nisbet, second ed. 1961).

_____. *The Interpretation of the Fourth Gospel* (Cambridge, 1953).

Flusser, D. *Israel Exploration Journal*, 9 (1959).

Higgins, A. J. B. "Son of Man-Forschung Since 'The Teaching of Jesus.'" *New Testament Essays*, ed. Higgins (Manchester, 1959).

_____. *Jesus and the Son of Man* (Philadelphia: Fortress, 1964).

Hooker, M. P. *The Son of Man in Mark* (London: SPCK, 1967).

Knox, John. *Christ the Lord* (New York, 1945).

Leivestad, Ragnar. "Exit the Apocalyptic Son of Man," *NTS*, 18.3 (1972).

Longenecker, Richard. *The Christology of Early Jewish Christianity*, SBT, 2.17 (London: SCM, 1970).

Marshall, I. H. "The Son of Man in Contemporary Debate," *Evang. Qu.*, 42.2 (1970).

Marxsen, W. "The Resurrection of Jesus As a Historical and Theological Problem" in *The Significance of the Message of the Resurrection for Faith in Jesus Christ*, SBT, II. 8 (London: SCM, 1968).

New Testament Theology: Vol. 1, *The Proclamation of Jesus* (New York: Scribners, 1971).

Tödt, H. E. *The Son of Man in the Synoptic Tradition*, ET (London: SCM, 1965).

Vorlesungen über neutestamentliche Theologie (Leipzig, 1864).

The Person and Ministry of the Holy Spirit

Kenneth C. Kinghorn
November 7, 1973

Introduction

In our time we are experiencing a tremendous renewal of interest in the Person and ministry of the Holy Spirit. Varieties of teachings abound, some of which seem non-biblical and some of which appear to be creative contributions. If various teachings abound, so do various methodologies, which are used to study and present the Spirit's nature and ministry. Methodologies ranging from subjective impressions to rigid systematic approaches are being used. Never has there been a greater need for a proper biblical understanding of the Holy Spirit and His ministry.

The methodology used in this paper has been to sift through the biblical references to the Holy Spirit and to determine the major emphases stressed therein. This paper does not attempt to examine various representative writers on the Holy Spirit. Consequently there are few footnotes referring to monographs on and treatments of the ministry of the Holy Spirit. Space limitations prohibit dealing with all the biblical references to or developments of the Holy Spirit. The responsibility for the choice of the three themes developed in the second half of this paper will, of course, be this writer's. Others doubtless would have chosen different emphases. However, the ones that will be dealt with in this paper seem to this writer to be the major ones developed in the New Testament.

The Person of the Holy Spirit

The Old Testament Hebrew word for Spirit is רוּחַ (ruah), which means wind or breath. The word used in the New Testament is πνεῦμα (pneuma), which also means wind or breath. πνεῦμα derives from the verb πνέω, which means *to blow* or *to breathe*. In the Old Testament the word spirit signified feelings and emotions (Genesis 41:8, 2 Kings 19:7, Judges 8:3, Proverbs 29:11, Isaiah 26:9, Daniel 2:3), intelligence (Exodus 28:3, Deuteronomy 34:9, Job 32:8, Isaiah 29:24, Malachi 2:15), attitude of will (Exodus 35:21, Jeremiah 51:1,

Haggai 1:14; Ezra 1:1, 1 Chronicles 5:26), and one's general disposition (Psalms 34:18, Proverbs 14:29, 16:2). But most important of all, the word *spirit* stood for life itself. For the Hebrews God pre-eminently has spirit. He is a breathing, living, acting God. The Old Testament writers hold it a matter of great wonder that in the miracle of creation God transmitted His spirit of life to His creatures. He breathed into man the breath—the spirit—of life (Genesis 6:3, Job 10:12, Psalms 104:30, Isaiah 44:3, Ezekiel 37:6, 9, 10)

For the New Testament writers the situation was basically the same. The Greek language has two words for the human spirit. One is νοῦς (nous), which means man's rational or intellectual being. The other is πνεῦμα (pneuma), which denotes the principle of life itself.

For the biblical writers God's Spirit is vital, dynamic, and life-giving. Even as man's spirit is his person in action, so God's Spirit is His Person in action. God's Spirit is God acting.

The Holy Spirit has been progressively understood by the people of God. Our perception of His nature and ministry has grown from the earliest biblical times throughout the fuller revelation of the Spirit in the period following Pentecost. The Old Testament prophets, in their dismay over Israel's unfaithfulness, looked forward to the time when God would move mightily in the midst of His covenant people so as to change their rebellion into worship and service. For these writers the best was yet to be. They longed for the time when God would intervene in the lives of persons to change them for good. Often these longings are seen in the light of the future work of the Holy Spirit.

For example, Moses said, "Would that all the LORD'S people were prophets, that the LORD would put his spirit upon them!" (Numbers 11:29). Ezekiel prophesied, "A new heart I will give you, and a new spirit I will put within you; and I will take out of your flesh the heart of stone and give you a heart of flesh. And I will put my spirit within you, and cause you to walk in my statutes..." (Ezekiel 36:26, 27). One of the classic Old

Testament passages regarding the future work of the Holy Spirit is found in Joel. "And it shall come to pass afterward, that I will pour out my spirit on all flesh; your sons and daughters shall prophesy, your old men shall dream dreams, and your young men shall see visions. Even upon the men servants and maid servants in those days, I will pour out my spirit" (2:28, 29).

The prophets saw a day when God's Spirit would perform a new creative act, not unlike what he did when he breathed life into Adam. They looked forward to the time when God would impart a new vitality to a people who were rebellious and sinful. Only God's Spirit could effect the necessary change.

That new day began to unfold when the Holy Spirit overshadowed Mary and she miraculously conceived a son, not of man but of the Spirit of God. For a witness for all to see, the Holy Spirit descended upon Jesus at the time of the beginning of His public ministry. The opening words of His first recorded sermon text were, "The Spirit of the Lord is upon me…" (Luke 4:18). Then He announced, "Today this scripture has been fulfilled in your hearing" (v. 21).

After Jesus' earthly ministry climaxed with His resurrection and ascension, the Holy Spirit came in His fullness on the Day of Pentecost. As Christians began to experience the Spirit's presence, they began to describe His working. And in the case of the Apostles they received and recorded new truth as to the nature of the Spirit's ministry in the Church.

Several fundamental ideas about the Holy Spirit began to emerge in the life and thought of the New Testament Church.

1. <u>The Holy Spirit is God's primary agent in working in the lives of persons.</u> The Holy Spirit was seen as the "Other Comforter" whom Jesus promised as His legacy to the Church. The New Testament avoids Gnosticism, which teaches that God is pure spirit and that a part of His spirit is a natural possession of man. By way of contrast, the New Testament teaches that the Holy Spirit of God is altogether other, and yet in response to our faith He does come to dwell within our lives. In other words

the Holy Spirit's coming to man is the gracious act of a personal God. The believer knows God through the action of His Spirit in whom we have our life and upon whom we continually depend.

2. <u>Outward manifestations of the Spirit are not necessarily meant to be normative but rather they are simply an indication that God has total claim over all areas of our lives.</u> No aspect of human personality lies outside the sphere of the Spirit's activity. Luke is more concerned than other New Testament writers about describing physical results of the Spirit's activity. For example, Luke writes of the Spirit's descent upon Jesus in bodily form as a dove (Luke 3:21) and the miraculous speaking in other languages at Pentecost, in the house of Cornelius, and at Ephesus (Acts 2:4, 10:46, 19:6). We need to remember that Luke was reporting events as a historian; he was not teaching doctrine, as was Paul. The meaning of the external phenomena reported by Luke is not to teach that they were to be standard experiences for all time. Rather they are illustrations of the decisiveness of the Spirit's ministry and the radical totality of God's working in human personality.

3. <u>The Holy Spirit is inextricably linked with the risen Lord and the reigning Father</u>. Paul, more than any other writer in the New Testament, emphasizes that the Holy Spirit is the Spirit of Jesus. For instance, he alternates "Spirit of God" and "Spirit of Christ" in Romans 8:9, 10. No distinction is made between the two. This usage harmonizes with Jesus' promise of the Spirit to come after His resurrection and ascension. At times Paul uses Father, Son, and Spirit together in the same passage because their ministry in the believer's life is one and the same. The best illustration is found in 1 Corinthians 12:4-6. "Now there are varieties of gifts, but the same Spirit; and there are varieties of service, but the same Lord; and there are varieties of working but it is the same God who inspires them all in everyone." (See also Romans 5:1-5 and Galatians 4:4-6.) Such passages demonstrate that the New Testament Church

saw both the Holy Spirit and the risen Lord as expressions of God the Father.

The biblical accounts of the activity of the Holy Spirit show us that the nature of the Holy Spirit is much more than merely subjective or applicative. Many theologians within the broad Reformation tradition have conceived of the Holy Spirit as directing our attention to Christ and opening our eyes to His work. His ministry is often restricted merely to an instrumental function. The result of much of this type of thinking is to relegate the Holy Spirit to a second-class reality, subordinating Him to Christ, limiting His work to the application of Christ's atoning work to the believer.

We have seen that the *function* of the Holy Spirit *is* primarily to exalt Christ and to mediate His living presence to the Church, but the *nature* of the Holy Spirit is that He is fully God in Himself. His nature is more than a subjective reflection of Christ's work. Christ Himself told His disciples that after His ascension the Holy Spirit would teach new things and continue His ministry in the Church. The Spirit's coming in His fullness at Pentecost marks a new event in the series of God's saving acts. The Holy Spirit creates a ministry of His own, not independent of Christ but complementary to His. The Spirit may be resisted, grieved, lied to, quenched, and sinned against. He also may be loved and obeyed. He effects our conversion and sanctification; He leads the Church in its task of mission. He organizes, prays, inspires, corrects, sustains, equips, creates, and empowers. Thus, the Holy Spirit is not only the agent of God Who exalts Christ and applies His "finished work" to the Church, He is also the source of new creative actions in the Church. He has His own ontology and He functions in His own unique way. Again, we must ever keep in mind that the Holy Spirit cannot be separated from Christ, for He is the Spirit of Christ (Romans 8:9).

Certain improper ways of viewing the Holy Spirit have always existed in the Church. One typical faulty view of the Holy Spirit is the identification of the Holy Spirit with inner impressions or outward manifestations. While the Holy Spirit doubtless does "speak" to the inner consciousness of man and while outward manifestations may sometimes be a part of His divine working, these in themselves should not be confused with the Holy Spirit. Hunches and outward acts do not necessarily stem from the Holy Spirit. Sometimes they are very much of "the flesh," or even from the Evil One.

An improper emphasis upon the Holy Spirit can lead to a "Cult of the Holy Spirit," wherein Jesus Christ is neglected and worship centers almost exclusively upon the Holy Spirit. When this shift occurs we run the danger of blurring the distinction between the human spirit and the Holy Spirit. If we push Christ into the background and make the Holy Spirit almost the exclusive object of our worship and attention we run the risk of making Christ merely the historic inspiration for a religious principle.

Too little emphasis upon the Holy Spirit therefore results in institutionally objectifying Him. And too much of the wrong kind of emphasis on the Holy Spirit results in individualistically subjectifying Him. In either case we have not properly understood His nature or realistically dealt with His work.

Any biblical understanding of the nature of the Holy Spirit requires that we think of Him as the Spirit of Christ. In His last teaching about the Holy Spirit Jesus said, "I will not leave you desolate; I will come to you" (John 14:18). Matthew gives the same idea when he reports Jesus as saying, "I am with you always, to the close of the age" (Matthew 28:20). Jesus is not only the possessor of the Holy Spirit; He is the One who dispenses the Spirit to the community of believing Christians (Luke 24:49).

The New Testament identifies the Holy Spirit as the Spirit of Christ, in which Christ Himself encounters His people (Luke 12:12, cf. 21:15, Acts 10:14, cf. 10:19). Paul plainly asserts, "Now the Lord is the Spirit" (2 Corinthians 3:17).

The goal of the Holy Spirit is to change our existence so that we may he conformed to the new manhood of Christ's resurrection. Christ's ministry, message, and nature constitute the starting point and goal of the Spirit's creative acts. "We all, with unveiled face, beholding the glory of the Lord, are being changed into his likeness from one degree of glory to another; for this comes from the Lord who is the Spirit" (2 Corinthians 3:18; see also 1 Corinthians 6:17 and Romans 8:9-11).

We come now to a definition of the Holy Spirit: the Holy Spirit is the divine third Person of the Holy Trinity whose function it is constantly to breathe creative life into the world and in a special way mediate divine things to the Church to the end that it may be formed after the image of the Son and serve as a principle witness of the grace of Christ to the glory of God the Father.

The Function of the Holy Spirit

Obviously in the space, which remains, it is not possible to list and discuss all aspects of the work of the Holy Spirit. For instance, we will not be able to discuss the Spirit's part in creation, sanctification, revelation, inspiration, eschatology, etc. We will, however, discuss three aspects of the work of the Holy Spirit. These three aspects of His working are all related to the Christian life in the Church today.

1. <u>The primary function of the Holy Spirit in the lives of human beings is to bring them into a living relationship with Jesus Christ.</u> The most basic work of the Holy Spirit is Christian conversion and the working out in human life the implications and dynamics of the new life in Christ.

Christian conversion, sometimes called the new birth, results in a new orientation of one's personality toward Jesus Christ. The human spirit, bound as it is by sin, cannot regenerate itself. If the human spirit is ever to come into a knowledge of God it will be as a result of the work of the Holy Spirit. As Paul wrote, "Anyone who does not have the Spirit of Christ does not belong to him" (Romans 8:9). And he also wrote, "No one can say 'Jesus is Lord' except by the Holy Spirit" (1 Corinthians 12:3).

The life of Paul illustrates the futility of seeking spiritual life apart from the work of the Holy Spirit. He felt in his pre-Christian life that true spiritual reality was found insofar as he proved himself obedient to the command of God as contained in the law. At the time he firmly believed that the law led to life (See Romans 7:10 and Galatians 3:21). The seventh chapter of Romans shows how the truth gradually dawned on Paul that instead of producing life, the law was incarcerating him in death. He finally came to the place where he cried, "Wretched man that I am! Who will deliver me from this body of death?" (Romans 7:24). Then he answers his own question by stating the greatest discovery of his life: "There is therefore now no condemnation for those who are in Christ Jesus" (Romans 8:1). Paul's birth in the Spirit produced a personal relationship with Christ, which brought him from spiritual death into spiritual life. He saw that his hope lay in Christ, not the law. What no human effort could accomplish, he found in a spiritual birth. Paul exulted, "You are not in the flesh, you are in the Spirit, if the Spirit of God really dwells in you" (Romans 8:9).

The New Testament presents a uniform picture of the dynamics involved in Christian conversion.

In the first place, the Holy Spirit brings us into relationship with Christ not because we have managed to achieve sanctification, but in order that we may be sanctified. Christ is the savior of sinners, not the righteous. The Holy Spirit does not wait until we are pure and holy to bring us into union with Christ; He does so in order that we may become pure and holy. He never comes to us in our unregenerate state with the demand, "Get clean!" Rather He comes with an offer, "I take you just as you are. Receive Christ and live."

After we have entered into a life-giving relationship with Christ, we are then called to a life of sanctification and holiness. We must keep in mind, however, that the Alpha point of Christian experience is Christ seeking us. And He seeks us in our sinfulness, because there is none righteous (Romans 3:10). In this connection we must remember that the Church that

Christ is presently sanctifying is not an "ideal" Church free of blemishes, but a Church consisting of imperfect people, yet on the way.

Secondly, the nature of our union with Christ is unique, quite superior to any other union. The Bible gives analogies of our union with Christ, using such terms as vine and branch, husband and wife, father and son. But none of these analogies can possibly express or explain our being in Christ. As splendid and wonderful as these relationships are, our union with Christ through the Holy Spirit is much more wonderful. In a mystical way the Holy Spirit infuses the divine life of the resurrected Christ into our human personalities. Paul described our relationship with Christ in this way: "We have this treasure in earthen vessels, to show that the transcendent power belongs to God and not to us" (2 Corinthians 4:7).

The New Testament writers generally and Paul particularly insist that the Christian life begins to flower when the Holy Spirit effects the miracle of Christian conversion. All else in the Christian life is predicated upon that divine-human encounter wrought in human life through the gracious working of the Holy Spirit in what Jesus called the new birth.

The power of the Holy Spirit provides a "plus" in the Christian's relationship with Christ that is not present in any other type of human relationship. It is qualitatively different from any other relationship. The Spirit makes available to the Christian the divine power of God for the living of daily life. This power affects our relationships to our neighbor, our vocation, and world. As Luke states it in a classic passage, "You shall receive power when the Holy Spirit has come upon you..." (Acts 1:8). In speaking of the Holy Spirit, Jesus stated, "It is the Spirit that gives life, the flesh is of no avail..." (John 6: 63). The Holy Spirit in the life of the Christian does more than merely inspire him to obey Christ and to live a "godly life." The Spirit mediates the divine life of Christ to the Christian, enabling him to live a life that is pleasing to God. He authors a relationship totally unique, quite superior to any other relationship.

And thirdly, the Holy Spirit works in the lives of Christians in a dynamic and relational way, not just in a static and theoretical way. Another way of saying the same thing is to say, "The Christian's *condition* is altered as well as his *relationship*."

While the Christian's union with Christ coincides with a covenant relationship to Christ, it is not identical with a covenant. Our human spirits are not absorbed into or subsumed under the Holy Spirit. Nevertheless, our bond with Christ carries with it the benefit of partaking of the Holy Spirit in a real way.

Since the Christian life is dynamic and not static, the Christian ought constantly to grow, gain new insights, receive new illumination and new experiences. Peter emphasized that a part of the work of the Holy Spirit in our lives is to impart new dreams and new visions, leading the Christian to experience an unfolding drama of realized redemption in wider and wider dimensions of human life.

Working in our lives, the Holy Spirit gives power to the words of Christian preaching (1 Corinthians 2:4, 1 Thessalonians 1:5, Romans 15:16). He guides the Church in its life (Acts 6:3) and supplies all the differing gifts that are necessary for its common life (1 Corinthians 12:4-30). The Holy Spirit leads the Church into all the truth (John 16:13). He guides the Church's worship and fellowship (1 Corinthians 14). To be in Christ, then, is to share in His Spirit, by Whom He was made flesh (Luke 1:35). It is, to use John's phrase, to have "an anointing from the Holy One" (1 John 2:20). "And by this we know that he abides in us, by the Spirit which he has given us" (1 John 3:24).

Having received the Spirit of Christ at conversion, Christians have access to the life of the Holy Spirit. The powers of the age to come are at work in us (Acts 2:17-21, 33, Romans 8:11, 23, Hebrews 6:4, 5). God through His Holy Spirit constantly seeks to perfect that which He has begun in us. By the Holy Spirit we are sealed unto the day of redemption (Ephesians 1:13, 4:30, 2 Corinthians 1:22) and in Him we have the foretaste, the earnest, and the first fruits of a new humanity and a new age.

These aspects of Christian life are but some of the implications of being in Christ through His Spirit. The grandest event in human existence is to come to know Jesus Christ through the miracle of the birth of the Holy Spirit. Once in Christ, God through the Holy Spirit begins the perfecting of the believer to the end that he will glorify God.

2. <u>Another important work of the Holy Spirit is to bring persons into a creative and harmonious relationship to the Body of Christ, the Church</u>. Man is made for community and belonging. Some observers of human behavior attribute man's longing for community to fear, survival, or the need for goods and services. These doubtless are a part of the reason that man is by nature a "joiner." But there seems to be a deeper reason that man reaches out for fellowship with others. Something within the nature of man, grounded in the *imago Dei*, urges him to stretch beyond himself for fellowship both with God and with God's creation.

The supreme provision for fellowship with God is, as we have seen, the new life in Christ wrought by the Holy Spirit, God's supreme provision for man's essential need of fellowship with his fellow man is found, I believe, in *koinonia*, or community within the Body of Christ, the Church.

Obviously Christianity is private and personal; but it is also social. The Christian relates upwardly to God and outwardly to others. In the Christian understanding of *Church*, the Christian belongs to all others who also belong to Christ. Phillips translates Romans 14:8: "The truth is that we neither live or die as self-contained units." In a special way, God reveals Himself through community or in what Bonhoeffer called "life together." When Christians are converted to Christ they are grafted into the one indivisible body of Christ, the Holy Catholic Church. The Holy Spirit both brings us into this unity and He helps us discover the implications and overtones of what it means to be a brother or sister to every Christian believer throughout the world.

The Christian inherits a special relationship with, and responsibility to, fellow believers who are also in Christ. Loss of fellowship and quarrelling among Christian believers are contrary to the work of the Holy Spirit. When true Christians are not in fellowship with each other the reason does not lie in the Holy Spirit because where the Spirit of the Lord is regnant unity exists.

An important part of the work of the Holy Spirit, therefore, is to rectify present disunity and to lead the Church to manifest her unity around a common Lord. It appears from this writer's point of view that one of the obvious activities of the Holy Spirit in present-day spiritual renewal is that He is replacing the bitter doctrinal and ecclesiastical strife of the post-Reformation era with a new sense of catholicity and brotherhood. This is even more significant when we observe that this growing sense of the unity of the Spirit is developing at the grass roots, among laymen and on a large scale. We are rediscovering the New Testament emphasis upon the unity of the Body of Christ. Perhaps one of the significant areas of study in the years ahead will be the relationship of the Holy Spirit to the study of ecclesiology.

A radical biblical ecclesiology is revolutionary—as are most aspects of the Gospel. In this connection, perhaps our main problem is that we have failed to recognize that carnal attitudes and self will have been a part of professional Church leaders as much as they have been a part of the laity.

One finds it easier to forgive churchmen for the man-made divisions that they have imposed upon their respective flocks when we remember that a cautious spirit has often been the result of the heavy burden of pastoral responsibility. It is right to be on guard for wolves in sheep's clothing who would do harm to the flock of God. But human nature being what it is, we have often tended to erect our own criteria for judging other Christians. Having our particular criteria for deciding with whom we can fellowship as brothers in the Lord releases us from the more demanding requirements of spiritual discernment and redeeming love. Man-made rules (justified by proof texts) give us sometimes a false security, and they can easily blind us to the fact that the Holy Spirit is free and sovereign, often creating new wineskins where older ones have not remained sufficiently pliable for His creative working. We sometimes forget that the Holy Spirit promises to the Church the necessary gifts by which His working can be discerned (1 Corinthians 12:10). The Holy Spirit, when allowed right of way, is creating a Church not ruled by the letter of written codes, but by the Holy Spirit Himself (2 Corinthians 3:4-6).

The basic principle is, of course, not hard to determine from Scripture. "By this you know the Spirit of God: every spirit which confesses that Jesus Christ has come in the flesh is of God, and every spirit which does not confess Jesus is not of God" (1 John 4:2, 3). Church history demonstrates, to be sure, that there is still room for error even with this safeguard. Nonetheless, the true discernment of the spirit can only come as the body of Christians lives in the Spirit. And in the Church there is only one body and one Spirit just as we were called to one hope (Ephesians 4:4). Whenever we seek to develop any sort of security against false brethren that can function apart from the present, active working of the Spirit Himself, we are living not by the Spirit but by the flesh. Orthodoxy is no substitute for the indwelling Holy Spirit. The Holy Spirit is not an abstract doctrine, but a living, vitalizing Presence. He is not a substitute for a resurrected Lord, but the divine Agent of His living presence.

When we allow the Holy Spirit to bring us into a creative and harmonious relationship with the Body of Christ, enormous benefits accrue to us.

1. We are greatly enriched by the multitude of Christian traditions that are but partial expressions of *the* Tradition. Along this line, we are also enabled to contribute to the Church our own unique understanding of Christian faith and life.

2. The Body of Christ functions harmoniously and it edifies all believers when they are in the unity of the Spirit. The Holy Spirit leaves no room in the Church for feelings of inferiority or pride. There are differing *functions* in the body of Christ, but there are no differences of *status*. To understand that the Church is one Body of the Lord of which we are all members is to be in a position to allow the Holy Spirit to erase from among us all traces of carnal competition. In the Church no one is "second class" and no one is superior. There are no underdogs in the Church nor are there any super-Christians. We are all one in the Spirit.

3. When we live in community in the fellowship of the Spirit our joys are increased and our burdens are made lighter. Mutual sharing replaces an uninvolved provincialism. We mature in Christ best in the community of the Spirit. God's promises are largely to His covenant people and to His Church. We participate in them as we participate in the fellowship of other Christian believers.

The Church is more than a witness to Christ; it is also the Body of Christ. It is not only a reporter of God's mighty acts of redemption; it is itself the bearer of God's redeeming grace as an object of His ministry of saving love. In the Book of Acts, to lie to the Church was to lie to the Holy Spirit (Acts 5:3) and to be in the Church was to be in Christ.

3. <u>The third major work of the Holy Spirit is to make of each Christian a living witness to the glory of God the Father</u>. A major misunderstanding of the nature of the work of the Holy Spirit in maturing Christians persists both inside and outside the Church. That misunderstanding is based on the notion that Christianity produces a bland sameness or sterile uniformity in people's lives. Unfortunately we in the Church have sometimes preferred the "safe" Christian to the creative Christian. Often, in the interests of discipling persons, we seek to mold them into identical patterns after the fashion of our particular group's perception of the Christian life. We should instead encourage

them to be taught by the Holy Spirit and shaped by Him into the full development of their own creative uniqueness.

The Holy Spirit never works the same in any two persons. We have often frustrated His working by drawing up blackboard models of "the work of the Holy Spirit." In attempting to force others into our categories we stand in the way of the Spirit Himself. Sadly, the Church has often insisted that her Davids wear the armor of Saul. This unbiblical approach has produced frustrated persons, guilty persons, and resentful persons.

For a biblical illustration of the variety of the working of the Holy Spirit look at Acts. The converts in Cornelius' house received the Holy Spirit before they were baptized in water, and those in Samaria were baptized in water before they received the Holy Spirit. Christian leaders in the early Church were wise enough to allow for variety. Paul wrote to the Corinthians, "There are varieties of working, but it is the same God who inspires..." (1 Corinthians 12:6).

To be sure, there *are* common characteristics, which belong to all Christians. In certain areas there is only *one* Christian response possible. Christians should be uniform in that each one should manifest the fruits of the Holy Spirit as listed in Galatians 5 (v. 22, 23).

Nevertheless, the Holy Spirit works in each life in a unique way because each person is a unique individual. God has given to every person special talents and unique abilities, and He has for each life a different plan. As the Holy Spirit works individually in the lives of Christians, He does so in order to produce a witness to the glory of God the Father. Paul wrote to some first-century Christians, "As for you, it is plain that you are a letter that has come from Christ a letter written not with ink but with the Spirit of the living God (2 Corinthians 3:2, NEB).

We glorify God most as we manifest the divine blend of our own personality with that of the Holy Spirit. God calls us to manifest our Spirit-filled individuality in the context of daily life. For some, daily life means the Christian pastorate; for others, it means the shop, the office, the classroom, or the farm. None of us has exactly the same vocation. But each one of us does have a divine call to be fully Christian and fully human at every level of our existence. The Holy Spirit beckons us to a continuing and growing relationship to Christ. And as we respond in obedience to the creative, customized, personal ministry of the Holy Spirit we grow into mature "epistles" seen and read by others.

Naturally, none of us in our lifetime fully realizes his entire potential. John wrote, "Here and now, dear friends, we are God's children; what we shall be has not yet been disclosed, but we know that when it is disclosed we shall be like him, because we shall see him as he is" (1 John 3:2, NEB). Although Christians are not yet perfect (Philippians 3:12), they are nevertheless on the way! And the continuing growth is part of the joy of being a disciple of Christ. As the Christian continues to respond to the Holy Spirit, the Spirit continues to release his uniqueness as He fills him with His Spirit of sanctity and power. The Holy Spirit applies personally the promise of our Lord, "If the Son makes you free, you will be free indeed" (John 8:36).

Becoming at once fully Christian and fully human rests not in following a program; it results from a relationship to a Person. That Person, of course, is Jesus Christ. The work of the Holy Spirit is to glorify Christ and to reveal Him to human beings at deeper and deeper levels. Telling His disciples of a soon-to-come Pentecost, Jesus spoke of the Holy Spirit. "I have yet many things to say to you but you cannot bear them now. When the Spirit of truth comes, he will guide you into all the truth; for he will not speak on his own authority, but whatever he hears he will speak, and he will declare to you the things that are to come. He will glorify me, for he will take what is mine and declare it to you" (John 16:12-15).

The Holy Spirit remains God's primary agent of making effective the redeeming and liberating ministry of Christ in our hearts. Our very lives must be lived out not by human might or secular power, but by Christ's Spirit. To have Christ's Spirit is to have Christ Himself. For this reason Paul urges the Ephesians,

"Be filled with the Holy Spirit" (Ephesians 5:18). The verb here is πληροῦσθε (present, imperative, requiring continuous action). The translation therefore might literally read, "Be continually being filled with the Holy Spirit."

No better advice can be given to the Church in our day or in any other day. To be full of the Holy Spirit is to experience Christ within and to enter a dimension of existence described by our Lord as the abundant life.

Justification
The Just Shall Live by Faith
Robert E. Coleman
November 20, 1973

Unless we can speak a definitive word here, however relevant we may seem in other areas, we have nothing to say that can meet man's ultimate need.

1) <u>The Heart of the Gospel</u> – Justification concerns man's relationship to God. When interpreted in its' larger dimension of grace, faith and personal holiness, it lies at the heart of the Gospel.

    The term itself normally has a forensic reference in scripture, indicating that God by His own sovereign will forgives our sin for the sake of His Son. "Imputation" and "reckoning" explain the way the merit and character of Christ is ascribed to the believer—"Reconciliation" focuses upon bringing together two parties that were once separated. The word "redemption" means to buy back and to loosen the bonds of a prisoner setting him free.

2) <u>Relation to the Atonement</u> – Running through all these terms is the vicarious sacrifice of Jesus Christ. He died in our place, not only as our example, but as our sin bearer. Interpretations of the atonement vary, but at its heart is the objective fact that Calvary covers it all.

3) <u>New Life in Christ</u> – More than a change of relationship is ours in Christ. Men dead in sin not only die with Christ on the cross, but are raised in the power of His resurrection to walk in newness of life. With justification comes regeneration of the human personality and adoption into the family of God. There is an actual transformation of the inner man through the impartation of the Holy Spirit. In this experience there is joyous assurance even as there is continuous growth in the realization of God's perfect will.

4) <u>Grace and Faith</u> – All who believe in Jesus Christ have title to this life now, for it is completely a gift

of God. Such faith, of course, is accompanied by repentance, which means a change of mind and purpose. In turn, grace in the heart brings forth good works to the praise of God. Roman Catholic, Calvinistic, and Arminian views at this point are considered.

5) <u>A Living Example</u> – The relationship between justifying faith and personal righteousness can be seen vividly in the experience of John Wesley.

6) <u>Always Contemporary</u> – What Wesley discovered at Aldersgate is always contemporary. How it happens is not important. But the personal reality of salvation by faith in Jesus Christ is God's design for every man.

When the titles for these scholarly papers were publicized, an alumnus of the Seminary expressed apprehension at the selection of subjects. He felt that the treatment of classical doctrines would be dismissed by the contemporary Christian world as "obscurantist." There was sincere concern that we come to grips with the real hurts of the world and the church, and not just run the old "clichés through the grinder again."

This astute minister makes a point, which we dare not ignore. Our Lord does not permit us the luxury of talking to ourselves in the cloistered retreat of an ivory tower while all around us the world goes up in flame. Nor will our despairing society excuse such academic immunity in the face of their burning woes. We are expected to be in the arena where people live and die.

But is this removed from the recurring task of clarifying our historic faith? Indeed, in this confused age of relativity, what is more needed than a sure basis for human redemption— in this world and in the world to come? If we can not speak a definitive word here, however relevant we may seem in other areas, we have nothing to say that can resolve man's ultimate problem.

The Heart of the Gospel

Crucial to the whole discussion of salvation is the doctrine of justification, or to put it in the Reformation motif—"*sola fide*," justification by faith alone. Contained in its truth is the basic issue of man's state before God. When interpreted in the larger dimension of grace, faith, and personal holiness, it lies at the heart of the Gospel. Luther called it "the principle article of all Christian doctrine, which maketh true Christians indeed."[1]

As used in Scripture, the words "justify" and "justification" normally have a forensic reference, closely related to the idea of trial and judgment (Deuteronomy 25:1; 1 Kings 8:32; Matthew 12:37; Romans 3:4; 1 Corinthians 4:3). That is, one is justified when the demands of the law have been fully satisfied.

But how could this ever apply to man? None of us is inherently righteous. We have all turned to our own way, transgressing the moral requirements of the holy law. Individually and corporately the whole human race has come under the just condemnation of sin and death. Obviously from any standpoint of merit or innocence, man cannot be justified before God.

Only then in the Gospel sense of pardon can this term apply to sinners. God simply by His own sovereign will forgives our sin for the sake of His Son who loved us unto death. In this figure, Christ is seen as the One altogether lovely taking unto Himself the judgment due a fallen race. As our Representative He assumed our legal liability when He suffered the consequence of our sin. The Father "made Him who knew no sin to be sin in our behalf, that we might become the righteous of God in Him"[2] (2 Corinthians 5:21; cf. Galatians 3:13; Romans 5:18).

By identification with the nature of His sacrificial act, we are declared just, and introduced into a state of righteousness. It is a decree from the high court of heaven establishing an entirely new relationship toward God. Both our relation to Him and His attitude toward us is changed through the cross. God's nature is not changed; He is forever the same. But the way He looks at us is different. He sees us as we are in Christ (1 Corinthians 1:30). In Him there is no condemnation (Romans 8:1). The justified person thus stands before God free of all sin. "Therefore let it be known unto you, brethren, that through Him everyone who believes is freed from all things, from which you could not be freed through the law of Moses" (Acts 13:38, 39).

"Imputation" or "reckoning" is a term used to explain the way Christ's merit and character is ascribed to the sinner. The word means that the righteousness by which we are justified is not our own; it is Christ's, and is accounted to the believer entirely by God's Word of grace. Paul cites Abraham's experience as an illustration of the principle. While Sarah was barren, God told Abraham that he would have a son though empirical reason seemed to the contrary. Yet the old patriarch did not stagger at the promise of God, being fully persuaded that what God said He would also perform. "Therefore, it was reckoned to him as righteousness" (Romans 4:22; cf. 3, 9, 23; Galatians 3:16; James 2:23; Genesis 15:6). Accordingly, Abraham was made the father of many nations "in the sight of Him whom he believed, even God, who gives life to the dead and calls into being that which does not exist" (Romans 4:17). In the same way, we are to believe when the Gospel tells us that we have been made righteous in Christ, who "was delivered up for our transgressions, and was raised because of our justification" (Romans 4:25).

Akin to this truth is the concept of "reconciliation" in Scripture. Here the focus is upon bringing together two parties that were once separated. That sin which kept us apart is now removed, for "God was in Christ reconciling the world to

Himself, not counting their trespasses against them" (2 Corinthians 5:19). The resulting relationship is one of harmony and friendship. "Having made peace through the blood of His cross," we who were "formerly alienated and hostile in mind, engaged in evil deeds," He has now "reconciled in His fleshly body through death" (Colossians 1:20-22).

The word "redemption" reflects much the same idea. As applied to man, it means to buy back and to loosen the bonds of a prisoner setting him free. Commonly the term in Jesus' day referred to the amount required to purchase the life of a slave; or in a slightly different rendering, it might be used in the context of ransom where a sum of money was supplied as the condition of release. Relating this concept to Christ's work, His blood is the purchase price of our redemption (1 Peter 1:18, 19; Hebrews 9:12; Ephesians 1:7; Colossians 1:14). Through His cross we are ransomed from death and hell (Matthew 20:28; 1 Timothy 2:6). The shackles of sin are broken. Satan has lost his hold. There is a change of ownership. We belong now to Him who gave Himself for us. As Christ's bondslaves we are His treasured possession— His to keep, His to use, His to enjoy forever.

> We bless Thee, Jesus Christ our Lord Forever be Thy name adored: For Thou, the sinless One, has died, That sinners might be justified.
> O very Man, and very God, Who has redeemed us with Thy blood; From death eternal set us free, And made us one with God in Thee.
> (C. Vischer)

Relation to the Atonement

Running through all these terms is the vicarious sacrifice of Jesus Christ. He died in our place. We were all sold unto sin, under the sentence of death. But in God's amazing love, Jesus offered Himself as our Redeemer. The life we now have in Christ is inseparable from His shed blood on the cross.

Forgiveness through grace does not mean that God mercifully overlooks sin as if it were of no consequence. Such a view may have appeal to people who sentimentalize God's nature of love. But it has no validity in Scripture. Sin as the repudiation of God necessarily invokes His judgment. Anything, which scorns His nature, cannot be ignored. Something must be done to remove the divine wrath incurred because of sin.

How this can happen is represented by the term "propitiation." In pagan religions, it usually had reference to what man could do to appease the offended deity. However, when used in the Bible, it is God who takes the initiative in removing His wrath. A gift is offered, but it is God who offers it in Christ. He gives His blood. The gift is pleasing to the Lord because it displays His own glory in that He sacrifices His life for the creature of His love.[3]

Christ's blood changes the whole nature of our salvation. God is seen as both the subject and the object of propitiation. His wrath is removed, not because we do anything, but because He did something. From beginning to end, it is a display of His sovereign grace.

God hates evil, but He loves man. His love blazes against that which would destroy His beloved—a love so pure that it would not let us go even while we were yet sinners. "In this is love, not that we loved God, but that He loved us and sent His Son to be the propitiation for our sins" (1 John 4:10; 2:2; Romans 3:25). Through the cross God discloses His love in terms consistent with His justice and holiness. By making Christ our Substitute, He satisfied Himself while at the same time forgiving us.

Regrettably, this concept of substitution is often ignored by modern theologians. Some relate it all to myth.[4] A more common approach, however, is to interpret Christ's death primarily as a revelation of love or self-dedication. The sacrifice is not regarded as changing the relationship of God to man, but as furnishing the basis for an appeal to the sinner. The force of the cross is directed man-ward, not God-ward.[5] A recent creedal formulation of this moral influence idea, reminiscent of ancient Socinianism, is the new doctrinal statement of the United Methodist Church.[6]

Certainly the cross does reveal God's love, just as it discloses Christ's perfect obedience to the divine will. In recognizing this truth, however, we dare not minimize the satisfaction of divine justice through Christ's willing sacrifice on our behalf. John Wesley put it bluntly when he said: "If, as some teach, God never was offended, there was no need of this propitiation. And, if so, Christ died in vain."[7] The founders of Methodism, as the Reformers and the most revered fathers of the church universal, have all recognized the full, complete, and perfect sacrifice of Christ for the sins of the whole world. Interpretations of the atonement may be different, but at its heart is the objective fact that Calvary covers it all. The "work is finished!" Through His blood we have a new and living way into the very presence of God.

> Arise, my soul, arise;
> Shake off thy guilty fears:
> The bleeding Sacrifice
> In my behalf appears:
> Before the throne my Surety stands,
> My name is written on His hands.
> He ever lives above,
> For me to intercede;
> His all-redeeming love,
> His precious blood to plead;
> His blood atoned for all our race,
> And sprinkles now the throne of grace.
> (Charles Wesley)

New Life in Christ

More than a change of relationship is ours in this new freedom. Men dead in trespasses and sins, not only die with Christ in the cross, but are raised in the power of His resurrection to walk in newness of life (Romans 6:4). With justification comes regeneration of the human personality and adoption into the family of God. There is an actual change of character in the heart of man through the impartation of the Holy Spirit. Justification may be viewed as Christ for us; regeneration may be described as Christ *in* us. Though different in nature, both belong to the miracle of conversion.

The Bible speaks of this transformation as a new birth, "born of the Spirit" (John 3:3-8); "born not of flesh, nor of the will of the flesh, nor of the will of man, but of God" (John 1:13; cf. 1 John 3:9; 4:7). It is "a new creation; the old things pass away; behold, new things have come" (2 Corinthians 5:17). The Old corrupted self is laid aside, and a new self is put on, "which in the likeness of God has been created in righteousness and holiness of the truth" (Ephesians 4:22-24).

Clearly something happens whereby the inner man is changed. This does not mean that God destroys human nature and ability. Rather He takes the natural powers of man and bends them to their true created purpose. In this sense, Christ enables one to fulfill his destiny as a man created in the image of God (Colossians 3:10, 11). Only a person indwelt by His Spirit can live for real.

Renewed by this new principle within, the soul embraces and delights in the holiness of God. To the extent that the heart is controlled by the Spirit of Christ, the mind, the emotions, and the will act in conformity to the divine will. Love motivates life so that obedience to the law becomes a joy. The love of God in turn moves one to love himself, which overflows love for his neighbor. Spiritual perceptions are heightened, and with it a whole new system of values comes into focus. That which brings glory to God is seen now as the chief end of man.

It all centers in Christ whom the indwelling Spirit exalts within the believing heart. He is "all and in all" (Colossians 3:11); not as some theological abstraction or creedal dogma, but as a living Reality. There is fellowship with a personal Savior, a mystical union so real that Christ can be said to live in us and we in Him (John 15:4; cf. 14:20; Galatians 2:20; Colossians 1:27;

3:4). Through His indwelling Presence the fruits of the Spirit savor our lives with something of His own life quality (Galatians 5:22).

Regeneration is only the beginning. Life in Christ is always roving "on toward the goal for the prize of the upward call of God" (Philippians 3:14); growing in "the knowledge of the Son of God, to a mature man, to the measure of the stature which belongs to the fullness of Christ" (Ephesians 4:13). There is no end to it. Whatever we may have experienced heretofore, the best is yet to be. What this implies is staggering to comprehend. "Beholding as in a mirror the glory of the Lord," relentlessly we are "being transformed in the same image from glory to glory, just as from the Lord, the Spirit" (2 Corinthians 3:18).

This process of conformity to Christ is called sanctification. It means that God's Spirit is continually working within our heart setting apart a people for Himself. Like any surgical operation, the undertaking is not easy. There are times of suffering and pain. As understanding of God's will enlarges, misdirected areas of our present experience, including our carnal disposition of self-centeredness, must be brought into harmony with the obedience of our Lord. But through it all, we may be assured that God is seeking our best interests. He intends to "present to Himself the church in all her glory, having no spot or wrinkle or any such thing; but that she should be holy and blameless" (Ephesians 5:27).

The secret of this ever-expanding life in the fullness of the Spirit is simply to walk in the truth of God's Word. "If we walk in the light as He Himself is in the light, we have fellowship with one another, and the blood of Jesus His Son cleanses us from all sin" (1 John 1:7). This requires a daily yielding of our lives to His control. It is the attitude of perfect delight in the Father's will. Why should we fear? He never makes a mistake. And "all who are being led by the Spirit of God, these are the sons of God" (Romans 8:14).

There is no doubt about it! For in Christ we "have received a spirit of adoption as sons by which we cry out, Abba! Father!" (Romans 8:15). This is not some supposition of hope, but a direct witness of the Spirit Himself with our spirit "that we are children of God" (Romans 8:16). With all other members of His family, breathtaking as it may seem, we are now the "heirs of God and fellow-heirs with Christ" (Romans 8:17).

Christians who do not rejoice in the assurance of their salvation are surely an anomaly to the New Testament church. For the Spirit testifies through the Word that our sins are forgiven—they are nailed to the cross (Colossians 2:13, 14). Delivered from the judgment of the law, we have peace with God (Romans 5:1). Fear of the future is gone. The grave has lost its hold. We have already passed from death unto life (John 5:24; 1 John 3:14). We do not know all the circuitous ways that our faith will be tested in this world, but we know Whom we have believed, and are sure that He will keep that which is committed unto Him (2 Timothy 1:12). Come what may, we are more than conquerors through our victorious Lord. And nothing can separate us from His love (Romans 8:37-39).

Little wonder than, an air of celebration surrounds the apostolic witness. Just to think that we are united with Christ in an eternal bond of love— chosen in Him before the worlds were made (Ephesians 1:4; 1 Peter 2:4). And whom God "foreknew, He also predestined to be conformed to the image of His Son" (Romans 8:29; Ephesians 1:5). In Him we "have obtained an inheritance," that we "should be to the praise of His glory" (Ephesians 1:11, 12) "He has made us to be a kingdom" (Revelations 1:16); "a chosen race, a royal priesthood" (1 Peter 2:9); possessing in Christ "every spiritual blessing in the heavenly places" (Ephesians 1:3).

What more can we say? God is for us! His infinite desire to "freely give us all things" can only be measured by His sacrifice at Calvary (Romans 8:32). Our finite minds cannot imagine the "breadth and length and height and depth" of such love. Yet, lost in its wonder, we know that God wants to fill us with His fullness. And He "is able to do exceeding abundantly beyond all that we ask or think, according to the power that works within us" (Ephesians 3:18-21).

> O for a heart to praise my God!
> A heart from sin set free;
> A heart that always feels Thy blood,
> So freely spilt for me;
> A heart in every thought renewed,
> And full of love divine,
> Perfect, and right, and pure, and good,
> A copy, Lord, of Thine!
> (Charles Wesley)

Grace and Faith

All who believe on Jesus Christ have title to this life, for it is entirely a gift of God. Whether only the elect have this enabling grace to believe, as classical Calvinists contend; or as Arminians insist, God's prevenient grace extends this ability to all men, the fact remains that "God so loved the world, that He gave His only begotten Son, that whoever believes in Him should not perish but have eternal life" (John 3:16). No other response to divine grace is expected. "As many as received Him, to them He gave the right to become children of God, even to those who believe in His Name" (John 1:12; cf. Acts 16:31; Hebrews 10:39; Romans 10: 4).

By this is meant that the atoning sacrifice of Christ "once and for all" at Calvary is believed to be just that— it is offered and accepted as my own. Saving faith is not an intellectual consent to the credibility of His work, nor a willingness for reformation of character; it is a complete reliance upon the Person of Jesus Christ, the Son of God, Who gave Himself for me.

Such faith, of course, is accompanied by repentance—a complete change of mind and purpose (Luke 13:3; Matthew 9:13; Romans 2:4; 2 Timothy 2:25; 2 Peter 3:9). Until there is godly sorrow for sin and the willingness to turn from it, one may

Robert E. Coleman | 115

question how genuine is faith. It is academic as to which comes first. What needs emphasis is that both are co-joined, and flow together from the gracious working of the Holy Spirit. The penitent man knows that in his own merit he is nothing, and confessing his guilt and corruption, casts himself upon the mercies of God. In this feeling of helplessness and dependence he lives thereafter determined to keep God's commandments.

Still it is God that makes it possible. From beginning to end redemption is the drama of *"sola gratia"*—grace alone. Resolution of amendment, noble deeds, high morality, fervent prayer, self-denial, sacramental rites—these good things are not unwanted by God; but finally nothing that man does himself can make him worthy of his Savior's justifying act. We simply say yes to God's will. "For by grace you have been saved through faith; and that not of yourselves, it is the gift of God; not of works, that no one should boast" (Ephesians 2:8, 9).

Theological friction between Protestants and Catholics becomes evident at this point. Official Roman doctrine asserts that justification comes partially through the infusion of supernatural grace at baptism. This has the effect of equating justification with sanctification, and allows to some degree divine bestowal of mercy because of what man is.[8] Justification is thus seen not as a completed action, but as a gradual process through life; faith is only the first act. The believer is progressively made righteous as he grows in sanctification. Not only does this view confound the biblical meaning of justification, but it also tends to make Christian growth the result of faith plus something else.

While evangelical Protestant theologians are agreed that salvation comes entirely by faith, there is an interesting difference between Calvinists and Arminians concerning its origin. Calvinists, following their view of the eternal decree, hold that the heart of man is "passive with respect to that act of the Holy Spirit whereby it is regenerated."[9] Only after the heart is awakened by God's exertion of creative power can the soul exercise saving faith. According to this position, a form of regeneration precedes justification, though in point of time it may be concomitant. This perspective stresses that regeneration is accomplished apart from human initiative, but it may also allow room for carelessness on the part of those who are not inclined to repent and obey the Gospel.

Arminians, on the other hand, believe that justification and regeneration are two sides of the same coin. It is contended that faith for righteousness is imputed by the grace of God, not the object of that faith. Such faith is not regarded as having any personal merit. Rather it is simply the free gift of God by which the righteousness of Christ is appropriated.

In fairness to all these views, no one wants to minimize the obligation to keep God's law. As James affirmed, "Faith, if it has no works, is dead" (James 2:17; cf. Matthew 25:34-46; Galatians 5:6). Even those like Luther who had a hard time with this passage still contend for faith expressing itself freely in obedience to the Word of God.[10] That we live entirely by grace in no way implies liberty to sin. Something is wrong with any concept of justification, which does not result in holiness of life. We must take exception to those who insist justification may be completely hidden with no evidence of personal transformation and outgoing concern for others. Such a view would be in contradiction to God's redemptive purpose and creative power. The pietists, and later Wesleyans, rose as a protest to this kind of scholastic maneuvering. However one may formulate a theological explanation for the divine act, the words of Isaac Watts express man's only reasonable response:

> When I survey the wondrous cross
> On which the Prince of Glory died,
> My richest gain I count but loss,
> And pour contempt on all my pride.
> Were the whole realm of nature mine,
> That were a present far too small:
> Love so amazing, so divine
> Demands my soul, my life, my all.

A Living Example

The relationship between justifying faith and transformation in Christ can be seen vividly in the experience of John Wesley. For years he had sought to know the reality of personal righteousness. Unsparingly he devoted himself to attain God's blessing through works of devotion and charity— he engaged in regular Bible study and prayer, entered into a small group to seek with others holiness of life, observed frequent attendance at Holy Communion, visited the sick and those in prison, gave generously of his means to the poor and naked, served as a minister of the Gospel at home and abroad— but all to no avail. He still had no assurance of salvation.

By the spring of 1738 Wesley was convinced that the cause of his "uneasiness was unbelief; and that the gaining a true, living faith was the 'one thing needful.'"[11] Still, as he put it, "I fixed not this faith in its right object. I meant only faith in God, not faith in or through Christ. Again, I knew not that I was wholly void of this faith, but only thought I had not enough of it."[12]

However, his honest searching of the Scriptures, and the supporting testimony of the confident Moravians, finally resolved all his doubts. He became "thoroughly convinced that a true living faith in Christ is inseparable from a sense of pardon for all past and freedom from all present sins," that this faith was "the free gift of God; and that he would surely bestow it upon every soul who earnestly and perseveringly sought it."

Not long after this at a little place on Aldersgate Street, at about a quarter before nine, his quest was fulfilled. While a layman was reading from Luther's Preface to the Epistle to the Romans, describing the change which God works in the heart through faith in Christ, Wesley said: "I felt my heart strangely warmed. I felt I did trust in Christ, Christ alone for salvation; and an assurance was given me that he had taken away my sins, even mine, and saved me from the law of sin and death."[13]

This simple, childlike trust in Jesus was the experience, which Wesley so long had sought. Yet his "strangely warmed heart" was not kindled by emotional pleas. Listen to some of the words John Wesley heard that day:

> The work of the law is everything that one does or can do, towards keeping the law of his own free will or by his own powers. But since under all these works and along with them there remains in the heart dislike for the law, and the compulsion to keep it, these works are all wasted and of no value. That is what St. Paul means when he says: 'By the works of the law no man becomes righteous before God...' To fulfill the law, however, is to do its works with pleasure and love, and to live a godly and good life of one's own accord, without the compulsion of the law. This pleasure and love for the law is put into the heart by the Holy Ghost. But the Holy Ghost is not given except in, with, and by faith in Jesus Christ. And faith does not come save only through God's word or gospel, which preaches Christ, that he is God's Son and a man, and has died and risen again for our sakes....
>
> Hence it comes that faith also makes righteous and fulfills the law; for out of Christ's merit it brings the Spirit, and the Spirit makes the heart glad and free as the law requires that it shall be... Faith, however, is a divine work in us. It changes us and makes us to be born anew of God (John 1); it kills the old Adam and makes altogether new and different men, in heart and spirit and mind and powers, and it brings with it the Holy Ghost. O, it is a living, busy, active, mighty thing, this faith, and so it is impossible for it not to do good works incessantly. It does not ask whether there are good works to do,

but before the question rises it has already done them, and is always at the doing of them Faith is a living, daring confidence in God's grace, so sure and certain that a man would stake his life on it a thousand times. This confidence in God's grace, and knowledge of it, makes a man glad and bold and happy in dealing with God and with all his creatures; and this is the work of the Holy Ghost in faith. Hence a man is ready and glad, without compulsion, to do good to everyone, to serve everyone, to suffer everything, in love and praise to God, who has shown him this grace; and thus it is impossible to separate works from faith, as impossible as to separate heat and light from fire.[14]

The compact between saving faith and experiential righteousness could scarcely be stated more clearly. That Wesley understood it is immediately apparent by the way he began with all his might to pray for those who had despitefully persecuted him, while also openly testifying to the transformation felt in his heart. Salvation was a personal experience. Not on the basis of anything he had done, nor because there was any inherent righteousness of his own, but only on the basis of what Christ had done for him through the cross. There was no diminishing of good works, but now they followed out of love in grateful obedience to his Lord.

> I build on this foundation—
> That Jesus and His blood
> Alone are my salvation,
> The true eternal good;
> Without Him, all that pleases
> Is valueless on earth;
> The gifts I owe to Jesus
> Alone my love are worth.
> (Paul Gerhardt)

Always Contemporary

Modern churchmen may look wistfully to the witness of John Wesley and lament that things are different in the twentieth century. Ironically, Wesley thought the same thing when Peter Böhler first tried to convince him of this saving reality. Even when he was persuaded that it was the teaching of the New Testament and the experience of the early Christians, he argued: "Thus, I grant, God wrought in the first ages of Christianity; but times have changed. What reason have I to believe he works in the same manner now?" He was only "beat out of this retreat," he says, "by the concurring evidence of several living witnesses who testified God had thus wrought in themselves."[15]

His confrontation at Aldersgate erased all doubt. What the New Testament and the "living witnesses" had taught him now became a personal reality. To be sure, times had changed, but He found that the Gospel of God's redeeming love is forever the same. "The same resources that were available to the first Christians were available to him. And the same resources are available still for us, by the same grace of God and the same 'living, busy, active, mighty faith' of Paul, of Luther, of Peter Böhler and the Wesleys."[16]

This is the message of justification that is always contemporary. It is a doctrine that must be experienced in the present with every generation. How it happens, its manner and mode, the cultural pattern it reflects is inconsequential. All that matters is that salvation by faith in Jesus Christ become a living reality. This experience in turn motivates the believer to proclaim the good news to those that have not heard.

The constraining impulse to tell the story is seen on that evening of May 24 when John Wesley burst into the room of Charles exclaiming, "I believe." The two overjoyed brothers, joined now in spirit as well as flesh, lifted their voices in song. And in that union of hearts we, too, can join a perpetual celebration of love.

Where shall my wondering soul begin?
How shall I all to heaven aspire?
A slave redeemed from death and sin,
A brand plucked from eternal fire,
How shall I equal triumphs rise,
Or sing my great Deliverer's praise?
O how shall I the goodness tell,
Father, which thou to me hast showed?
That I, a child of wrath and hell,
I should be called a child of God,
Should know, should feel, my sins forgiven,
Blest with this antepast of heaven!
And shall I slight my Father's love?
Or basely fear his gifts to own?
Unmindful of his favors prove?
Shall I, the hallowed cross to shun,
Refuse his righteousness to impart,
By hiding it within my heart?
Outcasts of men, to you I call,
Harlots and publicans and thieves!
He spreads his arms to embrace you all;
Sinners alone his grace receive;
No need of him the righteous have;
He came the lost to seek and save.
Come, O my guilty brethren, come,
Groaning beneath your load of sin!
His bleeding heart shall make you room,
His open side shall take you sin;
He calls you now, invites you home;
Come, O my guilty brethren, come!
(Charles Wesley)

Notes

[1] Martin Luther, *A Commentary on Paul's Epistle to the Galatians* (London: J. Clarke, 1953), p. 143.

[2] All Scripture quotations are from the *New American Standard Bible* (Carol Stream, Illinois: Creation House, 1971).

[3] The most competent recent study of this concept which I have seen is Leon Morris's, *The Apostolic Preaching of the Cross* (Grand Rapids: Wm. B. Eerdmans, 1955), pp. 108-274; cf. R. E. Coleman, *Written In Blood* (Old Tappan: Revell, 1972), pp. 104-113.

[4] Rudolf Bultmann would typify this school. Note, e.g., his *Kerygma and Myth*, ed. by H. W. Bartsch, trans. Reginald Fuller (New York: Harper, 1953), pp. 7, 8, 35, 37.

[5] Eminent scholars like C. H. Dodd, D. M. Baillie and Vincent Taylor are typical of this position. An insightful summary of the views of these men may be found in the chapters by Robert Nicole, "The Nature of Redemption," and Lorman Peterson, "The Nature of Justification," in *Christian Faith and Theology*, ed. Carl F. H. Henry (New York: Channel Press, 1964), pp. 193-221, 363-370.

[6] Entitled "Our Theological Task," this statement constitutes Section 3 of the Report of the *Theological Study Commission on Doctrine and Doctrinal Standards*, which was adopted at the 1972 General Conference of the United Methodist Church. In striking contrast to *The Articles of Religion*, and the standards of doctrine of historic Methodism, the new position avoids any reference to an objective vicarious atonement. All it affirms is that "in the midst of our condition of alienation, God's unfailing grace shows itself in his suffering love working for our redemption." The work of Christ is seen only as a "clue to God's redeeming love." This position is totally unfair to the witness of Scripture. Those who follow this new course digress from the faith of historic Methodism, as well as the avowed doctrinal commitment of Asbury Theological Seminary.

[7] John Wesley, *Explanatory Notes Upon the New Testament* (London: The Epworth Press, 1952, c. 1754), p. 530; cf. pp. 531, 532, 536, 742, 801, 879, 905. Wesley does not labor to formulate any particular theory of the atonement, but he consistently affirms the fact that "the offering of Christ, once made, is that perfect redemption, propitiation, and satisfaction for all the sins of the whole world" Article XX, *The Articles of Religion of the Methodist Church.*

[8] *The Catholic Bible Encyclopedia* defines righteousness as "the permanent state of those who are inherently righteous (just) or inwardly sanctified, because through the merits of Jesus Christ they have been justified by the real remission of their sins as well as by a true inward renewal and sanctification wrought by sanctifying grace intrinsically inhering in the soul" (New York: Joseph F. Wagner, 1955), p. 552.

[9] A. A. Hodge, *Outlines of Theology* (Grand Rapids: Zondervan, 1972, c. 1860), p. 460.

[10] There is considerable difference of opinion regarding Luther's position on justification and the resulting life of obedience. Some scholars like Karl Hall contend that Luther believed justification involved actual moral transformation of a sinner into a saint. Approaching the justification of man analytically, he held that God's judgment is viewed eschatologically on the basis of what man shall become. Theologians like Barth take strong exception to this interpretation, believing that it is little different than the Roman Catholic teaching. The problem centers in subjectivizing the act of God's grace. However, this does not have to be the case, it seems to me, if the norm of God's truth in Jesus Christ is kept clearly in focus. Perhaps it would be best, not to strain the basic forensic sense of justification, but to note the inseparable relation of justifying faith to regeneration and sanctification. Note the discussion of this issue in G. C. Berkouwer, *Faith and Justification* (Grand Rapids: Wm. B. Eerdmans, 1954), pp. 9-22.

[11] John Wesley, *Journal of the Rev. John Wesley*, std. ed., ed. by Nehemiah Curnock (London: The Epworth Press, 1938), Vol. I, p. 471.

[12] Ibid.

[13] Ibid., p. 475, 476.

[14] Martin Luther, *Works of Martin Luther*, Vol. VI (Philadelphia: Muhlenberg, 1932), pp. 449-452.

[15] John Wesley, *Journal*, op. cit., pp. 454-455.

[16] Philip S. Watson, *The Message of The Wesleys* (New York: Macmillan, 1964), p. 18.

Works Cited

Berkouwer, G. C. *Faith and Justification*. Grand Rapids: Wm. B. Eerdmans, 1954.

The Catholic Bible Encyclopedia. New York: Joseph F. Wagner, 1955.

Coleman, Robert E. *Written In Blood*. Old Tappan: Fleming H. Revell, 1972.

Henry, Carl F. H., ed. *Christian Faith and Modern Theology*. New York: Channel Press, 1964.

Hodge, A. A. *Outlines of Theology*. Grand Rapids: Zondervan, 1972, c. 1860.

Kittel, Gerhard. *Theological Dictionary of the New Testament*. Grand Rapids: Wm. B. Eerdmans, 1964.

Lampe, G. W. H., ed. *The Doctrine of Justification by Faith*. London: A. R. Mowbray & Co., 1954.

Luther, Martin. *A Commentary on Paul's Epistle to the Galatians*. London: J. Clarke, 1953.

_____. *Works of Martin Luther*, Vol. VI. Philadelphia: Muhlenberg, 1932.

Morris, Leon. *The Apostolic Preaching of the Cross*. Grand Rapids: Wm. B. Eerdmans, 1955.

Watson, Philip S. *The Message of the Wesleys*. New York: Macmillan, 1964.

Wesley, John. *Explanatory Notes Upon the New Testament*. London: The Epworth Press, 1952.

_____. *Journal of the Revelations John Wesley*, Vol. I. Std. ed., ed. by Nehemiah Curnock. London: The Epworth Press, 1938.

Wiley, H. Orton and Culbertson, Paul T. *Introduction to Christian Theology*. Kansas City: Beacon Hill Press, 1949.

Entire Sanctification

William M. Arnett
January 16, 1974

Introduction

In his illuminating study, *Revivalism and Social Reform*, Dr. Timothy L. Smith traces the permeating influence of the evangelical revival in the latter half of the nineteenth century. He tells us "the quest of personal holiness became in some ways a kind of plain man's transcendentalism, which geared ancient creeds to the shaft of social reform."[1] With irrefutable documentation Dr. Smith reveals that most of the great social reforms of that period grew out of the work of dedicated evangelicals, many of who were leaders in the holiness movement. Commenting on this revival that gave impetus to social reconstruction, Shirwood Wirt states that

> The evangelical preacher, the revivalist, the mass evangelist, carried the doctrines of holiness and Christian perfection into the seamy aspect of the day. They revealed a boundless passion for the welfare of humanity. Anything that stood in the way of making America great—and Christian—they opposed. Thus they spoke frequently for the friendless, the jobless, the drunkard, the illiterate, the Indian and the Negro, the widow and the orphan.[2]

The immoral climate of the last half of the twentieth century needs a like visitation from God with a similar penetrating moral revolution. Very recently, Bishop Paul W. Milhouse, resident bishop of the Oklahoma Methodist area was asked this question: "If you could cause one trend, or emphasis, or change, or program, or event, or attitude to develop across the United Methodist Church today, what would it be?" He replied, "I believe my answer can be stated best as an intensified concern for 'scriptural holiness', understood in its broadest sense."[3] In a recent television interview, Bishop Fulton J. Sheen of the Roman Catholic Church was asked what the greatest need of the Catholic Church is at this time. Bishop Sheen answered with just one word: "Holiness." Granted the difference with which these Episcopal leaders would interpret and apply this theme, the fact remains they declare the greatest need of our time is "holiness."

The subject of this paper, "Entire Sanctification," is a special area of the broad theme of sanctification. The term "sanctification" in a general sense means "the hallowing of the Christian believer by which he is freed from sin and enabled to realize the will of God in his life."[4] Whatever we may know concerning personal sanctity, however, has its source in what is revealed about the holiness of God. This must be our starting point, as the Scriptures plainly teach (1 Peter 1:15, 16).

I. The Holiness of God

Because the Israelites believed in a perfectly holy God they came to believe also that God's people should be holy. Their belief was not based on human ingenuity or discovery, but on Divine revelation. It has been divinely disclosed that holiness characterizes God's essential nature. He is uniquely and absolutely holy. The Old Testament, for example, rings with the thought of God's holiness. Leviticus 11:45, "I am holy"; 1 Samuel 2:2, "there is none holy as the Lord"; Psalms 145:17, "the Lord is holy in all his works"; Isaiah 6:3, "Holy, holy, holy is the Lord of hosts." These passages hardly begin the list.

Four elements revealed in the holiness of God are relevant to our topic, namely, the awesomeness of God, the glorious majesty of God, the moral purity of God, and the communicability of the Divine nature. Rudolph Otto calls our attention to these emphases.[5] Everything else that is said about holiness in the Christian revelation has its basis in one or the other of these four elements of the holiness of God.

These Divine elements are disclosed or experienced in various ways in the Old Testament.[6] The element of awe, for example, which produces in us a sense of fear and reverence, was experienced by Jacob at Bethel. "And Jacob awaked out of his sleep, and he said, surely the Lord is in this place; and I knew it not. And he was afraid, and said, how dreadful is this place! This is none other but the house of God, and this is the gate of heaven" (Genesis 28:16, 17). It is observed at the call of Moses at the burning bush: "And Moses hid his face; for he was afraid to look upon God" (Exodus 3:6). It appears also in the vision of Isaiah in the Temple (6:4), in the vision of Ezekiel (1:28), as well as by Job (13:21) and the Psalmist (114:7).

God's glorious majesty is described in the song of Moses after crossing the Red Sea (Exodus 15:11); in the cry of the Psalmist (99:2,3; 68:35); in the disclosures to Isaiah (40:25); in the teaching of Ezekiel (38:23); in the understanding of Amos (4:2). The moral excellence and ethical perfection of God's holiness were various revealed, for example, to the Psalmist (15:11 24:3,4); to Isaiah, whose vision of God's holiness made him conscious of his own impurity (6:5); and in God's Law and requirements (e.g., Leviticus 19). Finally— and this is the most glorious factor of all— God's holiness is communicable and available to man on certain conditions. That God's holiness is contagious and communicable is the pledge and promise that God's command can be realized: "Ye shall be holy; for I am holy" (Leviticus 11:44; 19:2).

II. The Holiness of Jesus

God is best revealed in Jesus, "the Holy One of God" (John 6:69). He is the One who has declared or exegeted God. "No man has seen God at any time; the only begotten God (Son), who is in the bosom of the Father, He has explained *Him*" (John 1:18 NAS). The Holy God who commanded the light to shine out of darkness "hath shined in our hearts, to give the light of the knowledge of the glory of God in the face of Jesus Christ" (2 Corinthians 4:6). Jesus came to live a holy life, to fulfill a holy vocation, and He is supremely the Holy Man of the world. Since man's primal fall, Jesus Christ is the only man who ever walked the earth who could ask without embarrassment the question, "Which of you convinceth me of sin?" (John 8:46).

The four basic elements in the holiness of God, which we noted above, burst forth in the holy life of Jesus.[7] The sense of awe is there, for frequently in his earthly ministry we come across an expression like this: "They were all amazed" (Mark 2:12). Peter experienced this after the unusual catch of fishes (Luke 5:8). Even the encroaching shadow of the Cross was the occasion for one of the most vivid pictures of awe resting on Jesus and His disciples, as Mark records: "And they were in the way, going up to Jerusalem; and Jesus was going before them: and they were amazed; and they that followed were afraid" (10:32).

The glorious majesty of our Savior is abundantly evident as we observe His stilling the storm, walking on the sea, healing the sick, and raising the dead. His moral purity and excellence are likewise evident. He not only was "without sin" (Hebrews 4:15), He was also "full of grace and truth" (John 1:14). The contagiousness of His holiness is also manifested. Mark, for example, tells us, "wheresoever he entered, into villages, or into cities, or into the country, they laid the sick in the marketplaces, and besought him that they might touch if it were but the borders of his garment: and as many as touched him were made perfectly whole" (6:56; cf. Matthew 14:35,36). Out of His innermost being flowed rivers of living water (John 7:38, a prophecy concerning Him and those who believe in Him that has been fulfilled across the centuries. Small wonder that J. Baines Atkinson concludes: "How great are the blessings that are bestowed through the holiness of Jesus— eternal life, everlasting rule, grace, anointing, utmost salvation, spiritual authority... the believer is sanctified in the sanctification of Christ."[8] Such is the meaning of Jesus' High Priestly prayer, "For their sakes I sanctify myself, that they themselves also may be sanctified in truth" (John 17:19). As P. T. Forsyth puts it so succinctly, "The same holiness which satisfied God sanctifies us."[9]

III. Sanctification in the Old Testament

Sanctification or holiness permeates the Old Testament.[10] Its prominence is reflected in the fact that the primary term for holiness, *qadosh*, occurs in the canonical books approximately 835 times. The basic meaning of the term is separation, that is, it implies being set apart from the common and unclean (Exodus 3:4,5; Numbers 6:5), and a dedication to the divine (Exodus 13:2; Deuteronomy 15:19; Numbers 6:5,6). The biblical term "sanctify" occurs 102 times in various forms in the Old Testament, and often has the meaning we have come to associate with "consecrate." It was in this sense that men were told to sanctify themselves, as well as places, garments, vessels, days, priests, and people to the Lord. The meaning, of course, is to separate or set apart as dedicated to God. Although the primary usage was in a ceremonial sense, the deeply spiritual and ethical significance was not lacking in regard to inner holiness or sanctification in the Old Testament (e.g., Psalms 51:7,10; Ezekiel 36:26-27; Isaiah 4:3; 6:7). Our survey must necessarily be limited to this brief digest.

In summary, then, sanctification or holiness in the Old Testament means (1) separation, (2) recognition of the divine, and (3) to purify or cleanse.

IV. Sanctification in the New Testament[11]

The New Testament teaching on sanctification or holiness is built solidly upon the Old Testament foundation. The Greek word *hagios*, the equivalent of the Hebrew word *qadosh*, and its cognate forms, convey the basic meaning of separation in the New Testament. It is the primary word used for "holy" in the Greek New Testament, and occurs a total of 234 times. Its use in the New Testament is illustrated by the fact that all Christians are described as saints, or "holy ones" (*hagioi*). The words "holy," "sanctified," and "saint" are used synonymously for all members of the Christian Church. 1 Corinthians 1:2 is typical of this usage, "sanctified in Christ Jesus, called to be saints" (Cf. Romans 1:7; 1 Corinthians 1:30; 6:11). It is important to observe, however, that "sanctified" in this context is not a description of a mature level of Christian experience, but of the initial stage of Christian conversion. The Apostle Paul was using the term in regard to Christians whom he later described as "carnal" (1 Corinthians 3:1,3,4).

Three areas of sanctification can be discerned in the New Testament: (1) Initial sanctification (1 Corinthians 1:2; 6:11); (2) Entire sanctification (1 Thessalonians 5:23; Ephesians 5:25-27); and (3) Progressive sanctification (1 John 1:7; 2 Corinthians 3:18). These areas will be analyzed or described later.

V. Entire Sanctification: (A) Definitions and (B) Distinctions

In order to ascertain the main elements in the experience of Entire Sanctification, several representative statements or definitions are given, and some important distinctions are made.

(A) Definitions

1. <u>John Wesley</u> – Entire sanctification, or Christian perfection, is neither more nor less than pure love; love expelling sin and governing both the heart and life of a child of God.[12] The Refiner's fire purges out all that is contrary to love.

Pure love reigning alone in the heart and life, —this is the whole of scriptural perfection.[13]

Perfection is another name for universal holiness: Inward and outward righteousness; Holiness of life, arising from holiness of heart.[14]

I believe one that is perfected in love, or filled with the Holy Ghost, may be properly termed a father.[15]

2. <u>The Book of Discipline of the United Methodist Church 1972</u> – Sanctification is that renewal of our fallen nature by the Holy Ghost, received through faith in Jesus Christ, whose blood of atonement cleanseth from all sin; whereby we are not only delivered from the guilt of sin, but are washed from its pollution, saved from its power, and are enabled, through grace, to love God with all our hearts and to walk in his holy commandments blameless.[16]

134 | Entire Sanctification

3. <u>Asbury College</u> – Entire Sanctification is that act of divine grace, through the baptism with the Holy Ghost, by which the heart is cleansed from all sin, and filled with the pure love of God. It is a definite, instantaneous work of grace wrought in the heart of a believer, through faith in the cleansing merit or the blood of Jesus Christ, subsequent to regeneration and is attested by the Holy Spirit.[17]

4. <u>Henry Clay Morrison</u> – Entire sanctification involves the baptism with the Spirit, applying the cleansing blood and the purging out the natural depravity, the indwelling, or natural, sin, restoring the heart of the believer to the original state of purity, as God created it.

As we have been taught and understand; entire sanctification not only embraces a gracious baptism with the Holy Ghost cleansing from all sin, but it also includes the shedding of the love of God abroad in the heart, and manifests itself in a most important and convincing way among one's fellow-beings.[18]

5. <u>W. Curry Mavis</u> – Entire sanctification is that work of the Holy Spirit, subsequent to regeneration, by which the fully consecrated believer, upon exercise of faith in the atoning blood of Christ, is cleansed in that moment from all inward sin and empowered for service. The resulting relationship is attested by the witness of the Holy Spirit and is maintained by obedience and faith. Entire sanctification enables the believer to love God with all the heart, soul, strength and mind, and his neighbor as himself, and prepares him for greater growth in grace.[19]

There are several important factors that are more or less common in each of these statements.

     1) It is a definite cleansing away of indwelling sin.
     2) It is subsequent to regeneration, hence for believers.
     3) It is the work of the Holy Spirit as Divine Agent.
     4) It is procured by the blood of Jesus Christ.

5) The heart is filled with the pure or perfect love of God.
6) It is attested by the witness of the Holy Spirit.
7) It prepares for greater growth in grace.
8) It empowers for service.
9) It is maintained by faith and obedience.
10) It is manifested in holy living, including interpersonal relationships.

(B) Distinctions

1. <u>Justification and Sanctification</u> — Broadly speaking, justification refers to the whole work of Christ wrought *for* us; sanctification, the whole work wrought *in* us by the Holy Spirit (Romans 3:24-26; 1 Peter 1:2). Justification is a relative change, that is, a change in relation from condemnation to favor; sanctification, in a broad sense, is an inward change from sin to holiness. Justification secures for us the remission of actual sins; sanctification in its complete sense, cleanses the heart from indwelling sin or inherited depravity. Justification is an instantaneous and completed act, while sanctification is marked by progressiveness, that is, it has stages and degrees (e.g. initial or partial sanctification and entire sanctification). Justification is a forensic and judicial act in the mind of God; sanctification is a spiritual change wrought in the hearts of men.[20]

2. <u>Three Phases of Sanctification</u> — (a) *Initial sanctification*, which is concomitant with justification and regeneration, signifies an initial cleansing from the acquired depravity that attaches to the actual sins of unbelievers, for which the sinner is himself responsible (e.g., Titus 3:5; Ephesians 5:26 "...having cleansed it by the washing of water with the word"). (b) *Entire sanctification*, a completed work, realized experientially in a definite, second work of grace (1 Thessalonians 5:23). (c) *Progressive sanctification* is a continuous relation to Christ and his atoning blood by faith whereby there is preservation in purity and holiness (1 John 1:7, e.g., 2 Corinthians 3:18). There is a sense in which a Christian

can have perfection in quality, but not in quantity, "remaining imperfect in that he has not the graces in sufficient intensity." Here is the distinction between purity and maturity.

Dr. Turner distinguishes three phases of sanctification in this manner: (a) Positional sanctification (Romans 1:2; 1 Corinthians 1:2; 3:1); (b) Actual sanctification (2 Peter 1:4; 1 Corinthians 6:11); (c) Entire sanctification, the negative aspect (2 Corinthians 7:1), and the positive aspect (cf. 2 Corinthians 8:6,11; Galatians 3:3).[21]

3. What It Is Not – John Wesley warned that to set Entire Sanctification or Christian Perfection too high was tantamount to driving it out of the land. He was careful to point out that it is not absolute perfection, accorded only to God, or the perfection of Adam prior to the Fall, or the perfection of resurrection glory, neither is it exemption from ignorance, mistakes, infirmities, temptations, or forfeitability.[22]

There are natural imperfections due to physical or mental limitations. Faulty judgment may arise from imperfect knowledge. Involvement in social injustices is possible because we do not live in a totally Christian environment, though a conscientious Christian does not or should not smugly acquiesce to the imperfections of our social order. Entire Sanctification or Christian Perfection is not freedom from trouble, or natural instincts (i.e., self, herd, sex), or growth. It is not sinless perfection. There is a difference in not being able to sin (i.e., sinless perfection) and being able not to sin (cf. Romans 6:22; 1 John 3:6,9; Luke 1:71,74,75; 2 Corinthians. 9:6). It is not a perfection of knowledge, judgment, memory, power or service. It does create in the believer a clean heart, and it does empower for witnessing and for service. We do have "this treasure in earthen vessels that the excellency ("greatness") of the power may be of God, and not of us" (2 Corinthians 4:7), for God has not "given us the spirit of fear (fearfulness); but of power, and of love, and of a sound mind" (i.e., a disciplined mind, 2 Timothy 1:7).

VI. Entire Sanctification: Terminology

The experience of Entire Sanctification is known by various terms representing its different phases, such as Christian Perfection, Perfect Love, Heart Purity, the Baptism with the Holy Spirit, and the Fullness of the Spirit, Full Salvation, and Christian Holiness. John Wesley used a variety of words or phrases to express it, though he preferred scriptural terminology or descriptions. More than twenty terms or expressions have been observed in his writings. For Wesley, the essence of Entire Sanctification or Christian Perfection is "perfect love."

VII. Entire Sanctification: Biblical Basis

There are important references in the New Testament where sanctification is referred to as "whole" or "entire," or is strongly and implicitly inferred. Of special significance is 1 Thessalonians 5:23,24, "And the very God of peace sanctity you wholly; and I pray God your whole spirit and soul and body be preserved blameless unto the coming of our Lord Jesus Christ. Faithful is he that calleth you, who also will do it." The context clearly indicates that Paul's prayer for the Christians of Thessalonica anticipates an advanced stage of sanctity or holiness. Prior to the Apostle's prayer in chapter five, there is evidence of his concern for a deeper work of grace. In 1 Thessalonians 3:10 Paul expresses a desire to see the recent converts in order that he might "perfect" what was lacking in their faith. Paul's burden breaks forth in the prayer that God might "establish your hearts unblameable in holiness before God" (3:13). The work of grace for which he prays in verses 12 and 13 is that these Christians may abound in love and be established in holiness.

Entire sanctification, it seems, is the concern of the Apostle in Ephesians 5:25-27 where the Greek verb form *hagiadzo* is used ("to sanctify").

> Christ loved the church and gave himself for her, That he might *sanctify* her, having cleansed

> her by the washing of the water with the word, that the church might be presented to him in splendor, without spot or wrinkle or any such thing that she might be *holy* and without blemish.

Jesus' prayer for his disciples in John 17:17,19 has a similar concern.

> Sanctify them through thy truth: thy word is truth... And for their sakes I sanctify myself that they also might be sanctified through the truth.

The Apostle's admonition in 2 Corinthians 7:1 implies full or entire sanctification, "let us cleanse ourselves from all filthiness of the flesh and spirit, perfecting holiness in the fear of the Lord." All of these foregoing passages anticipate a level of Christian experience beyond the elementary stages of conversion.

In addition to these passages, there was Jesus' command for his disciples to tarry in Jerusalem for the enduement of power (Luke 24:49) and the baptism with the Holy Spirit (Acts 1:5), which was realized on the Day of Pentecost when "they were all filled with the Holy Spirit" (Acts 2:4). Also in Acts 8 the Samaritans received the Holy Spirit as a second crisis, the chief significance of which was not power (Acts 8:10,19) but purity of heart (cf. Acts 15:9). Paul's summons to the Christians at Rome to "reckon yourselves to be dead indeed unto sin" (Romans 6:11) and "to present your bodies a living sacrifice, holy, acceptable unto God" (Romans 12:1) infers a deeper work of grace and a level of holy living beyond the initiatory stages of the Christian life.

There is implicit inference to Entire Sanctification in the following passages: Acts 20:32; 26:18; Romans 6:19,22; 15:16; 2 Thessalonians 2:13; 2 Timothy 2:21; Hebrews 2:11; 10:10, 14,29; 12:14; 13:12; and 1 Peter 1:2.

VIII. Entire Sanctification: Vitally Related Themes

(A) The Doctrine of Sin

George A. Turner warns that "no doctrine of sanctification is valid unless related to a sound doctrine of sin."[23] Indeed, the doctrine of Entire Sanctification rises or falls on whether or not sin is basically two-fold in nature: sins as acts or deeds, and sin as an attitude or disposition, a principle or instinct of indwelling corruption. Sins committed and the guilt incurred are clearly in mind when Paul wrote, "There is no difference: for all have sinned, and come short of the glory of God" (Romans 31:22b, 23). But when Paul said that "I am carnal, sold under sin" (Romans 7:14b) and spoke about the "sin that dwelleth in me" (Romans 7:17,20), he was not confessing wrong doing, but expressing an awareness of an inner disposition or condition of which he now was fully cognizant. John Wesley's significant sermons, "On Sin in Believers," "The Repentance of Believers," and "The Scripture Way of Salvation," probe this area of inner sin which exists as a latent correlation or state, a principle or propensity within rather than an activity.[24]

Various terms, biblical or historical, are used for this propensity: the carnal mind, the mind of the flesh, the flesh, the root of bitterness, the seed of sin, indwelling or inbred sin, original sin, or inherited depravity. This bias in human nature, or bent to evil, while dynamic, is not an entity in the strict sense of the term. God's remedy for inner sin is His sanctifying grace that cleanses "through and through" (1 Thessalonians 5:23).

In a discerning, scholarly discussion on "The Dual Nature of Sin," Merne A. Harris and Richard S. Taylor warn us concerning attenuated views of inbred sin or carnality. Their warning is so vital it is appropriate to include it in this discussion.

> The holiness movement needs constantly to be on guard against any gradual erosion of a clear-cut doctrine of inbred sin. To permit views to

> be disseminated among us, and finally pervade our literature and theology, which
>
> — think of the carnal nature as spiritual ignorance, which can be corrected by knowledge;
>
> — or as debility or weakness or infirmity, which can be corrected by discipline and growth in grace;
>
> — or as dislocated relationships, which can be set right by repentance and forgiveness;
>
> — or as estrangement from God, which is confusing the consequence with the cause;
>
> — or as the natural drive toward self-fulfillment of the normal personality, which is not in itself an evil but needs to be made a "living sacrifice" to the service of God;
>
> — or as an immature search for freedom, which will be chastened by maturity;
>
> — or as some form of mental illness, or physical disorder, which will respond to proper treatment and needs the counselor or physician more than the altar;
>
> — or as merely a habit-pattern toward selfishness acquired in infancy which needs to be replaced by new habit-patterns,
>
> — *is to surrender a key pillar in our doctrinal structure.*
>
> All such views are sub-biblical and sub-Christian.[25]

To ignore inbred sin or carnality, or to regard it superficially, results in spiritual shallowness.

W. Curry Mavis calls attention to two general classes of interior urges to wrongdoing: (1) there are the inborn tendencies toward wrongdoing, which the Bible calls the carnal mind (2) there are those urges and tendencies toward wrong that arise out of repressed complexes.[26] The first is inherited; the second is acquired. Dr. Mavis says both are rooted in the unconscious. Carnality is hostile to God, but repressed complexes generally are not. The latter may be resolved in a moment of faith, though this may not always be so. If not, the Holy Sprit can give guidance and insight into an understanding of the nature of the problem, or Christian counsel may prove helpful.

In regard to the acts of sin, it is important to discern the distinction between a legal definition and an ethical definition of sin.[27] In a legal doctrine of sin, the essence of sin is in the act, not the motive, intention, or knowledge behind the act. This normally is the Calvinistic view. In the ethical doctrine of sin, generally Wesleyan, "the moral quality of an act in the sight of God is primarily determined by the spirit and intentions of the agent in relation to his knowledge of God's will and his duty, and only secondarily by the act itself."[28] The legal view would virtually preclude the possibility of full deliverance from sin. But the Scriptures remind us that it is possible to be "free from sin" (Romans 6:7,18.22), to be cleansed from "all sin" (1 John 1:7) and from "all unrighteousness" (1 John 1:9), and our definition and understanding of sin should be consistent with this possibility.

(B) The Death of Christ

The death of Christ has as much to do with sanctification as it does with justification. "Wherefore Jesus also, that he might sanctify the people with his own blood, suffered without the gate" (Hebrews 13:12). "Christ also loved the church and gave himself for it; that he might sanctify it..." (Ephesians 5:25b, 26a). "By the which will we are sanctified through the offering of the body of Jesus Christ once for all... For by one offering he hath perfected forever them that are sanctified." (Hebrews 10:10,14).

One of the most significant questions in the Bible is asked in the book of Hebrews:

> For if the blood of bulls and of goats, and the ashes of an heifer sprinkling the unclean, sanctifieth to the purifying of the flesh: how much more shall the blood of Christ, who through the eternal Spirit offered himself without spot to God, purge your conscience from dead works to serve the living God? (9:13,14)

It is abundantly clear that Entire Sanctification has a vital part in God's scheme of redemption. The procuring cause of this gracious experience is the blood of Christ. What His nature requires, His grace has wonderfully provided.

(C) The ministry of the Holy Spirit

Sanctification is identified in the New Testament as being the special work of the Holy Spirit. We are "sanctified by the Holy Spirit" (Romans 15:16), and both Paul and Peter speak of the "sanctification of the Spirit" as the subjective aspect of salvation (2 Thessalonians 2:13; 1 Peter 1:2). Thus, viewed morally, salvation *is* sanctification. Salvation is subjectively the hallowing of our lives by the gracious work of the Holy Spirit. As John Wesley observed, "The Holy Spirit is not only holy in himself, but the immediate cause of all holiness in us." God has called His children to holiness and has given the Holy Spirit to effect sanctity of heart and life (1 Thessalonians 4:7,8).

It is generally believed in Wesleyan circles that Entire Sanctification is effected through the baptism with the Holy Spirit. The promise of this baptism was clearly enunciated by John the Baptist and his statement is recorded in all three of the Synoptic Gospels (Matthew 3:11; Mark 1:8; Luke 3:16). Matthew records: "I indeed baptize you with water unto repentance: but he that cometh after me is mightier than I, whose shoes I am not worthy to bear: he shall baptize you with the Holy Ghost, and with fire." When was this promise of Jesus' baptism with the Holy Spirit fulfilled? Obviously it occurred on the Day of Pentecost, and if not then, it was never fulfilled.

Paralleling the promise by John of the Holy Spirit's baptism as the prerogative of Jesus is the implied promise in the prayer of Jesus for His disciples: "sanctify them through thy truth: thy word is truth" (John 17:17). When was the prayer of Jesus for the sanctification of the disciples fulfilled? In view of the transformation wrought in the disciples in the Book of Acts, one would have to say the answer came on the Day of Pentecost. The obvious conclusion is that the promise of John the Baptist and the High Priestly prayer of Jesus were fulfilled on the Day of Pentecost and were but different aspects of the one experience.

Acts 1:5 records the promise of Jesus to his disciples: "Ye shall be baptized with the Holy Ghost not many days hence." The fulfillment of Jesus' promise is in Acts 2:4. "And they were all filled with the Holy Ghost." In this first instance, to be baptized with the Holy Spirit is to be filled with the Holy Spirit. This activity of the Holy Spirit is distinct from the Spirit's baptism mentioned in 1 Corinthians 12:13. "For by one Spirit are we all baptized into one body," which is an obvious reference to conversion when the believer is incorporated by the Holy Spirit into the body of Christ. As the Apostle Paul observed, there are diversities of gifts, but the same Spirit, and there are diversities of administration or ministrations, but the same Lord (1 Corinthians 12:4.5).

IX. Entire Sanctification: Vital Aspects of a Pauline Prayer

In 1 Thessalonians 5:23:24, we have the Apostle Paul's prayer for the sanctification (entire) and preservation of the recent converts at Thessalonica. We can only indicate the important aspects of this prayer as it relates to the petition, "And the very God of peace sanctify you wholly..."

1) It is a prayer for Christians, not for unbelievers or sinners.
2) It is the work of God, not the mere efforts of man.
3) It is a completed work, not a mere process.
4) It is a necessary work, not a mere option.

X. Entire Sanctification: (A) How Obtained and (B) How Retained

(A) How Obtained

Having made sure that one is in a clear saving relationship with Jesus, then briefly the human conditions are (1) full consecration to God (Romans 12:1), and (2) appropriating faith in Jesus Who suffered beyond the Jerusalem gate to sanctify His people. Appropriating faith involves seeking and asking: (a) earnestly (Luke 11:13), (b) yielding (Romans 6:13), and (c) believingly (John 11:24).

More elaborately, there is the necessity of (a) recognizing the need of a sanctified or pure heart; (b) a realization of God's provision for that need, first in the death of Jesus (Hebrews 13:12; Ephesians 5:25,26), and secondly, through the ministry of the Holy Spirit (Matthew 3:11,12; Acts 1:8); (c) facing courageously this spiritual crisis (d) confessing honestly and forthrightly the barriers, remembering the chief barrier is carnality or the carnal mind which hates God (Romans 8:7), and particularly any personal manifestation or manifestations of the carnal mind; (e) committing fully the self to God (i.e., full consecration), and (f) appropriating God's sanctifying grace by faith.

John Wesley's very wise advice was to "hold fast what you have, and earnestly pray for what you have not,"[29] in regard to Christian perfection or Entire Sanctification. Finally, "there is an inseparable connection between these three points, expect it *by faith*; expect it *as you are*; and expect it *now*."[30]

(B) How Retained

Very simply, Entire Sanctification is retained by faith and obedience. Obedience embraces the Holy Habits: feeding on God's Word, a vital prayer life, a faithful stewardship of time, talents and possessions, and fellowship and worship with God's people in the ongoing life of the Church, the Body of Christ.

H. Orton Wiley wisely suggests (a) there must be perfect and continuous consecration; (b) the cultivation of a spirit of watchfulness; (c) daily living as in the presence of God; (d) the cultivation of a spirit of faith; (e) the sharing of testimony on every proper occasion; (f) seeking more and more the mind of Christ; and (g) telling others of this gracious experience, with a view of leading them to the sanctifying Christ and the rest of faith (Hebrews 4:9,11).[31]

XI. Entire Sanctification: (A) Proclamation and (B) Interpretation

Two important aspects of our Christian task are to proclaim the Gospel of Christ and to interpret it to others. There is no greater responsibility than this, and certainly no more rewarding or gratifying service.

(A) Proclamation

There has never been a time of greater opportunity or need to proclaim the message of Entire Sanctification. It must be admitted, however, that the doctrine of sanctification has been a neglected truth, speaking of this theme in its broader perspective, Billy Graham declared, "God has called every Christian to a life of sanctification. Yet very few have any idea what it is all about. The subject of sanctification is one of the most neglected truths in the entire Scriptures."[32] Graham calls it a "precious doctrine," and says "silence in regard to sanctification, from both pulpit and pew, is doubtless responsible for the failure of many professed Christians to live separated, dedicated, disciplined lives."[33]

In volume one of *New Directions in Theology* (1966), William Hordern includes a chapter on "Sanctification Rediscovered" and stresses that the renewed interest in sanctification is an important development in recent theology.[34] The church generally pays a very high price for its neglect of truth in the long run. But the revived interest is a hopeful sign of encouragement.

(B) Interpretation

Equally challenging is the task of interpreting the Christian message. There is a great storehouse of vital truth concerning Christian holiness in the Holy Scripture. Explanation, exposition, and exegesis will always be a continuing challenge. There are dangers in the task of interpreting the doctrine of Entire Sanctification, and W. T. Purkiser sounds a discerning note of warning:

> There is a vast difference between explaining a truth and explaining it away. Some calls for "reinterpretation" seem not so much the desire for better understanding as the wish to get rid of the truth entirely. But we must be interpreters, not corruptors. We are to be translators, not transformers, of the truth. We are to explain and apply the doctrine, not change its content.[35]

Dr. Paul S. Rees concluded a sermon on "The Beauty of Holiness" by calling holiness "that three-petaled flower of doctrine, experience and life." That conclusion is an appropriate challenge for us today. Holiness, he said, is what

> some of us are commending and seeking to exemplify wherever we go. It is a radiant, reasonable, royal Christian reality of which I can never be ashamed. I ask you not to be ashamed of it. Believe it heartily. Accept it obediently. Experience it personally. Cling to it loyally. Witness to it joyfully. Live it consistently. Promote it enthusiastically.[36]

This many faceted challenge has its beginning with the heart – forgiven and redeemed, purified and filled with the Holy Spirit, through the workings of Divine grace. Christian holiness is shared by proclamation, and then understood more fully through explanation and interpretation. Thus the outreach of the holy life is fulfilled in obedience to Christ's Great Commission in a stewardship of the whole of life.

XII. Entire Sanctification: The Testimony of Experience

In a little more than a year prior to his death, Wesley made this observation: "Gradual sanctification may increase from the time you was [sic.] justified; but full deliverance from sin, I believe is always instantaneous—at least, I never yet knew an exception."[37] A similar observation is made in his sermon "On Patience," asserting that he had not found a single exception to instantaneous sanctification in either Great Britain or Ireland among the many who professed Entire Sanctification, and added: "Not trusting to the testimony of others, I carefully examined most of these myself; and in London alone I found six hundred and fifty-two members of our society who were exceeding clear in their experience, and of whose testimony I could see no reason to doubt."[38]

(A) Wesley's Indirect Witness

Writing to one of his preachers (Thomas Maxfield) who had fallen into error. Wesley gave his witness objectively to the instantaneousness of Entire Sanctification.

> I like your doctrine of Perfection, or pure love; love excluding sin; your insisting that it is merely by faith; that consequently it is instantaneous though preceded and followed by a gradual work), and that it may be now, at this instant. But I dislike your supposing man may be as perfect as an angel; that he can be absolutely perfect; that he can be infallible, or above being tempted; or that the moment he is pure in heart he cannot fall from it. I dislike the saying, This was not known or taught among us till within two or three years. I grant you did not know it. You have over and over denied

> instantaneous sanctification to me; but *I have known and taught it (and so has my brother, as our writings show) above these twenty years* (emphasis added).[39]

(B) E. Stanley Jones

An outstanding alumnus of Asbury College and renowned missionary to India, E. Stanley Jones bore joyful witness to God's sanctifying grace. Approximately one year following his conversion, which made a very decisive change in his life as a young man, he experienced an equally decisive filling with the Holy Spirit.

> ....Suddenly I was filled. Wave after wave of refining fire swept through my being, even to my finger tips. It touched the whole being, physical, mental, and spiritual. I could only pace the floor with tears of quiet joy streaming down my cheeks. The Holy Spirit had invaded me and had taken complete possession. He was cleansing and uniting at depths I couldn't control. The subconscious mind, which is the special area of the work of the Holy Spirit, was being purified and empowered and united with the conscious mind. So that now conscious mind and subconscious mind were under a single control—the Holy Spirit. Life was on a permanently higher level.[40]

(C) Henry Clay Morrison

There is one testimony to Entire Sanctification that has especial significance on this 50th Anniversary occasion. Just inside the main entrance to the Henry Clay Morrison Administration Building there is a plaque with this simple but significant message:

> Administration Building
> Erected 1947 in memory of Rev. Henry Clay

Morrison D.D.
Founder Asbury Theological Seminary
He preached and professed the experience of
entire sanctification as taught in the Holy
Scriptures and interpreted by John Wesley

Bishop Arthur J. Moore of the southern Methodist Church stated that his ministry was influenced more by Henry Clay Morrison than by any other man; he considered Morrison as the greatest champion of Entire Sanctification within Methodism. Here is a portion of Bishop Moore's eulogy:

> Throughout his lifetime he was the exponent and champion of the Wesleyan doctrine of entire sanctification as a second work of grace. He not only proclaimed but exhibited in his life this doctrine of perfect love. To him, more than to any other one man, we are indebted for keeping this original standard of Methodism alive in the modern church.[41]

What John Wesley's heart-warming experience at Aldersgate in 1738 was to the origin and growth of Methodism, Henry Clay Morrison's experience of Entire Sanctification is to the founding of Asbury Theological Seminary. It involves an obscure segment of religious history that has had remarkable significance. It contained in embryo the founding of this institution, the survival of Asbury College, and the eternal destiny of literally multitudes of people.

Actually, it can all be traced to a flash of spiritual illumination in the life of a young preacher in the year 1887. The immediate occasion of that burst of spiritual light was a revival meeting in the Highlands Methodist Church, located in what is now known as Ft. Thomas, Kentucky, overlooking the Ohio River. The recipient of the spiritual illumination was the young pastor of that church, Henry Clay Morrison. The truth illumined to his mind and heart was the doctrine of Entire Sanctification. Previously he had completely rejected this doctrine, which he had first heard presented by a preacher whose theology was a strange mixture of free grace, predestination, final perseverance, the higher life, and universalism. In the shaft of light that eventually shone across his path on that memorable day, "the vision of the whole truth came to him then and there. He saw the doctrine, and that it was for him," as C. F. Wimberly, his biographer, points out.[42] Concerning this significant experience, Morrison himself gave the following testimony.

> ...the truth broke in upon me like an inspiration; I saw the doctrine and experience of full salvation as clearly as the sun in a cloudless noonday sky. My whole heart said, "It is the truth," and I laughed and wept for joy. It seemed as if the following conversation went on within my breasts: "I am the Lord's child. Yes, but not his holy child. He wants me to be holy, but I cannot make myself holy. That is so, but he can make me holy." "Yes, he can," was the response of my whole heart. I saw clearly the reasonableness of it all, and the will and power of God in the matter.[43]

The ensuing spiritual quest resulted in the experiential reality of a "pure heart," another term for Entire Sanctification. Wimberly calls it "an epoch-making event" in the life and ministry of Henry Clay Morrison.[44] Not withstanding his gifts as a preacher, apart from this experience, Morrison, among others, was well on his way to obscure mediocrity, as Richard S. Taylor has correctly observed.[45]

Some significantly related factors should be delineated. Before he became established in this great truth, Morrison was to twice lose its glowing reality because of his failure to testify publicly to it. Though the event at Highlands was epochal, he had not yet paid down the full price. He was not yet willing to bear the reproach of Christ and holiness, as the writer to the Hebrews enjoins (Hebrews 13:13). The following year, 1888, while pastoring in Danville, Kentucky, Morrison tells us that the

Holy Spirit often spoke to him about the lost blessing, and put an impelling power upon him to seek anew the reality of God's sanctifying grace which he had forfeited. The issue became very sharply enjoined.

> One night in October I awoke with a great sense of fear—it was two o'clock, the town clock was just striking—and felt that I must get up at once and pray. I leaped out of bed and began to beg Christ to help me; He seemed to deal with me very positively; He impressed me with His great patience and forbearance, bore in upon my consciousness that I must loose from some things to which I seemed to be clinging almost unconsciously and enter into a closer and a more faithful relationship with Him, or there must be a final separation.[46]

There was all intensive struggle that followed, lasting fifteen days – a time of mental suffering, fasting, and prayer. This soul-searching, and at times, agonizing experience, had intermittent seasons of hope and comfort. There was an unusual degree of Divine unction on his preaching in this period, but the turmoil and struggle would be renewed when he stepped down out of the pulpit. Morrison frankly admits:

> I was in an awful school; it would hardly be lawful for me to go into details and tell what the Lord revealed to me of the nature of sin, and the hatefulness of it. He so withdrew all comfort from me and all witness of acceptance, that I had a foretaste of what it would be to be separated from Him forever. In addition, Satan buffeted, ridiculed, taunted, and tempted me almost beyond endurance.[47]

When the situation became virtually unbearable, Morrison sought the advice and counsel of Dr. Lapsley McKee, an elderly, highly respected Presbyterian minister and professor of theology, then residing in Danville. This pious, scholarly gentleman gave Morrison much comfort with these words:

> My young brother, the Lord has not forsaken you, but is leading you into what Mr. Wesley called "Christian Perfection," the Baptists call it "rest of faith," the Presbyterians call it the "higher life," or the "fullness of the Spirit."[48]

Further, Dr. McKee testified that he had received the same experience when he was a young pastor in Louisville.

Morrison was convicted, among other things, concerning his quick, evil temper, and a disposition to excessive levity. In addition, there was a strong desire to be a mighty preacher. "There was far more selfishness in these desires of mine than I knew of at the time, and I was startled and surprised when all the depth of my heart was laid open to me."[49] As Wimberly points out, there is no seeker of full salvation who has a harder death to die the a young preacher with gifts, graces, and a reasonable ambition. "This class of seekers must literally die out to the future— of place and promotions."[50]

In due time Morrison became fully rooted and grounded in the experience of Entire Sanctification. As a result of the process of sifting and refining, there was burned into the soul of Henry Clay Morrison the biblical truth of a definite, second work of grace. "Once Morrison became established, faces of clay, social and religious preferment, the tongue of criticism and ridicule were unable to move him," says Wimberly.[51] The needle was never truer to the pole star than he was to this great truth. It was out of the spiritual loins of this man that Asbury Theological Seminary was born with the avowed purpose "to prepare and send forth a well-trained, sanctified, spirit-filled, evangelistic ministry," and to propagate "a free salvation for all men, and a full salvation from all sin." In addition, it was this man who at one time saved Asbury College by accepting the presidency when the Board of Trustees was faced with the alternative of closing the College on account of financial difficulties. He is truly one of the great heroes of the Cross.

Morrison was a zealous proponent of evangelical Christianity, especially during the time of rising tides of liberalism and apostasy. It was the encroachment of these destructive forces of theological compromise and unbelief that prompted the founding of Asbury Theological Seminary. Morrison was the dominant personality on a committee which drew up the Articles of Incorporation which state that all instruction in the Seminary is to "truly recognize the fallen estate of mankind, the necessity of individual regeneration, the witness of the Spirit, the remains of the carnal nature, and entire sanctification as a definite second work of grace subsequent to regeneration."[52]

Our Seminary today is inseparable from that epochal, spiritual illumination which came to our founder in 1887. The doctrine of Entire Sanctification is our main distinctive, as well as our power and our glory. Our heritage and our stewardship for this precious biblical truth are very great, and to whom much is given, much will be required (cf. Luke 12:48).

Notes

[1] Timothy L. Smith, *Revivalism and Social Reform* (New York: Abingdon Press, 1957), p. 8.

[2] Sherwood Eliot Wirt. *The Social Conscience of the Evangelical* (New York: Harper & Row, 1968), p. 39.

[3] *The United Methodist Recorder*, 1, No. 46 (November 2, 1973), p. 2.

[4] Harris Franklin Rall, "Sanctification," *The International Standard Bible Encyclopedia* (Grand Rapids: Wm. B. Eerdmans Publishing Co., 1962), IV, 2682.

[5] Rudolf Otto, *The Idea of the Holy* (London: Oxford University Press, 1967), pp. 13ff.

[6] J. Baines Atkinson, *The Beauty of Holiness* (London: The Epworth Press, 1967), p. 16.

[7] *Ibid.*, p. 37.

[8] *Ibid.*, p. 43.

[9] *Ibid.*, p. 44. Quoted from *The Work of Christ*, p. 222.

[10] Cf. George Allen Turner, *The Vision Which Transforms* (Kansas City.: Beacon Hill Press, 1964), Ch. 1, "The Old Testament Witness to Holiness," pp. 13ff.

[11] *Ibid.*, Ch. 3, "Sin and sanctification in the New Testament," pp. 85ff.

[12] *The Letters of the Rev. John Wesley, A.M.,* John Telford, ed. (London: The Epworth Press, 1931), V, 223. Hereafter referred to as *Letters*.

[13] *The Works of the Rev. John Wesley, A.M.,* Thomas Jackson, ed. (London: John Mason, 1729), XI, 401. Hereafter referred to as *Works*.

[14] *Ibid.*, IV, 414.

[15] *Letters*, V, 229.

[16] *The Book of Discipline of the United Methodist Church* (Nashville: The United Methodist Publishing House, 1972), p. 60.

[17] The Articles of Incorporation, Asbury College, by Laws, Article II, Section 6.

[18] Percival A. Wesche, *Henry Clay Morrison, Crusader Saint* (Published for the Fortieth Anniversary Committee, n.d.), pp. 164-65.

[19] J. Paul Taylor, *Holiness the Finished Foundation* (Winona Lake: Light and Life Press, 1963), p. 14. This is Article Thirteen in the Articles of Religion of the Free Methodst Church. It was written by Dr. Mavis.

[20] H. Orton Wiley, *Christian Theology* (Kansas City: Beacon Hill Press, 1941), II, pp. 470-71.

[21] Turner, *op. cit.,* pp. 119ff.

[22] John Wesley, *A Plain Account of Christian Perfection* (London: The Epworth Press, 1952), pp. 28, 106.

[23] *The Distinctive Emphases of Asbury Theological Seminary* (Published for the Fortieth Anniversary Committee, n.d.), p. 78. Cf. Turner, *op. cit.,* pp. 65ff. Ch. 111, "Sin and Sanctification in the New Testament."

[24] *Wesley's Standard Sermons*, Edward H. Sugden, ed. (Nashville: Lamar & Barton, Agents, Publishing House M.E. Church South, n.d.), II, pp. 360ff., 379ff., 442ff. Hereafter referred to as *Sermons*.

[25] *The Word and the Doctrine*, Kenneth E. Geiger, comp. (Kansas City: Beacon Hill Press, 1965), p. 116.

[26] *Ibid.,* pp. 307f.

[27] *Ibid.,* pp. 94f.

[28] *Ibid.,* pp. 96, 97.

[29] Wesley, *Works*, XI, 426.

[30] Wesley, *Sermons*, II, 460. Sermon L, "The Scripture way of Salvation."

[31] H. Orton Wiley, "How to Retain Holiness of Heart," *The Flame*, XXVI, 31 (March-April, 1960).

[32] *The Word For This Century*, Merrill C. Tenney, ed. (New York: Oxford University Press, 1960), p. 88. Cf. Ch. 5 "Christ sin the Believer," pp. 87ff.

[33] *Ibid.*, p. 89

[34] William Hordern, *New Directions in Theology Today*, I, Introduction (Philadelphia: The Westminster Press, 1966), pp. 96ff.

[35] W. T. Purkiser, *Interpreting Christian Holiness* (Kansas City: Beacon Rill Press, 1971), p. 6, "Preface."

[36] Paul Stromberg Rees, *If God Be For Us!* (Grand Rapids: Wm. B. Eerdmans Publishing Co., 1944), pp. 64-5.

[37] Wesley, *Letters*, VIII, 190.

[38] Wesley, *Works*, VI, 491.

[39] *The Journal of the Rev. John Wesley, A. M.,* Nehemiah Curnock, ed. (London, Robert Culley, n.d.), IV, 536.

[40] *Flames of Living Fire* (Testimonies to the Experience of Entire Sanctification), Bernie Smith, comp. & ed. (Kansas City: Beacon Hill Press, 1950), p. 57.

[41] Percival A. Wesche, *The Life, Theology, and Influence of Henry Clay Morrison* (A Thesis submitted to the Graduate Faculty for the Doctor of philosophy degree at the University of Oklahoma, 1954). pp. 350-51, published in an abridged edition, Henry Clay Morrison, Crusader Saint, n.d., supra.

[42] C. F. Wimberly, *A Biographical Sketch of Henry Clay Morrison, D.D.* (New York: Fleming H. Revell Company, 1922), p. 95.

[43] Wesche, *op. cit., Theology, and Influence of Henry Clay Morrison,* p. 57.

[44] Wimberly, *op. cit.,* p. 96.

[45] Richard S. Taylor, *Preaching Holiness Today* (Kansas City Beacon Hill Press, 1968), p. 16.

[46] Wimberly, *op. cit.,* p. 97.

[47] *Ibid.,* pp. 97, 98.

[48] *Ibid.,* p. 98.

[49] Henry Clay Morrison, "My Pentecost" (Booklet), p. 6.

[50] Wimberly, *op. cit.,* p. 98.

[51] *Ibid.,* p. 99.

[52] The Articles of Incorporation, Asbury Theological Seminary, Article IV, Section D.

Works Cited

Atkinson, J. Baines. *The Beauty of Holiness*. London: The Epworth Press, 1955.

Brengle, S. L. *The Way of Holiness*. New York: Salvation Army, 1903.

Brown, Charles Ewig. *The Meaning of Sanctification*. Anderson, Indiana, The Warner Press, 1945.

Chadwick, Samuel. *The Way to Pentecost*. London: Hodder and Stoughton, 1972, 16th Printing.

Cook, Thomas. *New Testament Holiness*. London: The Epworth Press, 1963.

Cox, Lec G. *John Wesley's Concept of Perfection*. Kansas City: Beacon Hill Press, 1964.

The Distinctive Emphases of Asbury Theological Seminary. Published for the Fortieth Anniversary Committee, n.d. Digital copy freely available from First Fruits Press: <http://place.asburyseminary.edu/firstfruitsheritagematerial/29/>

Flew, R. Newton. *The Idea of Christian Perfection in Christian Theology*. London: Oxford university Press, 1934.

Hills, A. M. *Holiness and Power*. Cincinnati: N. W. Knapp, 1897.

Jessop, Harry E. *Foundations of Doctrine in Scripture and Experience*. Chicago: The Chicago Evangelistic Institute, 1938.

Lindstrom, Harald G. A. *Wesley and Sanctification*. London: The Epworth Press, n.d.

Morrison, H. C. *Baptism with the Holy Ghost*. Louisville: Pentecostal Herald Press, 1900. Digital copy freely available from First Fruits Press: <http://place.asburyseminary.edu/firstfruitsheritagematerial/1/>

Perkins, H. W. *The Doctrine of Christian or Evangelical Perfection*. London: The Epworth Press, 1927.

Purkiser, W. T. *Interpreting Christian Holiness*. Kansas City: Beacon Hill Press, 1971.

Rees, Paul S. *Addresses Delivered During Holiness Emphasis Week*. Asbury Theological Seminary 1948.

Rese, Delbert R. *A Theology of Christian Experience*. Minneapolis: Bethany Fellowship, Inn. 1948.

Ruth, C. W. *Entire Sanctification*. Chicago: Christian Witness Co., 1903.

Sangster, W. E. *The Path to Perfection*. New York, Abingdon-Cokesbury Press, 1943.

Smith, Bernie, ed. *Flames of Living Fire; Testimonies to the Experience of Entire Sanctification*. Kansas City, Beacon Hill Press, 1950.

Smith, Timothy L. *Revivalism and Social Reform*. New York: Abingdon Press, 1967.

Taylor, J. Paul. *Holiness—The Finished Foundation*. Winona Lake: Light and Life Press, 1963.

Taylor, Richard S. *Life in the Spirit*. Kansas City: Beacon Hill Press, 1966.

_____. *Preaching Holiness Today*. Kansas City: Beacon Hill Press, 1968.

Turner, George Allen. *The Vision Which Transforms*. Kansas City: Beacon Hill Press, 1965.

Wesche, Percival A. *Henry Clay Morrison, Crusader Saint* (Published for the Fortieth Anniversary Committee, n.d.), pp. 164-65. Digital copy freely available from First Fruits Press: <http://place.asburyseminary.edu/firstfruitsheritagematerial/24/>

Wesley, John. "On Sin in Believers"; "The Repentance of Believers"; "The Scripture Way of Salvation." Vol. 2, *Wesley's Standard Sermons*, Edward H. Sugden, ed. Nashville: Publishing House M.E. Church, South, n.d.

_____. A Plain Account of Christian Perfection. Kansas City: Beacon Hill Press, 1971.

Wimberly, C. F. *A Biographical Sketch of Henry Clay Morrison, D.D.* (New York: Fleming H. Revell Company, 1922), p. 95. Digital copy freely available from First Fruits Press: <http://place.asburyseminary.edu/firstfruitsheritagematerial/7/>

Wood, J. A. *Perfect Love.* Louisville, Ky.: Pentecostal Publishing Co. 1880.

Wynkoop, Mildred Bangs. *A Theology of Love.* Kansas City: Beacon Hill Press, 1972.

The Church

Howard F. Shipps
February 20, 1974

The Pattern of the Church, as Seen in the Acts of the Apostles

In the United Methodist form of worship the suggested introduction to the corporate affirmation of faith contains the following declaration,[1] *"Where the Spirit of the Lord is, there is the one true church*, apostolic and universal…"

The implications of this affirmation are numerous. For instance, it may be assumed from Scripture that the Spirit of the Lord is everywhere (Genesis 1, Psalm 139). Logically therefore it may be concluded that the church is everywhere. But immediately one realizes that such a general conclusion is quite contrary to the thought and intention of those who have formulated this introductory statement. Clearly they must have had in mind a far more limited concept of the church. It would appear that they held that the "one true church" is to be found only among believers whose lives are fully committed to the will of God and controlled by the direction of the Holy Spirit.

This concept of the church is helpfully illustrated by the figure which is used by Paul in his writing to the Colossians (1:18), "and he is the head of the body, the church." Undoubtedly the clearest and most important aspect of this figure is that Christ as the head of the body which is the church, is directing and controlling all the desires and activities of that body which is united to him. This union and resultant activity are dependent upon the life and ministry of the Holy Spirit in the life of the believer. Indeed, it is this relationship which makes him a part of the "one true church."

The Church and the Holy Spirit

Whenever the church is effective it is because the Holy Spirit has been allowed to remain in control. Substitutes for Him, no matter how splendid, important, and humanly perfect they may have been, have always initiated the decline of the church as a redemptive force in the purpose of God. The tendency to offer such substitutes has marked the history of the Christian community across the centuries. Repeatedly the growth and enrichment of the church in human skills and material possessions have persuaded her to believe that such things could assure her success quite independently from the presence and power and leadership of the great divine administrator.

Jesus (John 13:1-17, 26) in his final message to his church recorded by John chapters 13-17 forewarned his followers of this inherent danger. Throughout these five chapters Jesus outlines and describes the place and ministry of the Holy Spirit as the all-important element in the life of the individual Christian and in the corporate life of the Christian community. He speaks concerning five ministries which the Holy Spirit will accomplish in their behalf: (1) The abiding comforter and helper (John 14:16). In verse sixteen Jesus says, "and I will pray the Father, and he shall give you another Comforter, that he may abide with you forever" This perpetual Divine Power at the center of their inmost being would guarantee their success in effective witness and fruitful ministry. (2) The never-failing teacher (John 16:26). In verse twenty-six Jesus says, "But the Comforter, which is the Holy Ghost, whom the Father will send in my name, he shall teach you all things and bring all things to your remembrance, whatsoever I have said unto you." The lessons which they have learned and the truths which have been imparted to them during their years of association with Jesus, will be kept alive and reinforced throughout every day of their continuing ministries. (3) The supreme witness concerning Christ (John 15:26). In verse twenty-six of chapter fifteen Jesus says, "But when the Comforter is come, whom I will send unto you from the Father, he shall testify of me." And further in verse eight of chapter sixteen Jesus says (John 16:8), "And when he is come, he will convict the world of sin, and of righteousness, and of judgment." The emphasis here is that whenever and wherever the Holy Spirit is revealed to the world through the life of the believer He will become the most effective Evangelist. That revelation is raised to its highest point of effectiveness when the Spirit is in complete control of the individual, and giving undisputed leadership to the church. (4) The preserver of orthodoxy (John 16:13). In verse thirteen of chapter sixteen Jesus says, "Howbeit when he, the Spirit of truth is come, he will guide you into all the truth." He will continue to teach the church as Christ had begun to do. Thus the individual and the church will be safeguarded in all the elements which are essential for salvation and a fruitful Christian ministry. (5) The revealer of the beauty of Christ John 16:14). In verse fourteen of chapter sixteen Jesus says, "He shall glorify me." The fullness of the presence of the Holy Spirit in the life of the believer is the only assurance that through that person the beauty of Christ shall be revealed and that He shall be glorified. This is the only sure and adequate dealing with the constant problem of self. The self becomes the instrument through which the beauty and glory of Christ may be revealed to an unbelieving but hungry world.

Likewise the Holy Spirit is to be the revealer of Christ's beauty and glory through the collective life of the Christian community. Throughout the book of Acts, Luke speaks of persons and groups of persons as being "filled with the Holy Ghost," (Acts 2:4; 6:5; 7:55; 11:24, etc.) and as a result of this relationship the church is making new conquests.

When the need arose for the organization of the first administrative board as a body of laymen within the church, one of the major requirements was that they be men full of the Holy Ghost. The seven laymen who were chosen for this ministry performed their work so effectively in the power of the Holy Spirit that Luke reports Acts 6:7, 8), "the word of God increased; and the number of disciples multiplied in Jerusalem greatly; and a great company of the priests were obedient to the faith."

The general purpose of this treatise will be to describe the nature or pattern of the church as seen in the Acts of the Apostles. This portion of divine revelation is to be sure the first chapter of the history of the Christian church. But it is much more than that. It is an ideal which God has set before the eyes of His people for all time. It is not an unattainable ideal. Rather it is a norm or standard established. It is a practical realizable goal. Whenever the association of believers fails to realize such a norm it is failing to fulfill the desire and expectation which God has for it. More specifically, the story of the life and mission of the church as recorded in the Acts is the divinely appointed pattern by which the Christian community of any generation or geographic locality may determine the measure of its success.

Any consideration of the nature and life of the church should also be concerned with the nature of the kingdom of God as described by Jesus in his sermon on the mount as found in Matthew 5, 6, 7. In these three chapters the Messiah is proclaiming the basic principles of his kingdom. The laws of this kingdom are to be written upon the tables of persons' hearts. This is to be in fulfillment of the word of the prophet Ezekiel (Ezekiel 36:26, 27) when he foretold that the time would come when the law of God would be inscribed upon the heart of each person who had become a citizen of God's kingdom. Ezekiel foretold a new day for God's people (Ezekiel 37:26-28).

> Moreover I will make a covenant of peace with them; it shall be an everlasting covenant with them: and I will place them, and will set my sanctuary in the midst of them forevermore. My tabernacle also shall be with them; yea, I will be their God, and they shall be my people. And the heathen shall know that I the Lord do sanctify Israel, when my sanctuary shall be in the midst of them for evermore.

Also the author of Hebrews renews and confirms this prophetic word concerning the kingdom or the church (Hebrews 8:10).

> For this is the covenant that I will make with the house of Israel after those days, saith the Lord; I will put my laws into their mind, and write them

in their hearts; and I will be to them a God, and
they shall be to me a people.

Let us see then from these prophecies, and their fulfillment, that there is a very clear relationship, or perhaps even a complete identity, between this description of God's kingdom in Matthew and the account of the first chapter of the history of the Christian church as recorded by Luke in the book of Acts. The individual whose life is described in the gospel becomes the divinely chosen person by which the work of God is to be implemented in the church. He becomes the means in God's hands by which the ministry of the church is accomplished. So the redeemed person of Matthew becomes the divine material out of which the church is made, and by which it is enabled to perform its mission.

The Persons of Matthew 5, 6, 7

Matthew informs us in the latter part of chapter four that Jesus after his grueling temptation in the wilderness, went about all Galilee, teaching in their synagogues, and preaching the gospel of the kingdom. And he further states that there followed him (Jesus) great multitudes from Galilee, Decapolis, Jerusalem, Judaea, and beyond Jordan. Jesus takes this as an appropriate opportunity to announce certain aspects of his kingdom, which was soon to be known as the church.

In the three chapters which follow he describes the citizens of that kingdom, the persons who will constitute the church. These high standards of life and conduct are very demanding. It is immediately clear that such qualities of life will be possible only in those who have been supernaturally transformed into the likeness of God, and who gladly and enthusiastically yield themselves in obedience to the principles and spirit of the divine kingdom. The pattern of such a life is here set forth and described in considerable detail. The demonstration of such a life manifest in corporate expression is recorded by Luke in the story of the Acts of the Apostles.

Let us direct our attention to the description which Jesus gives of the nature of those who shall inherit this kingdom. First he speaks of them as the blessed ones. The term blessedness appears in both testaments, and in such classic passages which have to do with holy living, as Psalm 1 and this Sermon on the Mount. In this passage it is the Greek μακάριος. Vincent[2] in his Word Studies observes,

> In the Old Testament the idea involves more of outward prosperity than in the New Testament, yet it almost universally occurs in connections which emphasize, as its principal element, a sense of God's approval founded in righteousness which rests ultimately on love to God it becomes the express symbol of a happiness identified with pure character. Behind it lies the clear cognition of sin as the fountainhead of all misery, and of holiness as the final and effectual cure of every woe.

Alexander Maclaren in his commentary on the Psalms[3] discusses the meaning of blessedness. He says, "The secret of blessedness is self-renunciation," a love to lose my will in His and by that loss be free. In an age when the pace of life was much more calm than it is today, nearly a century ago MaClaren was proclaiming, "Men live meanly because they live so fast. Religion lacks depth and volume because it is not fed by hidden springs."

This blessedness is a state of being or condition of life which is the end hoped to be attained by all men everywhere. It is the state of life to be desired above all others. It is the goal of true human endeavor. Thus God has revealed some laws which are to be observed if man expects to arrive at this state of perfect contentment and satisfaction.

In summary, the idea of blessedness seems to imply four major elements, namely: immortality, satisfaction, fruitfulness, and service. The foreverness of life assures its meaning. Being made in the likeness of God, man is called to live with Him now and in the ages to come. Again the life of blessedness is one of satisfaction. This is not an attitude of complacency, but rather a sense of having the approval of God in the daily activity of life. A further evidence of blessedness is that of fruitfulness. As Jesus had said in John (John 15:5, 16), "He that abideth in me, and I in him, the same bringeth forth much fruit...and I have chosen you and ordained you, that he should go and bring forth fruit, and that your fruit should remain." Service is an inherent part of Christ likeness. The disciple finds fulfillment only as he serves God and man in the name of and for the sake of Christ. Jesus at the very beginning of his message to the church (John 13) assumes the role of a servant. And thus by precept and example he stresses that the life of the disciple as well as his own must be that of a servant.

In an expanded description of blessedness Jesus says such a person is poor in spirit or humble, sorrowful because of his sin, meek, a seeker after righteousness, full of mercy, pure in heart, a maker of peace, persecuted for doing good, salt of the earth, and light of the world.

Following this introduction concerning the nature of those who will inhabit his kingdom Jesus lists twelve qualities of life which these persons possess.

1) They are purged within—5:17-32.
2) They are willing second-milers—5:38-47.
3) They are perfect even as their heavenly father—5:48.
4) They are sincere, devoid of all sham—6:1-4.
5) They are always ready to forgive—6:14-15.
6) They are no fakers—6:16-18.
7) They do not covet—6:19-21.
8) They are single-minded, united in purpose—6:24.
9) They are confident in God's mercy—6:25-34.
10) They are not judgmental—7:1-5.
11) They are persistent in prayer—7:7-11.
12) They are doers of God's will—7:21-27.

This in brief is the description of the persons of whom the church is made. These are they whose lives and activity demonstrate the church in action. The story of Acts is a record of their service for God in the first generation of the Christian community. Among the characteristics of this community as portrayed in Acts may be found the following.

1. <u>A Divine Fellowship</u>. The second chapter (Acts 2:41-47) indicates that the first generation of believers established a joyful and lasting togetherness. It was a fellowship of teaching and study of the word; a fellowship of intercession; a fellowship of sociability; a fellowship of economic requirement; a fellowship of worship; a fellowship of effective witness.

It should be noted also that this "fellowship of the redeemed," by which name the early Christian community has long since been known, begets a unity which reaches beyond all chronological, geographical, national, cultural, or racial limitations. The saints of every age are united to God and to one another because they are committed to the accomplishment of the purpose of God, each in his own generation; and yet at the same time participating in that unity of faith which shares in God's work for all time.

Geographically this fellowship begins at a given point when two believers enter a compact of mutual trust, and share with each other the joy of that redemption which they have found in Christ. But this fellowship which begins at home will ultimately reach to the ends of the earth. Whoever is united with Christ is united with every other believer in bonds of Christian love. Thus all barriers of time, space, culture, tradition, or race are destroyed by the universal fellowship of faith. As John Mackay observes in is work on Ecumenics,[4]

> The Christian church, when true to its nature, is a *koinonia*, a fellowship. It was as a fellowship that it first came into being. Following the Ascension of Christ, a group of one hundred and twenty people who spoke of themselves as 'brethren,' and who were made up of the

apostles, the mother and brothers of our Lord, and others who had been His friends and disciples were accustomed to meet together daily for prayer in anticipation of the Spirit's coming. To this first nucleus of the primitive church three thousand more were soon added. The latter were converted after the Holy Spirit had descended at Pentecost time upon the original group of Christ's followers and inspired thereby Peter's famous sermon. The apostolic utterance led to the radical change in life and outlook that immediately became manifest among those who heard it.

Mackay further affirms that we must seek to validate the assumption that it is the church's glory, as the society of the redeemed, as Christ's friends, partners, and joyous servants, to fit into God's purpose for the world.[5] He suggests then that there are two questions which should follow: (1) What is God's purpose for the world? The answer in brief is that Christ should be known, loved, and obeyed throughout the whole world. (2) How can the church accomplish this purpose? The answer to this question is twofold. (a) To make the gospel known to all nations. (b) To live the gospel in every sphere and phase of its earthly life.

2. <u>A Spiritual Force</u>. The story of Acts is a continuing demonstration of the power of God effectively working through the instrumentality of the militant church. It is a magnificent fulfillment of God's promise through His servant Zechariah (Zechariah 4:6b) saying, "Not by might, nor by power, but by my Spirit, saith the Lord of Hosts."

The record in chapter four describes the imprisonment of Peter and John by mandate of the Jewish Council. Their offense was that they had witnessed to the resurrection of Jesus. This was surely a time of crisis for the church so newly begun. But notice that it neither panicked nor fled. Rather this new company of the way turned this threat to their lives into a greater triumph.

This crisis was met by the church moving into action and laying hold of divine resources (Acts 4:31-33). The initial action was togetherness in prayer. They prayed until it was possible for God to do in them and with them all that He desired. The result of their intercession is stated as the place being shaken where they were assembled. It also says that this company was fully in the will of God, being all filled with the Holy Spirit. It also speaks of their unattached relation to material things; neither said any of them that ought of the things which he possessed was his own. Ownership for them had been transformed into stewardship. They also spoke the word with freedom of speech, and witnessed to the resurrection with great power. In the midst of this very great conflict with evil the church was demonstrating a loveliness, beauty, and charm of which the world was taking note. The author in describing what the world noticed about them says (Acts 4:33b), "And great grace was upon them all." This divine radiance was much in evidence among those who esteemed it a high privilege to suffer for righteousness sake. It is seen likewise in the life of Stephen as he is brought before the council and charged with blasphemy (Acts 6:15). Here we are told that all who sat in the council, looking steadfastly on him, "saw his face as it had been the face of an angel." The church's witness is at its highest and best only when the radiance of its divine life shines through in sufficient measure to dispel the clouds of persecution.

3. <u>Persecuted, but Never Defeated</u>. The historian Luke in the eighth chapter of the Acts describes the church at Jerusalem as it confronts its initial general persecution. This is a typical illustration of the Christian community living and growing under the leadership of the Holy Spirit, and making its witness effective because it is channeling divine resources to meet the needs of the society in which its life is cast.

Let us now observe and evaluate the principle events and activities in the life of this church. (1) As a result of a great persecution many were scattered abroad. They were driven to the south, west, and north; and as they went they preached the word. Thus they transformed persecution into a spiritual awakening and an interracial revival. (2) There was concern for adequate organization, choice of leadership, and assignment of responsibility. The apostles chose to remain at Jerusalem to maintain the necessary structure of the church in order that it might continue to function. (3) The church provided for a meaningful burial service for the first of its members who had died in the triumph of faith. Here is a mighty thrust of evangelism which the contemporary church needs to recover. Wesley said of the Methodists of his own generation, "Our people die well." (4) It found its leadership among its enemies. Saul, the key potential leader during this awakening, was making havoc of the church, but the persistent lingering influence of Stephen's testimony was destined to bring him to his Damascus road shock. Here the church had another servant, Ananias, whom God could use in the completion of Saul's conversion and his designation as "God's chosen vessel" to bear His name before the Gentiles, and kings, and the children of Israel. (5) The church also initiates a lay witness campaign. It was Philip, a layman, to whom the word of the Lord came directing him to proceed toward the south where he was to find an unusual evangelistic opportunity. The conversion of this Ethiopian eunuch is not only lay evangelism at its best; it is also a significant step toward foreign missions. It is also to be observed that the preaching of Philip was given a responsive hearing. Luke records that the people (heathens) with one accord gave heed unto those things which Philip spoke (Acts 8:6). (6) There was administration of discipline in order to preserve the purity of the church. Simon as a pretended believer reveals selfish motivation and evil desire which may be among the "converts" to the faith. This evil is corrected by speaking the truth in love by messengers who are under the control of the Holy Spirit. There can be no expression of revenge or administration of carnal authority. Simon repented because he heard God speaking. (7) The church acted with supernatural (divine) authority. Neither the authority (ἐξουσια) or the power (δύναμις) to be employed by the church is ever derived from human resource, manipulation, or organization. Either of these can only be effective when it is clearly a manifestation of the presence and work of God. Meyer[6] in speaking of the coming of Peter and John to Samaria lays stress upon the two conditions upon which the power of God was given. These were (1) intercessory prayer and (2) laying on of hands. Meyer insists that the former of these was the more important though both were necessary. The coming of the Holy Spirit to accomplish His mission in and through the church was primarily dependent upon the intercession of the church. It is this quality of intercession about which Luke is writing when he says, "And when they had prayed, the place was shaken where they were assembled together," (Luke 4:31). (8) Complete healing brought great joy to the city. Luke affirms in chapter eight, seven and eight (Acts 8:7, 8) that evil spirits were driven out, many were healed of physical diseases, and there was great joy in that city. The church in any community when it is fulfilling its mission will bring great joy. It should be in constant conflict with evil and in such conflict will frequently be persecuted, but gladness and well-being are the inevitable consequences of the presence of the people of God in any community.

4. It Is Holy. No doubt in our oft-repeated affirmation in the historic creed of the church we have failed to give sufficient attention to the phrase, "I believe in the holy catholic church." As we do give more serious consideration to this statement we are confronted with difficulties in describing the church as holy as we see it in the world today. Webster in his definition of the word in English, says that in the church to be holy is "to be dedicated to religious use; belonging to or coming from God; consecrated; sacred; to be spiritually perfect or pure; untainted by evil or sin; saintly." This clearly indicates that for the individual or the church to be holy, perfection, in an absolute sense is not to be required. Yet nevertheless, it is appointed by

God that those who walk in His ways shall be properly designated as holy persons; and that the assembly of all such persons shall constitute His church which shall be properly designated as holy.

This aspect of the nature of the church is described by Schaff[7] in his study of the Christian life of the apostolic church. He says,

> Practical Christianity is the manifestation of a new life; a spiritual (as distinct from intellectual and moral) life; a supernatural (as distinct from natural) life; it is a life of holiness and peace; a life of union and communion with God the Father, the Son, and the Spirit; it is eternal life, beginning with regeneration and culminating in the resurrection. It lays hold of the inmost center of man's personality, emancipates him from the dominion of sin, and brings him into vital union with God in Christ; from this center it acts as a purifying, ennobling, and regulating force upon all the faculties of man—the emotions, the will, and the intellect—and transforms even the body into a temple of the Holy Spirit.

Hans Kung in his volume *The Church*[8] discusses this element of the nature of the church at some length. In the section entitled, "The Church is Holy", he emphasizes two affirmations. (1) That the only holiness of the church must be found in the purity of the lives of its members. And (2) that this holiness is always the work of God wrought in the life of the believer.

> Believers are 'saints' in so far as they are 'sanctified.' The concept of sanctification is usually passive in Paul; he speaks of those who are 'sanctified in Christ Jesus' (1 Corinthians 1:2) and 'sanctified by the Holy Spirit' (Romans 15:16). These are no self-made saints, only

those who are 'called to be saints' (1 Corinthians 1:2; Romans 1:7; cf. 1:6; 1 Corinthians 1:24) 'saints in Jesus Christ' (Philippians 1:1), 'God's chosen ones, holy and beloved' (Colossians 3:12). Only through divine sanctification can men actively become holy— holy in the ethical sense, familiar from prophetic literature and the Psalms. 'As he who has called you is holy, be holy yourselves in all your conduct; since it is written, 'You shall be holy, for I am holy' (1 Peter 1:15 f.; cf. Leviticus 11:44) God's will is the basis and goal of our continuing sanctification: 'For this is the will of God, your sanctification' (1 Thessalonians 4:3; cf. 4:1-8; Romans 6:19, 22; 1 Timothy 2:15; Hebrews 12:14; Revelations 22:11).

The New Testament knows nothing of institutional sanctity, of a sacred 'it'; it does not speak of a church which invests as many of its institutions, places, times, and implements as possible with the attribute 'holy.' The only kind of holiness at issue here is a completely personal sanctity. It is the believers who have been set apart from the sinful world by God's saving act in Christ and have entered a new Christian existence who make up the original 'communion sanctorum'; they constitute the church of the saints and hence the holy church. The church is holy by being called by God in Christ to be the communion of the faithful, by accepting the call to his service, by being separated from the world and at the same time embraced and supported by his grace.

Wesley[9] may be found to be in agreement with the position of Kung. In his sermon on the church we find the following definitive paragraph. Many reasons have been given for calling the church holy, such as Christ its head is holy, or because its ordinances are designed to promote holiness, or because our Lord intended that all its members should be holy. But Wesley concludes that

> The shortest and plainest reason that can be given, and the only true one, is: — The church is called holy because it *is* holy: because every member thereof is holy: though in different degrees; as he that called them is holy. How clear is this! If the church, as to the very essence of it, is a body of believers, no man, that is not a Christian believer, can be a member of it. If this whole body be animated by one Spirit, and endued with one faith, and one hope of their calling; then he who has not that Spirit, and faith, and hope, is no member of this body. It follows, that not only no common swearer, no Sabbath breaker, no drunkard, no whoremonger, no thief, no liar, none that lives in any outward sin; but none that is under the power of anger, or pride; no lover of the world; in a word, none that is dead to God, can be a member of his church.

5. <u>It Is United and Universal In Its Faith and Its World Quest.</u> In numerous passages from Acts (Acts 4:32; 20:21; etc) we are reminded that it was faith in the risen Christ which gave unity to the Christian community, and made the witness which they bore effective. Edwin Hatch[10] affirms, "There is no proof that the words of Holy Scriptures in which the unity of the church is expressed or implied refer exclusively, or at all, to the unity of organization." As Paul admonishes in his instructions to the Ephesians elders, the basis of Christian fellowship is a changed life— repentance toward God and faith toward our Lord Jesus Christ. Or again to emphasize such faith as the basic element in Christian unity Clarence Tucker Craig observes:[11]

The historic life of Jesus ended with good Friday. The Christian church was born when his disciples were convinced that this was not the end, but God had raised him from the dead. Without that belief Jesus would have remained a forgotten Jewish teacher who has supposed that he would be the Messiah. Without that belief there never would have been a Christian church. Surely it is no exaggeration to say that belief in the resurrection of Jesus is the best-attested fact of ancient history.

The church is a meeting of God with people, united by Christ, and under the direction of the Holy Spirit. It must have a tie with the past, and also a meaningful understanding of its mission today, and of the nature of the present generation to whom it is called to minister. It is better understood as a spiritual force rather than as an institution. In this sense the church is invisible. Man has never seen the church any more than he has seen God. Its manifestation is often visible indeed, but its real essence has never been seen. Organizations may be formed to facilitate its outreach, but such organizations are quite distinct from its real being. Or, as Bishop J. Williams[12] has so well said,

> The church is not an abstraction, but an institution embodying a living power and charged with a wonderful mission. It is to be God's appointed agent in carrying on to its final issues the work of man's redemption. It is to be God's family, into which men are to be adopted; His school, in which men are to be trained; His hospital, in which they are to be cured of their manifold diseases. It is to embrace in its beneficent work all human needs of body or of soul.

If the church is to heal the world it must have a very direct and meaningful identification with the world's hurt. Hans

Kung[13] a decade ago has described the mission of the church concisely and yet comprehensively.

> The church is the royal, priestly and prophetic people of God, called by him out of the world and sent by him into the world. She is built up on the foundation of the apostles and prophets, and she is led by Christ, acting through all the multiplicity of spiritual gifts and ordered ministries and offices. She has her center in the liturgical assembly, with the proclamation of the word of God and the Lord's Supper; we are incorporated into her by baptism. Thus she is the one, holy, catholic and apostolic community of those who believe in Christ; the Bride of Christ, awaiting him and yet already espoused to him, the Body of Christ and the Temple of the Holy Ghost, at once visible and invisible in this world. As the people of God, travelling on, believing, struggling, suffering, and also sinning, the church passes through time towards the judgment and the fulfillment of all things.

And now as we conclude this general discussion of the church let us share in the thought of J. W. C. Wand[14] when he affirms, "As the human body is the instrument of the personality, so is the church the instrument of the personality of Christ." And later[15] he continues,

> Here is the heart and core of the whole matter. The church is the church because in it believers are put into direct relationship with Christ and because its members are incorporated into him. Such a claim is not capable of proof but it is capable of experience. It has been the assertion of millions in every age since the time when Jesus lived on earth. They claim that this relation to Christ is precisely what they themselves have felt and known.

Notes

[1] *The Book of Worship*, The Methodist Church, p. 180, Nashville, 1964.

[2] Marvin R. Vincent, *Word Studies in the New Testament*, Vol. I,

[3] Alexander Maclaren, *The Psalms*, Vol. 1, p. 4.

[4] John A. Mackay, *Ecumenics: The Science of the Universal Church*, 1964, p. 47.

[5] Ibid., p. 51.

[6] Heinrich August Wilhelm Meyer. *Critical and Exegetical Commentary on the New Testament.* Vol. I, *Critical and Exegetical Handbook to the Acts of the Apostles.* New York: Scribner, Welford and Strong, 1877, pp. 229, 230.

[7] Philip Schaff, *History of the Christian Church*, Vol. I. 1950, p. 432.

[8] Hans Kung, *The Church*, 1967, p. 319.

[9] John Emory, *The Works of the Reverend John Wesley, A.M.* Vol. II, Sermons, 1856, p. 160.

[10] Edwin Hatch, *The Organization of the Early Christian Churches*, p. 186.

[11] Clarence Tucker Craig, *The Beginning of Christianity*, p. 133.

[12] J. Williams, *Studies in the Book of Acts.* New York, 1888, p. 52.

[13] Hans Kung, *The Council in Action*, 1963, p. 221.

[14] J. W. C. Wand, *The Church Today.* Baltimore, Maryland, Penguin Books, Inc., 1960, p. 112.

[15] Ibid., p. 117.

Works Cited

Armstrong, Anthony. *The Church of England, the Methodists and Society 1700-1850*. London: St. Paul's House, 1973.

Ayer, Joseph Cullen, Jr. *A Source Book for Ancient Church History* (From the Apostolic Age to the close of the Conciliar Period). New York: Charles Scribner's Sons, 1949.

Buttrick, George Arthur (Commentary Editor). *The Interpreter's Bible*. Volume IX, (General Articles on the New Testament—St. Matthew, St. Mark). New York: Abingdon-Cokesbury Press, 1951.

Craig, Clarence Tucker. *The Beginning of Christianity*. New York: Abingdon-Cokesbury Press.

Emory, John. *The Works of the Revelations John Wesley, A. M.* Volume II, New York: Lane & Scott, 1850.

_____. The Works of the Revelations John Wesley, A. M. Volume II, *Sermons*. New York: Carlton & Porter, 1856.

Erdman, Charles R. *The Acts*. Philadelphia: The Westminster Press, 1924.

Hatch, Edwin. *The Organization of the Early Christian Churches*. New York: Longmans, Green, and Company, 1895.

Homrighausen, Elmer G. *I Believe In The Church*. New York: Abingdon Press.

Inge, William Ralph (collected essays by). *The Church In The World*. New York: Longmans, Green and Company, 1927.

Johnston, George and Wolfgang Roth (eds.). *The Church In The Modern World*. Toronto: Ryerson Press, 1967.

Johnston, George. *The Secrets of the Kingdom*. Philadelphia: The Westminster Press. 1954.

Kirkpatrick, Dow (ed.). *The Doctrine of the Church*. New York: Abingdon Press, 1964.

Küng, Hans. *The Church*. New York: Sheed & Ward, 1967.

_____. *The Council in Action* (Theological Reflections on the Second Vatican Council). New York: Sheed and Ward, 1963.

_____. *Truthfulness: the Future of the Church*. New York: Sheed and Ward, 1968.

Latourette, Kenneth Scott. *A History of The Expansion of Christianity*. Volume I, *The First Five Centuries*. New York: Harper & Brothers Publishers, 1937.

Mackay, John A. *Ecumenics: The Science of the Church Universal*. Englewood Cliffs: Prentice Hall, Inc., 1964.

Meyer, Heinrich August Wilhelm. *Critical and Exegetical Commentary on the New Testament*. Volume I, *Critical and Exegetical Handbook to the Acts of the Apostles*. New York: Scribner, Welford and Strong, 187.

Newbingin, Leslie, *The House of God*. New York, Friendship Press, 1953.

Nygren, Anders (ed.). *This Is the Church*. Philadelphia: Muhlenbert Press, 1952.

O'Grady, Colm. *The Church in Catholic Theology: Dialogue with Karl Barth*. London: Geoffrey Chapman, 1970.

Richardson, Cyril Charles. *The Church Through The Centuries*. New York: Scribner Press, 1938.

Schaff, Philip. *History of the Christian Church*. Volume III, *Nicene and Post-Nicene Christianity*. Grand Rapids: Wm. B. Eerdmans Publishing Company, 1950.

_____. *History of the Christian Church*. Volume IV, *Medieval Christianity*. Grand Rapids: Wm. B. Eerdmans Publishing Company, 1950.

_____. *History of The Christian Church*. Volume VII, *The History of the Reformation*. Grand Rapids: Wm. B. Eerdmans Publishing Company, 1950.

Schmidt, Karl Ludwig. *The Church*. London: A. and C. Black Limited, 1950 (translated from the first edition, 1938).

Streeter, Burnett Hillman. *The Primitive Church*. New York: The MacMillan Company, 1929.

Walker, Williston. *A History of the Christian Church.* New York: Charles Scribner's Sons, 1959.

Williams, J. *Studies in the Book of Acts.* New York: Thomas Whittaker 2 and 3 Bible House, 1888.

Wood, A. Skevington. *The Inextinguishable Blaze.* Grand Rapids: Wm. B. Eerdmans Publishing Company, 1960.

Apologetics

Harold B. Kuhn
March 6, 1974

The term 'Apologetics' and the discipline which it indicates are rooted in the usages of antiquity. The *apology* finds its first formal origin in the legal procedures of the city state of Athens, in which the plaintiff (an individual or the polis itself) brought an accusation, and in turn the accused might make a reply, called an *apologia*—literally a "speaking off" of the charge. Thus the basic meaning of the term came to be *defense*; it was in this sense that Socrates spoke in his own behalf before his accusers.

If a word of explanation is fitting at the outset, it would be this: the word 'apologetics' sometimes carries a negative, even unpleasant connotation. This is due, in part, to the fact that it is customary to make an apology for some social miscue, or some word spoken in haste. Not only so, but some tend to regard the *bona fide* apologist as an unduly aggressive and personally defensive individual, who seeks primarily to shout down his opponent. But making allowance for unfortunate usages, the term apologetics has a long and respectable history, and the practice which it suggests has been, as we hope to show, an intrinsic and beneficial part of the Christian proclamation.

As classical philosophy came increasingly to be religious in tone, the element of apology came to increasing prominence in antiquity. Many of Plato's religio-philosophical discourses are quite clearly designed to persuade. Insofar, especially as these writings were concerned with the refutation of the current polytheism, they were clearly apologetic in tone. Thus the term *apologia*, as well as the procedures which it connotes, were in use in pre-Christian times. Near the beginning of the Christian era, Judaism made a determined effort to relate itself affirmatively to the systems of Hellenism. This was exemplified particularly in the Hebrew community in Alexandria, where Philo Judaeus (c. 20 B.C.- c. 42 A.D.) felt constrained to present an affirmative case for his historic faith before the intellectual spokesmen for the multi-stranded academic culture of the Egyptian metropolis.

Philo, as is well known, saw the Old Testament as the greatest and wisest of books, and Moses as the prince of teachers. By means of allegorical methods of exegesis, he attempted to show that the Old Testament was not only harmonious with the best in Hellenistic thought, but also that it contained a wisdom more lofty and certain than the best in non-Christian systems. By means of the concept of the Logos he sought to connect the major cosmological ideas of the Hebrew Scriptures with those extant in the Greco-Roman world.[1] The result was a powerful synthesis of Mosaic faith and Hellenism. He felt, incidentally, that philosophy was God's special gift to the Greek world, so that its best thinkers were able to discover by reason alone a great deal of that which was given to the Jewish people by special revelation.[2]

It is proposed to deal with the general subject of Apologetics under four rubrics: first, attention will be given to the apologetic element in the writings of the New Testament; second, brief consideration will be given to the development of apologetics during the early Christian centuries, when the exigencies of the occasion seemed to be the major driving force behind apologetic activity. The third division will examine the early forms of apologetic models, and to note something of the dynamics of model making. The final section will attempt to deal briefly with several forms of structured or modeled apologetics, and if possible, to point the way to the type of apologetic thrust which the conditions of our own century might dictate.

1

There is a surprisingly large degree of attention given to the element of apologetics in the New Testament. The term *apologia* and its verbal form *apologeomai*, appears four times in the New Testament (Acts 19:33, Acts 22:1, Philippians 1:7 and Philippians 1:17). The concepts which these terms bear appear far more widely than the terms themselves. This is true of the Gospels, as well as in the Pauline and Petrine writings. Our Lord himself is shown to have made a reply to representatives of three major Jewish elements of his time, Pharisees, Sadducees and 'Lawyers' (Matthew 22:15ff; 23ff; and 35ff). Paul's apologetic activity is described in the closing chapters of the Book of Acts, in which he undertook a defense before the mob in Jerusalem (Acts 22:1ff), before the council (Acts 23:1ff), before Felix (Acts 24:1ff) and during his hearing before Festus and Agrippa (Acts 26:1ff). Echoes of this same motif appear in his Epistles, notably in the Corinthian correspondence (1 Corinthians 9; 2 Corinthians 13) and in the Epistle to the Galatians (Galatians 1 &2). To this we would certainly add his masterly apologetic discourse at the Areopagus in Athens (Acts 17:22-31).

One of the discernible forms of apologetic activity in the New Testament is that which centers in the use of Old Testament materials by New Testament writers. It may be said, as an aside, that this is an aspect of early Church apologetics that is frequently overlooked. It goes without saying that the Evangelist Matthew makes the most conspicuous use of materials from the Hebrew Scriptures in his Gospel. Some thirty times the formula, with slight variations, occurs there: "...that it might be fulfilled which was spoken by..." (Matthew 1:22; 2:15; 2:23; 13:14; etc.). The purpose of this and similar usages was, of course, to support the claim of Christianity against objectors, (in this case perhaps non-believing Jews). The manner in which Scripture was employed to this purpose, and the shift of the mode of employment of it is discussed by Father Barnabas Lindars;[3] considerations of time forbid any detailed consideration of this more minute question.

While the use of the Old Testament for apologetic purposes by New Testament writers is most visible in St. Matthew's Gospel, the Epistle to the Hebrews is in some respects even more noteworthy for its reasoned employment of Old Testament motifs with a purpose to persuasion. A. B. Bruce has called this Epistle "the first apology for Christianity."[4] The writer seems to have been in correspondence with Christians of

Jewish origin who stood in peril of slipping quietly away from their Christian faith and back into Judaism. Against the tempting possibilities that Old Testament faith was being abandoned, that suffering and death were unworthy of a divine Messiah, and that the lack of ritual in the Christian Church represented a loss of vital visibilities in Judaism, the author of Hebrews made a three-fold defense. First, far from losing the essential features of the divinely given Faith channeled to the Patriarchs and Fathers, Christianity was shown not only to fulfill the inner core of Judaic religion, but to surpass all of its usages. Likewise, the sufferings of Christ were, far from being an argument against the dignity of the Messiah, the normal expectation of the *Hebrew* prophetic message. Further, our author points out that while the ritual system of Tabernacle and Temple were no longer observed, they have found a far more satisfying fulfillment in the priestly work of our Lord.

Thus the apologetic thrust of the Epistle to the Hebrews continues that which is both implicit and explicit in the Gospels. It carries that thrust further by showing that Christianity is the perfect Faith, fulfilling and surpassing all that the "Law and Prophets" contained and prefigured. The use of the *a fortiori* form of argumentation was 'a natural' to this mode of apologetic.

Much more ought to be said at the point of the employment of the apologetic method by writers of the New Testament. For a careful survey of the methodology of the several New Testament writers, the reader is invited to note especially the section "Apologetics in the New Testament" in Fr. Avery Dulles' work, *Theological Resources: A History of Apologetics*.[5] The following is an excerpt from the conclusions which Father Dulles reaches:

> While none of the NT writings is directly and professedly apologetical, nearly all of them contain reflections of the Church's efforts to exhibit the credibility of its message and to answer the obvious objections that would have

> risen in the minds of adversaries, prospective converts, and candid believers. Parts of the NT—such as the major Pauline letters, Hebrews, the four Gospels, and Acts—reveal an apologetical preoccupation in the minds of the authors themselves.[6]

It seems clear, in the light of the foregoing, that the apologetic mood, which here and there rises to objective expression, is pervasive of the writings of the New Testament. It should be added, that the resurrection of our Lord occupied a place of unique importance in the overall New Testament apologetic thrust. This event seemed to the New Testament writers, especially Paul, as the crowning manifestation of God's mighty and supernatural activity within human history. As such, it formed not only the basis for the *kerygma* of the primitive Church, but also a major point of reference and appeal as that Church stood at the cutting edge of history, tremulous but confident that it possessed a Faith worthy of universal acceptance.

2

The first two centuries of Church history were marked by a continuation of the apologetic activity begun by our Lord and by the Apostles. Two sets of circumstances called this forth. First, the Church faced, upon repeated occasions, persecution at the hands of the Imperial power— persecutions of varied fierceness, which at times decimated the Church and at most times during the second and third centuries formed a living threat to all who professed to be part of The Way. The second set of circumstances came to the fore as forms of teaching incompatible with the Christian Evangel were advanced within the Christian body (e.g., heresies). Thus was shaped the two-fold character of early Christian apologetics.

Chief among the Greek apologists of the ante-Nicene period were Justin, called The Martyr (died 166) and Irenaeus, Bishop of Lyons (140-202). While the causes of the Imperial persecutions were many, one causative factor was the slander directed against believers by both Jews and pagans. Another factor was, we feel certain, the general uneasiness which pervaded the Empire as a result of the constant incursions of the Germanic barbarians from the north and the east. This led to the psychological phenomenon of scapegoating. It was a concern of both Justin and Irenaeus, not only to refute such charges as those of cannibalism and of sexual license among Christians, but to convince the Imperial power of the reliability of Christian believers as citizens. High officials were assured that the presence of Christians within the prevailing society served only beneficial purposes. Thus, far from being responsible for the troubles of the Empire, Christians through their prayers actually served to hold the Empire together. The objective was, of course, to secure civil toleration for the Christian body. We do not know whether such apologetic writings actually reached the Emperors or not. Probably they had their largest effect at lower levels of the Imperial administration.

As the Christian body came to include many persons who were educated in the science of the time, early Greek apologists sought to relate the Christian Evangel to the prevailing knowledge of the age. Justin sought to show that Christian truth, particularly as it centered about the teaching of the *Logos*, carried forward to completion the major themes of Greek thought. In this, Justin laid the groundwork for much of later apologetics, in pointing out to objectors of all levels the essential affinities between Christianity and the best of prevailing thought. Greek philosophy was thus recognized as the *praeambula fidei*, preparing the way for the Christian Revelation.

Irenaeus developed an apologetic primarily designed to deal with the increasing currency of teachings which threatened the primary teachings of Christianity. His work *Against the Heresies* is not only a defense of Christianity; but it is as well a major source of information concerning heretical movements, notably Gnosticism. Tertullian (c. 160-245) likewise did an important work in his *Apologetic* and his two books *To the Nations*. The latter was a well-reasoned treatise in defense of the Christian message against the prevailing paganism. To the list we might add his work *On Idolatry* in which he exposed the unwisdom of the worship of idols against the backdrop of Christian theism. His works suggest a dual form of opposition, namely the bitterness of the Jewish communities toward the Christians, and the mocking attitude of the pagan thinkers of the period. Tertullian is brilliant in his application of the principles of Roman law and Roman justice to the defense of Christianity.[7] Incidentally, the Jews were not ignored in this period; Justin addressed an apologetic to them under the title of *Dialogue with Trypho the Jew*, in which, in the spirit of the Epistle to the Hebrews, he points out that the New Covenant has abrogated the Old, and urges Jews to turn to Christ as the source of the completion of their ancient faith.

Origen (185-254), usually regarded to be the greatest of the Alexandrian apologists, undertook a defense of the Christian faith in terms of a head-on refutation of the prevailing currents of pagan thought. Drawing upon the insights of his great teacher Clement of Alexandria (c. 150-214), Origen sought to elaborate a philosophical base for the several doctrines of Christianity. Unfortunately many of his writings have not survived. We do possess his major work, *On Principles* (in a Latin translation) and of course his *Contra Celsum*. While Origen was basically a Platonist, he did not attempt to erect his apology upon a thorough acceptance of Platonic thought.

It is significant that Origen's greatest apologetic work was elicited by the ablest criticism of Christianity which paganism could mount, that by the Platonist Celsus. If one were to paraphrase a homely phrase, it might read: "It takes a Platonist to catch a Platonist." In any case, it was in his engagement with Celsus that Origen produced "the keenest and most convincing defense of the Christian faith that the ancient world brought forth, and one fully worthy of the greatness of the controversy.[8]

To trace in any detail Origen's apologetic system would expand this paper beyond tolerable limits. It must be said, in sum, that with Origen, Christian apologetics reached a new level of clarity, and a new stage of approach to the subject. He no longer plead with authorities for mere toleration, but took the counteroffensive against the prevailing currents of thought. He, above all his colleagues, knew well the range of pagan thought and could speak as an authority in his own right, and not merely as a defensive thinker. He was a maker of synthesis, by which he demonstrated to the mind of his day that the Christian message not only includes all that is valid in pagan systems, but also embodies and engenders a wisdom more comprehensive and profound than any rival religion or any philosophy not resting on revelation.[9] In this sense, Origen was a creator of an apologetic model; as such he summed up in himself the best of ante-Nicene apologetics.

3

With Aurelius Augustine (354-430) there began a new era, not only in biblical interpretation, but as well, in theological discourse and in Christian apologetics. If it may be said that Origen moved far in the direction of an apologetic model, only reaching it at the end of his work, it may be said with equal plausibility that Augustine made from the beginning a systematic use of such a model.

It should be noted at the outset that Augustine imposed no logical order upon his writings. Many of them overlap, and later ones frequently develop or make explicit ideas only implicit in earlier ones. Also, he drew no sharp line of demarcation between philosophy and psychology, or between theology and philosophy. The major writings which concern apologetics are four: *The City of God*, *The Confessions*, *On the Trinity*, and *The True Religion*.

As a germinal thinker, Augustine's writings not only introduce new answers to old questions, but also project new forms of both methodology and content. The range of his researches encouraged this. He not only knew Plato and the Neo-Platonists as did Origen, but he also knew Aristotle, as well as both the original and the later Hellenistic forms of Stoicism and Epicureanism. We would note as an aside that he held Aristotle in high esteem.[10]

Against what he felt to be the excessive exaltation of reason by the Stoics, Augustine set himself to relate reason to will *and* to faith. Against the irreligiousness of the Epicureans, he insisted that religion, not irreligion, lay at the very root of correct reasoning. Thus he appears in the role of one who will meet all comers—not in an attitude of braggadocio, but from a posture of deep conviction of the validity and finality of the Christian faith.

His apologetic model concerned itself with three major and interlocking problems: 1. the nature of knowledge; 2. the relation of knowing to theology; and 3. the relation of God to the cosmos. These he treats in their interrelationships. Basic to his epistemology is his belief that all mental activity is from God. As he says in *The True Religion*, God is "the unchangeable substance which is above the rational mind."[11] In other words, knowledge of God is integral to any human knowledge. By cultivating, therefore, a knowledge of God, one will find illumination of the mind which will affect affirmatively all knowing.[12] If it be held that this is a deliverance of faith, not of reason, Augustine would say that the two are correlated, built into man and inseparably linked. Thus faith and reason are held to be reciprocal in activity. For this reason, Augustine would contend, the existence of eternal ideas in the mind leads logically to the affirmation that God exists.

Today's objector would no doubt say that it constitutes an unwarranted inference to move from the existence of truth to the existence of God. Augustine's reply would be, it seems clear, that the identification of truth (with a small letter) with

Truth itself (i.e., God) was self-evident. To Augustine the quest for God was not merely intellectual and analytic, but ultimately a moral quest— i.e., a question of will. The will, in turn, stands not only in a reciprocal relation to reason, but is itself the instrument through which God makes his presence indisputably known. It is evident that Augustine's theory of knowledge was neither systematic nor dialectical, but existential. That is to say, he developed it within a functional theological or religious context. As John A. Mourant writes, speaking of his epistemology:

> Its principle features are an activist theory of sensation, the function of imagination and memory, the nature of learning, the celebrated theory of the divine illumination, and the distinction between science and wisdom.[13]

In summary, Augustine's apologetic centered in the assumption (held as a conviction by him) that the nature of human thought presupposes God's existence, and that this guaranteed the validity of the thinking process and implied also God's activity in all parts of the universe, including the area within man. It is not to our purpose to determine the validity of his conclusions, but to note that Augustine formulated a model which was grand in its conception, existential in its methodology, and (to him) coercive in its power. In sum, to Augustine God was not a problem to be solved by logic, but a mystery to be apprehended by faith. As he says in one place, "He is more truly thought than expressed; and He exists more truly than He is thought."[14]

From the viewpoint of the actual source of his apologetics, it must be noted that the major work is his *City of God*, Books I to X. He here covered, in the grand manner, the historical bearings of Christian faith against the backdrop of paganism, and dealt with the Hellenistic paganism in such a way that he probably disposed of most of the prestige which it still enjoyed.[15] In Books VIII to X, he defends most of the major doctrines of the Christian faith. It is significant that the *City of*

God is still regarded as a powerful book, and more specifically, a relevant tract for bad times.

One of the most venturesome, if less well known, attempts at an apologetic during the era imprecisely known as the early Middle Ages, was undertaken by an unnamed Old Saxon writer. Writing about 830 during the reign of Louis I, eldest son of Charlemagne and known as 'The Pious,' this author produced the Saxon *Heliand*. The title was, of course, the Saxon equivalent for the modern high German word *Heiland* meaning Savior. The *Heliand* was directed primarily toward Germanic pagans marginal to the Christian tradition, as well as to Saxon converts, and manifested many interesting qualities of a modeled or structured apologetic. It demonstrated both affirmative qualities of the apologetic effort, and as well, some of the perils which beset such effort.

The *Heliand* was produced by a poet trained at the monastery of Fulda in Germany. Basing his work, not on the Vulgate but upon the Gospel Harmony of Tatian, the unnamed author wrote in simple but powerful contours; he portrayed the Gospel narrative in terms of old Germanic usages. The Christ of the *Heliand* is a warrior-hero, while his disciples are *theganos* or thanes—noble vassals who render their Lord unquestioning loyalty. The narrative does, of course, reflect the tribal ways of the Saxon people.

The landscape is that of Lower Saxony, with its flat fields, its forests, and its castles. The cities of the Gospels are known as 'castles'—thus Nazarethburg, Bethleemaburg, Jerusalamerburg, Rumerburg, vivid portrayals of Nazareth, Bethlehem, Jerusalem and Rome, as if they were Rhenish citadels. The evangelists' narratives are portrayed with typical German realism. Its personages live as Saxon retainers of the fourth and fifth centuries, sworn to lifelong *triuwe* (or reciprocal fidelity) to their Lord.

The *Heliand* is the last great poem in western Germanic speech employing alliterative verse. Its author describes, among other scenes, Herod's feast, the storm on Gennesaret, and the fall of Jerusalem. What is significant is, that he made a radical adaptation of the Gospel narratives to the thought-idiom of his own age. It may not please our Puritan ears that he made of the marriage in Cana a Germanic-type drinking bout. It does intrigue us that he sought to meet the mentality of the time on its own ground. At times our author was solemn and stately, as many of his lines will indicate.[16] For example, he made the Sermon on the Mount to be spoken by a Hero whose heroism was adorned with gentleness and mercy. The deviations from the Gospel accounts were so made as to establish contact with the writer's people. The life of our Lord was thus assimilated into the thought of Saxon people, some recently converted to Christianity, others as yet unreached.[17] The strategy was masterly, the language powerful and vivid.

In assessing the apologetic significance of the *Heliand*, one must take into account much more than the actual content of the work itself. It is, that is to say, necessary to note that the author had a governing ideal, a model, namely, of effecting a synthesis of Germanic form with Christian content. The objective was the enlisting of the inner loyalties of a people just emerging from a rugged form of paganism, for the Savior. Two specialists in Germanic life and literature, O. S. Fleissner and E. M. Fleissner, estimate the impact of the work thus:

> In the ninth century, under the successor of Charlemagne, Louis the Pious, there originated a great, Christian, low German literary work; the *Heliand*. The author tells therein of the life of Jesus, in old Germanic form. Jesus is a hero and leader, the disciples are his followers. As the life of a German prince, so was Jesus portrayed, bold and dramatic, awakening the love of his warriors. For this reason, certainly the *Heliand* has served greatly to assist the spread of Christianity because he blended together the known and that which was loved by the people, with the new and the unfamiliar.[18]

These points of greatness mark the *Heliand* as one of the great apologetic works of the medieval world. If its awkward concessions to prevailing practices and usages point out a peril to apologetics, its effective contact with the life and thought of those to whom it was addressed manifest the aptness of its conception and the validity of its model.

Anselm of Bec (1033-1109), the Benedictine abbot who became Archbishop of Canterbury in 1093, is an important link in the apologetic series. He represents the methodology of the high Middle Ages, and is important to the present study for his clearly defined apologetic model. This model embodied three major elements:

        1) The relationship between faith and knowledge;
        2) The possibility of demonstrating God's existence; and
        3) His objective view of the atonement.

Anselm's epistemological datum, *credo ut intelligam* (I believe in order that I may know) is fundamental to his entire apologetic system. He chose to begin with faith— with belief— accepting as true what is declared by scripture and tradition. He utilized reason as a means to the achievement of an analytic understanding of what is already believed. Thus he employed a rational methodology for inquiry; and where philosophical understanding was concerned, he began with what he deemed to be self-evident rational principles.[19] What is vital here is, that he found faith to be a light unto understanding, whether it concerned principles of theology, or whether matters essential to philosophy.

With reference to the question of God and his existence, Anselm elaborated in his *Proslogium* an argument which, while of debatable validity, has been the springboard of discussion, over and over again. If the ontological argument has not proved to be coercive, it has had a remarkable survival value. In essence, this argument seeks to argue, from *within the concept of God* to God's objective existence. Its weakness consists in its "leap" from logical order to ontological reality, from mental existence to extramental reality.

Probably this argument was underlain by a hidden assumption, namely that logical understanding is capable of grasping objective reality. This is, it seems clear, a specialized application of the view that faith leads to understanding— i.e., that faith is linked inseparably to the objectively real. This belief has its origin in the *imago dei* by which man, even in his fallen state, can conceive *and* love God.[20] There is also a close linkage between this assumption and the basic assertion of Augustine, to the effect that knowledge of God is part of man's knowledge in general.

With respect to soteriology, Anselm in his *Cur Deus homo*? (Why a God-man?) sought to establish the necessity of a redemptive Incarnation. Here again, he dealt with a form of analogy which is typically medieval; he sought to show from reason that redemption, with all it involved of incarnation and reconciliation, is as Revelation has indicated it to be. In the briefest, his doctrine of the atonement is strongly objective, and as such rested upon the belief that when man fell, he violated the Divine honor in such a manner as to disturb the entire moral, order.

In Anselm's view, if man were to be restored to fellowship with God, One must be found with sufficient intrinsic dignity (i.e., both as being Divine and as being sinless) to offer himself a satisfaction to the Divine honor and to remove the affront to it posed by man's disobedience. What is of permanent value in this view is, not his medieval analogy, but the principle of objectivity of the God-man relationship, and the consequent necessity of an adequate restoration of the fractured relationship.

Anselm's apologetic model was thus faith-oriented. As its formulator, he became the progenitor of a long line of apologists who sought to ground major biblical motifs in forms of objectively necessary arguments.[21] His contribution to soteriology cannot be overestimated, particularly when one understands the relative poverty of theology at this point prior to his time.

The apologetic of Thomas Aquinas (1225-1274) appears chiefly in his *Summa contra gentiles*, written near the end of his life. He seems to have produced this work at the request of Raymond of Pennafort, master-general of the Dominican order, as a refutation of the doctrines of infidels, a work "by which both the cloud of darkness might be dispelled and the teaching of the true Sun might be made manifest to those who refuse to believe."[22]

Aquinas' apologetic is too massive to be surveyed in small compass. His model is, basically, that of the development and treatment of his famous *classes* or levels of truth, and the apologetic consequences which flow from that development. He held that the human mind, while of limited competence, can establish beyond reasonable doubt the existence of one personal God and other important truths related to it (this is truth of *class one*). But with the assistance of Revelation, the mind can, asserts Aquinas, attain to truth beyond the investigative power of rational inquiry (this is truth of *class two*).

To Thomas Aquinas, apologetics assumes different forms, depending upon the type or class of truth which is to be established. For those areas of truth which lie beyond the range of rational inquiry (e.g., the Trinity, the resurrection of the body, the final judgment, etc.) he cites the authority of Revelation, appealing especially to the miraculous.[23] His apologetic rests, it seems clear, not primarily on the understanding of history (as in Augustine) but upon metaphysics. He appears to question Anselm's view, that Trinity and atonement may be demonstrated by rational investigation, and turns to his favorite view of extrinsicism— the appeal to authority outside man.

Some object that he is inconsistent, in his appeal to intrinsicism as a basis for establishing truths of *class one*, while resorting with such confidence to extrinsicism in dealing with *class two* matters. But be that as it may, St. Thomas has presented a massive apologetic, and has adduced some very carefully reasoned and persuasive arguments (we would stop short of saying 'proofs') for the validity of the Christian faith. If his *apologia* has weaknesses, they follow from the general limitations upon his *Weltanschauung* and from his mode of argumentation. From the modern point of view, these limitations lie primarily in the areas of that which he takes for granted.

In the period commonly known as the Modern Era, or more precisely, in the centuries following the Protestant Reformation, the apologetic task has been undertaken by a variety of thinkers, representing as many approaches and/or models. In this section, it will be necessary to treat representative writers— and each of these with tantalizing brevity— with a view to locating the major apologetic lines. It is hoped, however, that the selective survey may yield some guidelines for the possible erection of an apologetic edifice for our own time.

Blaise Pascal (1623-1662) had a decisive conversion in 1655, and devoted the remaining years of his life and his unquestioned genius to the cause of making the Christian religion understandable to the France of his day. In 1656, he projected a massive apologetic, which he never completed. There have been those who have tried to discern the precise lines which this work would have taken from a study of his *Pensées*.

His apologetic writings come to us in the form of brief sentences or paragraphs, many in epigrammatic form. Some were dashed off in haste; others appear to have been chiseled out with great care. His *Pensées* do not, of course, present a connected system, but consist largely of materials aimed at giving a sort of "shock treatment" to the religiously indifferent of his day.

Pascal countered the Deists with a view of God which he contended was hidden to sinful man. Nor could this God be found by the use of reason, at least by reason as understood in the Cartesian sense. His reasoning was dialectical, centering in his famous "wager," which runs thus: If Christianity be true (he told his objector) you have everything to gain by embracing it; if it is false, you have yet lost nothing.[24] As for reason (the shibboleth of the French Enlightenment), Pascal contended that nothing is more reasonable than for reason to submit to authority.[25] In a decision to submit, he declared, reason is guided in the best possible way— i.e., by "reasons of the heart"[26] which was to him an intuitive form of logic.

The thrust of Pascal's Wager (which is central to his apologetic) is, that the stakes are high, involving life itself. He makes frank reference to the professional gambler, noting that he takes risks on life which he would never take at the roulette table. Maintaining that the spiritual wager is inevitable, he exhorts his readers to take the line of common prudence. His apologetic aim was, of course, to shatter the complacency of the typically Gallic mentality of his day— we would say, to cause the skeptical person to "blow his cool." He stings and shocks the indifferent, and faces him with the claims of Jesus Christ, whom he feels to be inescapable. His is an apologetic marked by a deep grasp of the needs of the heart; it is small wonder that it has exerted a profound influence in the West.

Joseph Butler (1692-1752) directed his apology against the Deism of the British enlightenment. His *Analogy of Religion* was written in an age in which Christianity was adjudged to be irrelevant to the educated person. His appeal was, understandably, to the reasonable man or to reasonable men. His analogical method begins with the assumption that the Christian system rests upon a series of principles (or facts) for which there are convincing analogues in the general course of nature. Thus, objections leveled against the former are no more valid than the same when alleged against the latter. Conversely, of course, those presuppositions which are regarded as valid with respect to the general structures of nature are shown to be equally viable as applied to the principles of Christian faith.

He worked in close relationship to experienced facts, and shows the feasibility of following probability as a guide of life. His appeal is to minds which are serious, for he felt that it is to such, and such alone, that God makes His appeal. Thus he urges the men of the Enlightenment to lay aside frivolity, passion and prejudice. The importance of the *Analogy* for its time may be judged by the fact that it went through no less than 28 editions in Britain and over 20 printings in the United States. Even David Hume termed it the best defense of Christianity which he had ever encountered, while Cardinal Newman termed it the highest expression of Anglican theology.

Friedrich D. E. Schleiermacher (1768-1834) approached apologetics in a totally different spirit. The title of his major apologetic work, *On Religion: Speeches To Its Cultured Despisers*, might well have been used by Tertullian or Origen! Attacking the suavity and coldness of the *Aufklärung* in Germany, Schleiermacher sought to shear away from Christianity what he felt to be the excess baggage of traditional dogma. In this respect, his apologetic was basically negative; he sought to re-interpret Christian theology in such a manner as to remove all stumbling blocks to its acceptance by modern men of his time.

His theological system, outlined in his *On Religion* and sketched more fully in his *Glaubenslehre* (*The Christian Faith*) is far too sophisticated to be surveyed here. The most that can be done is to expose for further exploration his basic point of departure, and to indicate directions in which he sought to work from this point. To him, religion consisted, not in a set of articulated doctrinal statements, but in what he termed man's "feeling of absolute dependence."

As one committed to the Kantian epistemology, he makes no attempt at any rational argumentation for the existence of God, or for the corollaries of revelation, freedom or immortality. He maintains that man's religious sense finds its highest achievement in Christianity, defined, of course, in his way. Piety is seen in terms of man's immediate consciousness of absolute dependence, which in turn guides man to what is essential in theology. His is thus an inward and subjective form of apologetic, which makes faith to be something exercised from *the inside*. Under the influence of Christ's redeeming power, the Christian can apprehend God's existence and providence, and redemption through Jesus of Nazareth. Much of this is to be found in his less-known work, *Brief Outline on the Study of Theology*. Here his insistence is upon the Christian community as an association for the achievement of piety, for he felt that there is no religion apart from social religion.[27]

The full effects of Schleiermacher's radical redefinition have not yet been felt in the Christian world. His *On Religion* was the magna carta of modern liberalism, while his methodology has furnished impetus to similar apologetic attempts, notably by Albrecht Ritschl and Rudolf Otto.

A generation later Maurice Blondel (1861-1949) undertook in France a similar neo-Kantian apologetic, directed especially against the Enlightenment. In his work *L'Action*, he sought to legitimate for the thinking man and woman the claims of the supernatural. He based his presentation upon man's craving for communion with God, and upon the view that knowledge of God must be reciprocal, with God's giving of himself preceding man's dedication to Him. It is not possible here to discuss his "method of immanence"; it needs to be noted that he summarizes his view of the central core of Christian faith in these terms: "Only practical action, the effective action of our lives, will settle for each one of us, in secret, the question of the relations between the soul and God."[28]

His apologetic was one of reaction against extrinsicism, and was thus in reality a romantic defense of the validity of the appeal to inwardness, both as a source of faith in relation to the supernatural in general and to miracles in particular, and as a means for the inward apprehension of the gifts of grace.

Blondel's influence was confined largely to Catholic circles, where it excited much debate, and at times laid him open to attack both from conservative Catholics and from the Catholic modernists, Alfred Loisy and George Tyrrell.

The work of the Jesuit philosopher and paleontologist, Pierre Teilhard de Chardin is too complex and too sophisticated to be discussed here. Mention should, however, be made of two factors: first, the contemporary revival of interest in his writings in Catholic circles; and second, the fact that, quite apart from the question of the validity of his conclusions, he did pose, ahead of his time, the question of the relation of the Sacred to the Secular.

Thus far, apologists have been chosen from more recent centuries whose works have proved relatively effective, for their times and in subsequent periods. Turning now to our own century, we note that few apologetic writers have, due either to structural inadequacies of their systems or to the shortness of elapsed time, yet proved their permanent value. This is, we believe, true of the dialectical theologians, most of whose theological formulations are slanted toward persuasion— that is, are apologetic in tone and thrust. This is true of the systems of Karl Barth, Emil Brunner, Paul Tillich, and in some measure of Reinhold Niebuhr. It should be pointed out also, that the work of Rudolf Bultmann could quite fairly be termed a *non-apologetic*. In the volume *Kerygma and Myth*, Bultmann in his section "New Testament and Mythology" virtually wipes off the theological slate our Lord's pre-existence, his incarnation, his sacrificial death, his resurrection, the atonement, his exaltation, and his second coming, as well as the major aspects of the doctrine of the Church.[29]

Bultmann accomplishes this by the dogmatic assertion that *"Man's knowledge and mastery of the world"* [italics his] makes the historic formulation of these doctrines impossible of acceptance by any serious thinker of our time.[30] His reformulation of what remains is accomplished upon an existential base, and by any fair evaluation results in a form of

Christianity which, in the light of both Scripture and historical formulation, is a gnostic distortion.

Bultmann's pupil, Ernst Käsemann, adds to the teaching of his master the dimension of a radically pluralistic understanding of Scripture—the view that the New Testament abounds in contradictions, so that any unitary doctrinal formulation based upon it is unacceptable. This comes through clearly in his *Exegetische Versuche und Besinnungen*, particularly in his exegetical analyses of Matthew 15:1-14 and of Philippians 2:5-11,[31] and his discussions of the Church and of *Nichtobjektivierbarkeit*[32] (roughly translatable as "a quality of being incapable of being objectified"). His insistence upon multiplicity as an ultimate category for the interpretation of Scripture will continue to be a prolific source of mischief for the theological world.

Special mention is due to several who have undertaken, whether formally or informally, the apologetic task in recent years. The most influential lay apologist in recent decades has been, of course, C. S. Lewis, who by a variety of intriguing approaches demonstrated the plausibility of the historic Christian understanding of things, especially the view of God as transcendent, personal and concerned for man. In addition, he utilized the fanciful and the satirical to puncture many current objections to traditional Christianity.

Alan Richardson and the late Edward F. Carnell both undertook formal apologetic formulations. To Richardson, historiography appears the chief bulwark of an apologetic for today's men and women. He sees history as sufficiently broad, provided it be interpreted properly, to make a place for the miraculous, notably the resurrection of our Lord. He believes that the Christian *Weltanschauung* provides a view of history more nearly adequate to the facts of the human enterprise than rival systems. Unhappily his conclusions are vitiated for the Evangelical by his interpretations of some of the New Testament writings.

Edward F. Carnell, whose death seems to us to have been untimely, was searching for an apologetic during his last years. Those who knew his thinking feel that his volume on the subject was really but a tentative beginning. In this connection we might note that John H. Gerstner's volume *Reasons For Faith* suggests that its author has it in his thinking to do further apologetic work. The wide sweep of Carl F. H. Henry's theological researches impresses one also with the possibility that he may one day bring together his materials into an apologetic which might well be the most significant production of our time.

Finally, what does the history of apologetics suggest to us concerning the matter of the defense of the Faith for our day? We are persuaded that it is trying to tell us something concerning approach, method, and content. Certainly we would not wish to see a repetition of some older attempts which serve largely to convince those who already believe of the wrongness of their opponents. Equally certain it is, that no apologetic can be effective which adopts the stance of the antagonist who is "spoiling for a fight." It goes without saying that the use of straw men is futile.

The experiences of some apologists of the past suggest to us the peril of making undue concessions to the spirit of the times. The author of the *Heliand* affords us a genial warning in his over-Saxonizing of the Gospel records. More serious is the warning furnished by Schleiermacher and Bultmann, who insist, not only upon a re-formulation of Christianity, but as well, upon the normative quality (for their times at least) of this re-formulation. Now, would it not be singular indeed if the world had to wait until 1800 or until 1950 to learn what Christianity really is?

An effective apologetic must understand the objector better than the objector understands himself. Its writer needs to be able to think through *positions* to their logical and final consequences, and what is more important to identify himself with the doubts of others.[33] This calls for a measure of sympathy, of elasticity, and of winsomeness which only the Holy Spirit can engender.

The apologetic attempts of the past also speak to us concerning the content of a viable apologetic enterprise. It seems clear that a significant part of apologetic activity consists in the prudent selection of issues. Two perils arise at this point: the first is, that of selecting a front so broad that nothing really effective is accomplished with respect to any phase of Christian truth; the second peril is that of adopting a too-narrow base for the apologetic. Typical of the latter danger is the "one issue" apologetic, typified by such slogans as: "Revelation is event," or "Revelation is history."

The selection of the breadth of the front is thus crucial. We would suggest that the most effective selection involves the singling out of an issue sufficiently central to carry with it naturally and without any evident or artificial forcing, of related issues which are also of high significance. It may well be that in our time the central issue is that of the *Supernatural*, the question whether our universe manifests, and can be explained in terms of, a single order (i.e., the natural) or whether a valid interpretation of its phenomena demands the recognition of another range of reality. Implied here is, of course, the position that the same God is Lord of both orders, and that He shapes both to his purposes.

The relation of a rather wide range of data to this issue seems evident. Upon its validity hangs the issue of revelation itself, and of course the entire redemptive order, with its inevitable involvement of the structure of Incarnation-Atonement-Resurrection. The validity of this structure is vital in that it involves not only the Christian system, but the eternal hope of our race.

Should we in our time "contend earnestly for the faith?" There is abroad a romantic notion, to the effect that Christianity needs no defense, but only proclamation. History, however, suggests rather clearly that the Christian enterprise involves the harnessing of the talents of the finest and best of men and women, not only to declaration but as well, to the formulation and projection of reasons for the hope which is in us. This task has enlisted some of the best minds for nearly two millennia; we are persuaded that today and tomorrow the Lord of the Church will make no less demands upon the faithful, and especially the talented faithful.

Notes

[1] Williston Walker, *A History of the Christian Church*, rev. ed., New York, 1959, p. 17

[2] Avery Dulles, *A History of Apologetics*, New York, 1971, p. 24.

[3] Barnabas Lindars, *New Testament Apologetic: The Doctrinal Significance of the Old Testament Quotations*, London & Philadelphia, 1961, pp. 194-199.

[4] Dulles, *op. cit.*, p. 13.

[5] *Ibid.*, pp. 1-19.

[6] *Ibid.*, p. 19.

[7] *Ibid.*, p. 40.

[8] Walker, *op. cit.*, p. 75.

[9] Dulles, *op. cit.*, p. 38.

[10] Augustine Aurelius, *City of God*, VIII, p. 12.

[11] John A. Mourant, *Introduction to the Philosophy of Saint Augustine*, University Park, Pennsylvania, 1964, p. 70.

[12] Paul Glenn, *The History of Philosophy*, St. Louis, 1929, p. 161.

[13] John A. Mourant, *op. cit.*, p. 15.

[14] *De Trinitate*, VII, p. 4, 7

[15] Dulles, *op. cit.*, p. 67.

[16] J. G. Robertson, *A History of German Literature*, 4th ed., New York, 1962, p. 26.

[17] Kurt Reinhardt, *Germany: 2000 Years*, I, revised edition, New York, 1961, p. 57

[18] O. S. and E. M. Fleissner, *Deutsches Literaturlesebuch*, New York, 1968, p. 19 (transl. mine).

[19] Glenn, *op. cit.*, p. 194.

[20] *Proslogion*, Part 1.

[21] Dulles, *op. cit.*, p. 80.

[22] *Ibid.*, p. 87.

[23] Thomas Aquinas, *Summa contra gentiles*, I, p. 6.

[24] Blaise Pascal, *Pensées*, New York (Modern Library), 1941, Section III, 233, pp. 79-84.

[25] *Ibid.*, Section IV, 269-272, pp. 93f.

[26] *Ibid.*, Section IV, 277, p. 95

[27] Friedrich D. E. Schleiermacher, *On Religion*, trans. by John Oman, New York, 1958, p. 148.

[28] Maurice Blondel, *Letter On Apologetics*, trans. by A. Dru and I, Trethowan, New York, 1964. pp. 163f.

[29] Hans Werner Bartsch, editor, *Kerygma and Myth*, New York, 1961, p. 2.

[30] *Ibid.*, p. 4.

[31] Ernst Käsemann, *Exegetische Versuche und Besinnungen*, Gőttingen, 1964, pp. 237-241; 51-95.

[32] *Ibid.*, pp. 214-136.

[33] C. G. Schweitzer, "Praktische Apologetik (Apologie)," *Die Religion in Geschichte und Gegenwart*, Tűbingen, 1957, p. 490.

Works Cited

Blondel, Maurice. *Letter On Apologetics*, trans. by A. Dru and I, Trethowan, New York, 1964.

Fleissner, O. S. and E. M. *Deutsches Literaturlesebuch*, New York, 1968. (transl. mine).

Käsemann, Ernst. *Exegetische Versuche und Besinnungen*, Göttingen, 1964.

Lindars, Barnabas. *New Testament Apologetic: The Doctrinal Significance of the Old Testament Quotations*, London & Philadelphia, 1961.

Mourant, John A. *Introduction to the Philosophy of Saint Augustine*, University Park, Pennsylvania, 1964.

Pascal, Blaise. *Pensées*, New York (Modern Library), 1941.

Reinhardt, Kurt. *Germany: 2000 Years*, I, revised edition, New York, 1961.

Robertson, J. G. *A History of German Literature*, 4th ed., New York, 1962.

Schleiermacher, Friedrich D. E. *On Religion*, trans. by John Oman, New York, 1958.

Schweitzer, C. G. "Praktische Apologetik (Apologie)," *Die Religion in Geschichte und Gegenwart*, Tűbingen, 1957.

Walker, Williston. *A History of the Christian Church*, rev. ed., New York, 1959.

The Use and Abuse of Power
A Study of Principalities and Powers
Gilbert M. James
April 17, 1974

Hypothesis

"–the biblical description of principalities and powers and the sociological nature of massive institutions bear more than analogical relationship to each other and that an understanding of the relationship of prophetic witness to this present world of massive power structures should be informative to those who take seriously God's charge to man to be responsible for the world."

Power as a Biblical and Sociological Concept

Power is one of the more significant concepts in theology and sociology. To understand the Christian faith there must be a grasp of the meanings of the *power of God*, the *power of love*, the *power of evil*, the *power of death*, and the *power of nature*.

To understand the nature and function of society and its institutions it is necessary to locate the sources of power, how it is generated, and who controls it. The power of social norms, mores, and customs can control and give order to a society. To be socially competent one must know who has the power, its limits, and the goals and intentions of its wielders. Legitimate and illegitimate power must be distinguished.

Life cannot exist without power; it can sustain life or destroy it. Power can bring about needed changes or it can stifle and suppress. Even the voice of prophetic witness can be stilled. Power can destroy by violence or smother by reaction. It can exercise its will through secrecy, gossip, blackmail, threat, and falsehood. It can rob a poor man to enrich the wealthy man. Power can be used to keep whole communities or groups of people powerless, and by their very powerlessness increase the power of those who exploit them.

The subject of this paper is *The Use and Abuse of Power, A Study in Principalities and Powers*.

The purpose is to attempt to discover the nature of the Principalities and Powers described in the New Testament and their possible relationship with massive institutions in the world. The stated hypothesis is that the biblical description of principalities and powers and the sociological nature of massive institutions bear more than an analogical relationship to each other, and that an understanding of the relationship of prophetic witness to this present world of massive power structures should be informative for those who take seriously God's charge to man to be responsible for the world.

Principalities and Powers

According to John Howard Yoder, recent theologians have given considerable attention to the biblical subject of principalities, powers and elemental spirits, and a growing body of literature in this area has emerged during the past 25 years. In these present times when scholars no longer believe in spooks, poltergeists, and leprechauns, there is some reluctance and embarrassment in treating the subject of "powers" as they are described by Paul. Nineteenth century scholars tended to set aside these embarrassing concepts as out of date, and turned their attention to more scholarly pursuits in the philosophy of history and the theology of culture.[1]

In Berkhof's *Christ and the Powers* the author attempts to discover St. Paul's meaning of the terminology: *the powers*. He assumes that Paul did not invent the terminology which he used; a vocabulary which may sound obtuse and meaningless to *this* age was very clear and significant to Paul's readers. The problem that Berkhof attempts to solve is, how did Paul understand the cosmic language, which he employed? When he spoke of powers, what content did he give them, and was it the same content that was current among his readers? Berkhof, having stated the problem, summarizes:

> ...what was essential to the view of the powers found in the apocalyptic and rabbinic writings. Two things are always true of the powers: (1) they are personal, spiritual beings, and (2) they

influence events on earth, especially events within nature.[2]

To pursue his investigation of Paul's understanding of the content of the cosmic language which he employed, Berkhof starts with two familiar texts, Romans 8:38 and 1 Corinthians 3:22:

> 'For I am sure that neither death nor life, nor angels nor principalities, nor present nor future, nor powers, nor height nor depth, nor any other creature, will be able to separate us from the love of God, which is in Christ Jesus, our Lord.'[3]
> Obviously. Paul means to name a number of realities, which are part of *our earthly existence*, and whose role is one of domination 'Whether Paul, Apollos, or Cephas; whether world, life, or death, whether present or future, all is yours.'

In this second reference the names of the angelic powers are omitted, but Paul tends to group the names of experienced realities that dominated the lives of the Corinthians. The ease with which Paul weaves together in other references the names of angelic powers with a list of such empirical human experiences would indicate that Paul is not emphasizing their personal-spiritual nature, but rather the fact that *powers condition earthly life*.[4]

Oscar Cullman, in his work on Romans 13:1, insists that whatever views we hold about the invisible powers, "we must conclude…that these powers in the faith of primitive Christianity, did not belong merely to the framework *'conditioned* by the contemporary situation.' It is these invisible beings who in some way— not, to be sure, as mediators, but rather as executive instruments of the reign of Christ— *stand behind what occurs in the world.*"[5]

It is well to remember that the principalities and powers are indeed God's creation, for in Christ "everything in heaven and on earth was created, not only things visible but also the invisible orders of thrones, sovereignties, authorities, and powers…" (Colossians 1:16). There is no doubt that these powers were good forces, obedient to the will of God, just as human beings; also, however, like human beings they were subject to the fall. These fallen powers *now* have evil tendencies but they are still used of Christ, for all things "subsist" in Him. The word *subsist* has the same root as the modern word for system, and it is in Christ that all things are ordered and held together (Colossians 1:16-17). The whole realm of nature, the earth, the universe, society, and culture cannot exist without structures of order and regularity.

The principalities and powers that Paul speaks of were considered as "in between agents" or the functional structures between Christ and the visible world. In other words, creation has its visible "front stage" of human affairs; and the "back stage," made up of principalities, powers, thrones, dominions, and authorities, provide structures for the order that resists the chaos. Although these powers, like human beings, are rebellious and fallen, yet they are under the Lordship of Christ and are not free from divine sovereignty. They are subject to Christ and are used by Him. These powers are the related structures of unified corporate life; at the same time, they tend to separate men from the love of God.

Borg, Berkhof, Cullman, and Yoder have ventured to name examples of structures that are used of God in modern concrete forms.[6] *The state, politics, public opinion, social struggle, religious dogma, news media, ecclesiastical forms, commerce, and industry*—all institutional and corporate life may be subject to the powers, whether a seminary, a university, or a local school board, a bank, a brewery, or a bakery. From this limited list it is possible to discern two distinct evil results of institutional life: one is the latent evil within the structures and methodologies themselves, and the other is the manifest product. For example, a food producer may be canning and distributing healthful foods; but its labor practices may be exploitive and dehumanizing, and it's labeling and advertising policies deceptive. A distillery may have commendable working conditions with adequate compensations, and its financial arrangements with its outlets may be fair and equitable; but its *product* is contributing to one of America's most serious mental and physical health and accident problems.

The list of structures is endless, structures through which order is maintained in the world, and life is preserved and enhanced. Institutions of government, religion, education, and production have made great contributions to freedom, ethics, science, technology, and the producing, processing, and distribution of vast quantities of food, medicine, building materials, and means of transportation and communication. The contributions of these institutions to the good life in some parts of the world, such as Japan, Europe and America can hardly be measured. But the powers tend to selfishness and injustice. The same powers that produce food, work the very lives out of field hands, cannery workers, and migrants with little or no concern for their welfare. John Steinbeck's *Grapes of Wrath*, and especially the more recent play by Tennessee Williams, *The Migrants*, are reasonably accurate portrayals of the suffering of tens of thousands of families who help produce the fresh fruits and vegetables for the American table.

Production lines in American industry have produced an abundance of labor saving devices, and other products for human comfort and fulfillment; but the exorbitant price for these luxuries has been the alienation of two generations of workers by the monotonous and stultifying routine of unfulfilling work.

Principalities and Powers as "Creatures"

The Bible consistently speaks of principalities as "creatures." Christians generally refuse to recognize that massive organizations have a distinct nature of their own, and a style of life that is more or less independent of the human functionaries within the corporate structures. The following quotation from the book *America Inc.* is an example of what St. Paul calls "the wisdom of the world." The authors write:

> There is nothing sacred about the corporation. No process of God or Nature controlled the evolution which produced it. Rather, it developed as a method for accumulating capital and for shielding the user of that capital from individual liability. Thus, it is a mere legal device.[7]

William Stringfellow disagrees with this oversimplified description of the origins of Powers. He cannot be sure of the specific nature of the creatureliness of institutions, any more than he can know the secret of *human* creature-hood. "The creaturely status of principalities," Stringfellow writes, "comes not from men but from God."[8] John Howard Yoder reinforces this view in these words, "These structures are not and never have been a mere sum total of the individuals composing them. The whole is more than the sum of its parts. And this 'more' is an invisible Power, even though we may not be used to speaking of it in personal or angelic terms."[9]

Nature of Corporate Behavior

Perhaps a brief description of corporate entities might give insight into the "creatureliness" of institutions and their tendencies to selfishness. In the first place, no one person or group of persons can of their own volition create a corporation. The state, and the state alone can create a corporation; it is, and as long as it exists, it is a creature of the state. Furthermore, it cannot die or go out of existence without the specific action of the state. The assets may have totally disappeared, every scrap of paper or record destroyed, and every member of the corporation may have died, but that corporation *cannot* die until the state wills it.

The corporation has protections, rights, and privileges granted to it by the state that are not granted to individual citizens. *Under special conditions* it cannot be forced to fulfill some financial obligations, but individuals could be legally punished for the same dereliction.

According to research done by the Library of Congress, the legal literature supports the conclusion that a corporate director must use his judgment, influenced only by what is best for the corporation. Many courts have ruled that a director's loyalty is to be undivided and his allegiance influenced in action by no other consideration than the corporation's own welfare.

> Bernard D. Nossiter has said, 'there is nothing in the logic or practice of concentrated corporate industries that guides or *compels socially responsible decision-making.*' To be even blunter about it, the rule of thumb is that if conscience is operative in a corporation it is because conscientious conduct pays, and if conscience is absent it is because *that* pays.[10]

Dr. Milton Friedman of the University of Chicago, warned corporation officials as follows:

> Few trends could so thoroughly undermine the very foundations of our free society as the acceptance by corporate officials of a *social responsibility* other than to make as much money for the stockholders as possible.[11]

A pharmaceutical house may knowingly produce, advertise, and distribute a drug with dangerous side effects. But by the time the slow and cumbersome machinery of governmental regulation has banned the drug, months or even years have passed, and in the meantime the manufacturer has made a huge profit. At the worst, the company will be fined for its actions, although thousands of innocent victims may have suffered, been disabled, or died as a result of the company's actions. Successful lawsuits against the offenders seldom are commensurate with the profits which have been reaped.

Individuals Against the Powers

The tragedy is that the majority of good people seem to be oblivious to the subtle and overpowering control which corporate creatures exercise over human options, rendering millions of people nearly powerless. And, unfortunately, prestigious figures such as Billy Graham publicly reinforce the damaging folklore that saving individuals will change the evil nature of institutions.

In an article entitled "What Ten Years Have Taught Me," Graham writes: "Social sins, after all are merely a large scale projection of individual sins."[12] This statement reflects a serious lack of understanding of "principalities and powers," and it fails to take into account that they are not merely sums of men's sins. The nature of corporate beings may be analyzed from a strictly biblical and theological point of view or studied within a purely secular sociological model, but although the vocabulary may differ, the concrete results are the same. Massive institutions are capable of both *good* and *evil*. They are not mere sums of people, they have an existence of their own; they tend to separate men from God (theologically), and they tend to alienate men from their humanity (sociologically).

This point of view is often confronted with the argument, "But if enough saved individuals go into the institutions of industry, business, organized labor, and government, will they not change the nature of these institutions so drastically that they will become just and honorable?" The more pertinent question to face is this: If social, economic, and political institutions were to get a number of Christians in the upper echelons of responsibility where the believers' survival and promotions are dependent upon loyalty to the institutions, would not the institutions change these individuals so drastically as to render them powerless as Christians? It is more accurate, in general, to say that institutions change individuals, than to say that individuals change institutions.

Hans Gerth and C. Wright Mills write:
Institutions not only select persons and eject them; *institutions also form them*...Thus, institutions imprint their stamps upon the individual, modifying his external conduct *as*

well as his inner life. For one aspect of learning a role consists of acquiring motives which guarantee its performance.[13]

The Ethics of Corporate Power

Some theorists are interested in finding the means of limiting the power of large-scale bureaucracies, but such a pursuit requires a definition of the phrase, misuse of power. This is hard to come by, as the various beneficiaries of the products of power are prone to get their full share. The stockholders, the managers, the employees, the advertising media, the suppliers, the distributors, and the consumers are only a few of the many interest groups who are intent on getting a part of the increment.

This internal distribution of rewards is but a part of the power problem. Externally, large corporations negotiate or plunder other companies, foreign governments, labor unions, and especially domestic governments for trade-offs of power and advantage, but always with the intent of getting more than they give. As a result of these trade-offs, those with the most power are apt to get more power, while those who are incapable of participating in the power exchanges are those that are hopelessly trapped at the bottom. And the *welfare system* in this country does its bit to keep them there.[14]

What makes all this seem incredible to the general public is the studied effort of large corporations and governments to keep from the people any knowledge of the organization's activities. There are strong efforts to avoid unfavorable publicity that might arouse the people, that would in turn motivate the political sector to move against a business enterprise or a branch of government. An oil company advertised, "We want you to know," but when asked by a Congressional committee what their profit margin was, responded, "We *don't* want you to know."

An even more difficult roadblock to the limitation of power on the grounds of misuse of power is the question: who has the power and who is responsible for its implementation? There is perhaps no better example than the Watergate affair to illustrate the difficulty in pinpointing the misuse of power. Those who have been already convicted of crimes in this scandal and those who are under indictment seem utterly bewildered that they should be charged with any wrongdoing, since what they did seemed to them no different than what both parties, in consort with business and industry, had been doing for years. There were two major differences: First, the enormity of the scheme and second, they got caught!

A number of those who are awaiting trial are professed Christians; one, for example, admits that he was involved in breaking and entering, wiretapping, and burglary, but he insists he is not guilty of any crime!

We must leave to the duly appointed investigation agencies, the judicial and legislative branches of government to decide what illegal use of power may have occurred and who is to be held responsible for it. The public does not have sufficient information to make a judgment. But this we may be sure of: that in massive bureaucracies such as the Federal Government, III, General Motors, or Standard Oil, the pinpointing of firm responsibility in any surreptitious exercise of power is almost impossible. With the massive growth of business and government in recent decades it became necessary for technological reasons and growing complexity to engage in "collective leadership." This, according to Harlan Cleveland, led to the widest possible diffusion of powers. Cleveland writes:

> Corporate decisions of great moment are increasingly hard to pin on any individual: the process by which they are made is deliberately made complex by the erection of collective decision-making systems.[15]

Out of the many lessons to be learned from Watergate, for the purpose of this paper two very important insights emerge. *First*, the ethic of personal piety carries little weight for Christian involvement in the great structures of power, regardless of religious profession. *Second*, there is a desperate need for the development of a social ethic relevant to corporate, bureaucratic power.

Considering the evasiveness of massive power, and the almost total absence of any ethic except a public image of respectability, the biblical description of "principalities and powers" becomes acutely meaningful to daily lives, and to the future of nations.

Are men but hapless victims of capricious powers or do they have a responsibility for the world, as private citizens and as members of the body of Christ? What ought the Church to be doing?

The Christian's Responsibility in the World

If we are to know God, we must know about His purposes and His acts. How do we know that He is good, or that His creation is "good"? Langdon Gilkey reminds his readers that experience alone might cast doubt on the goodness of creation if men did not have some inside clues. The Christian belief in the meaning of creation comes from the revelation of God's will in the prophets and Jesus Christ, and the central proclamation is that God is at work restoring and recreating that which was lost in the fall through man's misuse of freedom.[16] If God's will is motivated by the same love revealed through the teaching, healing ministry, and the death of Jesus Christ, then the creative will in the beginning must have brought forth a good creation.

> Through the God-in-history is seen the love of God at the beginning of time and history. And thus because God is known to be 'good' in Christ, the world He made is known to be 'good' in Creation.[17]

This Christological stance is essential to any search for man's responsibility in the world. Plans or strategies cannot be deduced from natural laws or inherent human rights. As Bonhoeffer says, "The only human and natural rights are those which derive from Christ..."[18] Consequently, whatever the

Church has to say to the world is in preparation of His coming. And whenever the Church speaks about or to institutions, what is spoken, whether in religious or secular vocabulary, must be derived from the preaching and teaching ministry of Jesus Christ.

The present question is: how do Christians, as individuals and as members of the body of Christ, respond to the powers? This subject is extremely complex and deserves more treatment than either the length of this paper or the wisdom of this speaker will permit. But to raise the issues of powers and their consequences for the Church and for millions of people outside the pale, demands that at least an effort be made to stimulate Christian minds and hearts to search the scriptures and the wisdom of the Church for deeper insights into man's responsibilities for the world.

Adam's Mandate

The first Adam's responsibility was simple and very clear. He was to reproduce mankind, to have dominion over everything that moves upon the earth, to name the creatures, and to till the soil. His humanity was completed by God's gift of another human being to be beside him, and they were to become one flesh.

As a result of the fall, man and the earth suffered the curse of brokenness and alienation. The ecological chain was snapped at every link. Man and woman's relationship was strained by accusation; they now knew shame. Earth's abundance was now limited by earth's reluctance, to be overcome only by man's labor. The whole realm of nature was out of "sync."

Man had been given the charge to manage and have lordship over the earth, but by disobedience man failed and all creation suffered. However, there is no hint that man was any less responsible for the earth than before his disobedience. The psalmist writes:

> Thou madest him to have dominion over the works of thy hands; thou hast put all things under his feet.
>
> Psalm 8:6 KJV

The writer to the Hebrews, quoting from the Septuagint, and in somewhat different words, repeats God's mandate to his people.

> For it is not to angels that he has subjected the world to come, which is our theme. But there is somewhere a solemn assurance which runs:
> 'What is man, that thou rememberest him, or the son of man, that thou hast regard to him? Thou didst make him for a short while lower than the angels; thou didst crown him with glory and honor; thou didst put all things in subjection beneath his feet.'
> For in subjecting all things to him, he left nothing that is not subject. But in fact we do not yet see all things in subjection to man. In Jesus, however, we do see one who for a short while was made lower than the angels, crowned now with glory and honor because he suffered death, so that, by God's gracious will, in tasting death, he should stand for us all.
>
> Hebrews 2:5-9 NEB

God, by His gracious will, through Christ's death provides a "stand in" for all men. Man's assigned lordship now belongs to Christ, but the redeemed are His brothers. "For a consecrating priest and those whom he consecrates are all of one stock; and that is why the Son does not shrink from calling men his brothers..." Hebrews 2:11 NEB.)

The Message of Reconciliation

There is no implication in the Lordship of Christ that man's earthly responsibilities have been rescinded. Rather, as a result of man's failure to fulfill his destiny. Christ is achieving it through His death. Obedient men are Christ's brothers (Mark 3:35) and they are co-laborers with God (1 Corinthians 3:9). Dean Traina teaches that Jesus is doing the works of His Father, even at the risk of breaking the codal law. Christ's brothers and co-workers must focus on the works of God, especially the works done in Christ. And *we* must do what *He* is doing.

What God is doing through Christ in the cosmic sense is reconciling to himself all things.

> [Christ] is the image of the invisible God, for in Him all things were created, in heaven and on earth, visible and invisible, whether thrones or dominions or principalities or authorities— all things were created through Him and for Him.
>
> Colossians 1:15-16 RSV
>
> For in Him all the fullness of God was pleased to dwell, and through Him to reconcile to Himself all things, whether on earth or in heaven, making peace by the blood of His Cross.
>
> Colossians 1:19-20 RSV

Believers, then, must be His instruments of reconciliation; that is, if they are indeed new creatures in Him, and this is essential to obedience.

> Therefore, if anyone is in Christ, he is a new creation; the old has passed away, behold, the new has come. All this is from God, who through Christ reconciled us to Himself and gave us the ministry of reconciliation; that is, God was in Christ reconciling the world to Himself, and entrusting to us the message of reconciliation.
>
> 2 Corinthians 5:17-19 RSV

The second chapter of Colossians speaks of the nature and behavior of the powers and elemental spirits. From verse eight through the remainder of the chapter the writer encourages the saints to resist their bondage, which is described as "philosophy and empty deceit, according to human tradition, according to the elemental spirits of the universe…"

"Let no one pass judgment on you in questions of food and drink or with regard to a festival or a new moon or a Sabbath." Anything, in fact that attempts to "squeeze you into its own mold" should be resisted, but let God renew your mind— set you free, and keep your primary loyalty to Christ. Beware of unqualified commitments to a political party; even loyalties to denominations and to one's own country must be *secondary*, and subject to criticism and rebuke when the powers become oppressive or dehumanizing.

Beware of institutions, especially religious, where "authority" and status power is more important than leadership and community, where control is maintained by *secrecy* and where criticism of the powers is forbidden. Beware of ideologies, isms or absolutes that *demand* uncritical loyalty.

Making Known God's Will to the Powers

The church has the responsibility to inform the powers of the wisdom of God. Paul writes:

> To me, though I am the very least of all the saints, this grace was given, to preach to the Gentiles the unsearchable riches of Christ, and to make all men see what is the plan of the mystery hidden for ages in God who created all things; that through the church the manifold wisdom of God might now be made known to the principalities and powers in the heavenly places.
>
> Ephesians 3:8-10 RSV

Paul declares that it is God's will that the Church make known to the powers what *is* the wisdom of God. This does not necessarily imply a religious vocabulary or theological jargon, but whatever the Church has to say to the powers, whatever the vernacular employed, it must be deduced from the words of Jesus.

Suggestions for Action

Radical Evangelism That Will Unite Personal and Social Aspects of Christian Obedience

First, there is a need for radical evangelism that will reunite the personal and social aspects of Christian experience. It should emphasize total obedience to Christ in every category of life. This means that the new creature in Christ is not only prepared to proclaim the good news to men and women everywhere, but he is concerned about the powers that limit the life options of people whom Christ loves. The Christian must be prepared to take his stand against racial, ethnic, and sex discrimination, corrupt politics, and immoral and exploitive business practices. He must be willing not only to help make known to the powers the will of God for His world, but to join with others through whom He is speaking and acting.

C. Wright Mills is quoted by Marcus Borg as saying:
If you don't specify and confront real issues, what you do will surely obscure them. If you do not alarm anyone morally, you will yourself remain morally asleep. If you do not embody controversy, what you say will be an acceptance of the drift to the coming human hell![19]

The Christian in Conflict

Second, in a world of rapid change, group conflicts are inevitable. It is imperative that responsible Christians be keenly alert to these areas where conflict further oppresses the poor and the powerless, or where government policies defy God's law. The Christian can be God's agent of change by placing himself in the areas of public conflict that impinge upon the quality of life in the community.

The Church Renewal and Bearing Witness to the World Even at the Risk of Being Wrong

Third, in spite of the tendency of institutions toward selfishness, the fact remains that God works through organizations. The Christian's responsibility is not to retreat or to reject them, but rather to be alert to their objectives, behavior, and responsibility. Organizations, particularly religious ones such as churches and seminaries, should have built-in ongoing programs of renewal, analogous to personal renewal.

Oswald Chambers reminds us that:

> Organization is an enormous benefit until it is mistaken for the life... When their purpose is finished [God] allows them to be swept aside, and if we are attached to the organization, we shall go with it. Organization is a great necessity, but not an end in itself, and to live for one organization is a spiritual disaster.[20]

Spiritual responsibility can be agonizing, as there is always the hazard of being wrong. But this is part of the risk of responsibility. The Church cannot refuse to witness as best it can simply because of the possibility of error. Its dependence is not in its own wisdom, but in the leadership of the Holy Spirit and God's mercy and forgiveness when it fails.

Notes

[1] Berkhof, p. 4.

[2] Ibid, p. 10-11.

[3] See Yoder's, Trans, note on translations, Berkhof, p. 57, note 1.

[4] Berkhof, pp. 13-14.

[5] Cullman, *Christ and Time*, p. 192.

[6] Borg, p. 62; Berkhof, p. 50; Cullman, *Christ in Time*, p. 193; Yoder, pp. 139-140.

[7] Mintz et al., p. 357.

[8] Stringfellow, p. 80.

[9] Yoder, *Politics of Jesus*. p. 146.

[10] Mintz et al, p. 257.

[11] ICUIS – Institute, p. 1.

[12] Lockhart, p. 97.

[13] Gerth and Mills, p. 173.

[14] Ryan, p. 265.

[15] Cleveland and Lasswell, p. XXX.

[16] Gilkey, p. 218.

[17] Ibid., pp. 272-273.

[18] Bonheoffer, p. 361.

[19] Borg, p. 16.

[20] Chambers, pp. 118-119

Works Cited

Arthur, William. *The Tongue of Fire.* Winona Lake: Light and Life Press, Reprinted from 1856

Barth, Karl. *Against the Stream.* New York: Philosophical Library, 1954

Berkhof, H. *Christ and the Powers.* Trans by John Howard Yoder Scottsdale, Pennsylvania: Herald Press, 1962.

Bonheoffer, Dietrich. *Ethics.* New York: The Macmillian Company, 1965.

Borg, Marcus. *Conflict and Social Change.* Minneapolis, Minnesota: Augsburg Publication House, 1971.

Brown, Dale. "The Powers — A Bible Study," The *Post American*, III (January, 1974), p. 3.

Caird, G. B. *Principalities and Powers.* Oxford: Clarendon Press, 1956.

Chambers, Oswald. *The Shadow of an Agony.* London: Oswald Chambers Publications and Marshall, Morgan and Scott, 1934.

Cleveland, Harlan and Harold D. Lasswell. *Ethics and Bigness* New York: The Conference on Science, Philosophy and Religion in their Relation to the Democratic Way of Life, Inc, Harper and Brothers, 1962.

Cullman, Oscar. *Christ and Time.* Trans. by Floyd Filson. London: SCM Press LTD, 1962.

_____. *The State in the New Testament.* New York: Charles Scribner's Sons, 1956.

Faris, Robert E. L., ed. *Handbook of Modern Sociology.* Chicago, Illinois: Rand McNally, 1964.

Epstein, Edwin. *The Corporation in American Politics* Englewood Cliffs, New Jersey: Prentice-Hall, Inc, 1969.

Gerth, Hans and C Wright Mills. *Character and Social Structure.* New York: Harcourt, Brace and World, Inc., 1953.

Gilkey, Langdon. *Maker of Heaven and Earth.* Garden City, New York: Doubleday and Company, Inc., 1965.

Harkness, Georgia. *The Ministry of Reconciliation*. Nashville: Abingdon Press, 1971.

Heuvel, Albert H. van den. *These Rebellious Powers*. New York: Friendship Press, 1965.

ICUIS – *Institute on the Church in Urban Industrial Society.* (800 Belden Ave., Chicago Illinois)

Kuitert, H. M. *Signals From the Bible*. Grand Rapids: Erdmans, 1972.

Lockard, David. *The Unheard Billy Graham*. Waco, Texas: Word Books, 1971.

MacGregor, G. H. C. "Principalities and Powers: the Cosmic Background of Paul's Thought," *New Testament Studies*, I, 1954-55.

Michels, Robert. *Political Parties*. New York: Dover Publications Inc., first published 1915, first Dover edition, 1959.

Mintz, Morton and Jerry S. Cohen. *America, Inc.* New York: Dial Press, 1971.

Morrison, Clinton. *The Powers That Be*. Naperville: Alec R. Allenson, Inc., 1960.

Muelder, Walter. *Foundations of the Responsible Society*. New York: Abingdon Press 1956

Niebuhr, Reinhold. *The Nature and Destiny of Man,* I New York: Charles Scribner's Sons, 1941, 1964.

O'Meara, Thomas, O. P. *Holiness and Radicalism in Religious Life.* New York, New York: Herder and Herder, 1970.

Ramm, Bernad "Welcome 'Green Grass' Evangelicals," *Eternity* (March, 1974), 13.

Rauschenbusch, Walter. *A Theology for the Social Gospel.* New York: Nashville, 1917.

Rupp, Gordon. *Principalities and Powers.* London: Epworth Press, 1963.

Ryan, William. *Blaming the Victim*. New York: Pantheon Books, a Division of Random House, 1971.

Schaller, Lyle. The *Change Agent.* Nashville: Abingdon Press, 1972.

Schlier, Heinrich. *Principalities and Powers in The New Testament*. New York: Herder and Herder, 1961.

Simon, Herbert A. *Administrative Behavior*. New York: The Macmillan Co., 1957.

Stringfellow, William. *An Ethic for Christians and Other Aliens in a Strange Land*. Waco, Texas: Word Books, 1973.

Trebing, Harry M., ed. *The Corporation in the American Economy*. Chicago: Quadrangle Books, 1970.

Visser T. Hooft. *The Background of the Social Gospel in America*. St. Louis: The Bethany Press, 1928.

Whiteley, D.E.H. *The Theology of St. Paul*. Philadelphia: Fortress Press, 1964.

World Council of Churches The Division of Studies. *The Lordship of Christ Over the World and the Church*. Geneva, 1957

Yoder, John Howard. *The Politics of Jesus*. Grand Rapids, Michigan: Wm. B. Eerdmans Publishing Co., 1972.

Eschatology

Delbert R. Rose
May 1, 1974

Introduction

Eschatology is the doctrine of "last things." a study of those events, which conclude time and commence eternity. It is not an area of interest and inquiry peculiar to Christianity. For both philosophers and non-Christian religionists, ancient and modern, have asked: What is the individual's final destiny? Where is the human race headed? and What is its final goal? Numerous answers to these inevitable questions have been offered through the centuries.

Biblical eschatology is perhaps best classified under two broad headings: (1) Personal or Individual Eschatology which includes Physical Death, the Immortality of the Soul, and the Intermediate State. (2) World or Cosmic Eschatology which studies the Return of Christ, the Resurrection of the Dead; the Kingdom of God and its Consummation; the Kingdom of Satan and its Collapse; and the Eternal State of the Wicked or Hell (*Gehenna*), and of the Righteous or Heaven.

Throughout this study let it be remembered that from the standpoint of experience "the future is the sphere of the radically unknowable." While men may speculate about the future and strive to shape it in every way possible, it is our Christian conviction that only supernatural, divine revelation can give us any certitudes concerning those unexplored tomorrows. However, affirms Emil Brunner, "...the whole content of the Christian faith is oriented toward the *telos*, the end." And it is precisely at this point that "Christian faith is distinguished from all other religions in that in it faith and hope are inseparably linked, indeed almost inextricably one. Faith is the foundation of hope, hope is that which gives content to faith. But both faith and hope are rooted in the revelation of God in Jesus Christ."[1] Brunner further declares, that "teaching concerning the last things... is not merely an appendix to Christian doctrine. Rather faith makes no affirmatives but such as ever imply the Christian hope of the future."[2]

No century of mankind has been more aware of the future and man's role in shaping it— making it happen through political, social, technological, and biological engineering— than this generation. From the Second Assembly of the World Council of Churches in 1954, to the Jesus Movement of the 1970's, and from the oft-quoted theologians of the era, such as Paul Tillich, to the aggressive cultists, such as Jehovah's Witnesses, eschatology has been in the foreground.[3] The whole "occult movement" now sweeping across the Western world is interested in the future both of particular persons and the world as a whole.

"Twenty years ago the study of predictive prophecy was seen as a dying endeavor," writes J. Barton Payne. But that did not dissuade the young scholar from starting his 754-page *Encyclopedia of Biblical Prophecy*, published by Harper & Row in 1973.

Dr. Payne claims one of the major reasons for the rebirth of interest in Bible prophecy is reflected in biblical statistics. In his own critical research of the Old Testament he found that out of 23,210 verses in its thirty-nine books, 6,641 verses, or 28½% (plus) "involved predictive matters." Out of the New Testament's 7,914 verses, he found 21% (plus— or 1,711) of them contained predictive elements.[4]

As might be expected biblical prophecy focuses on Jesus Christ. In fact, "the testimony of Jesus is the spirit of prophecy" (Revelations 19:10). From the proto evangel of Genesis 3:15 through "to the forecast of His eternal reign in Revelation 20-22," there are 191 distinct prophecies (not including types) "that have personal reference to Jesus." Payne believes he has located forecasts of Christ's second coming in twenty-nine of the Bible's sixty-six books.[5]

In his volume *Biblical Religion and the Search for Ultimate Reality,* Paul Tillich affirmed: "Biblical religion is eschatological. It thinks in terms of a complete transformation of the structure of the... earth, the renewal of the whole of reality. And this new reality is the goal toward which history runs, and with it the whole universe, in a unique, irreversible movement."[6]

To cope with the problems and pitfalls inherent in prophetic study the following have been my guidelines for this paper.

1) Let exegesis determine theology rather than use theology to determine exegesis.
2) Follow a time-tested hermeneutical principle: "Unless there is some reason intrinsic within the text itself which requires a symbolical interpretation, or unless there are other Scriptures which interpret a parallel prophecy in a symbolic sense, we are required to employ a natural, literal interpretation."[7]
3) Interpret difficult passages in the light of the more easily understood, and not vice versa.
4) Expect to find a "prophetic harmony" within the Word when it is rightly understood since the Holy Spirit, the Spirit of truth, is the divine author of all Scripture (2 Peter 1:20-21; 2 Timothy 3:16)
5) Use the fulfilled prophecies within the Scripture— record, and/or early Christian history— as models for what we can expect in the future, as prophecies continue to be fulfilled.
6) Do not insist on a crisis-fulfillment of that which God may choose to accomplish through a process, nor extend to a process what God has promised as a crisis-event. God did not always give the prophets and apostles the "time perspective" when they wrote prophetically. Therefore much of biblical prophecy is written without this "dimension of depth" (distance into the future) being included (compare Isaiah 61:1-3 with Luke 4:17-21)
7) Remember that some prophecies will only be understood as we approach the period of their actual fulfillment (see: Daniel 12:1-4).

8) Expect to find the principle of progressive revelation both relevant and necessary in grasping the eschatology of both Testaments.
9) As I turn to the body of this study, you should know that I am developing much of my personal credo concerning "last things" rather than merely reciting what others have believed and taught on the subject.[8]

Personal Eschatology

Death

Until very recently the talk of death among Americans except for poets and novelists was widely repressed. Now university graduate-level courses are offered, which include planning one's funeral, filling out one's death certificate, and a visit to a mortuary and a state morgue.[9]

One of the very popular books today is Dr. Elizabeth Kubler-Ross' *On Death and Dying*. Yale University's eminent psychiatrist, Dr. Robert Jay Lifton, claims Death is the most important question of our time."[10] In contemporary films, music, poetry, and fiction, death "has emerged as a dominant theme."[11]

Why this growing preoccupation with death? Modern medicine and technological devices have lengthened life expectancy. Men are almost feverishly devising ways to extend life by means of heart and other organ transplants, drugs, and mechanical instruments. All these call attention to man's attempt to prolong life— to evade death.

Yet in spite of this death is the most universally imminent of the various phases of eschatology. It is a mystery that cries out for interpretation. "If man is truly the crown of the divine handiwork," asks E. F. Harrison, "why should he have a shorter existence than some forms of plant and animal life? ...Why, if man is made in the image of the eternal God, should he perish at all?"[12]

The biblical answer is that man has transgressed God's will and law, thereby bringing death as a penalty for his sin (Genesis 2:17; Romans 6:23). As a term, death carries the idea of separation, whether used literally or figuratively. When man sinned he died in three senses of the word. He became dead in sin— cut off from spiritual life and fellowship with God (Luke 15:24, 32; Colossians 2:13). He became subject to physical death (Hebrews 9:27). In physical death the body and soul are separated. He became liable to "eternal death." Those who reject the provision for eternal life are destined for "the second death" which is separation from God and his new, righteous creation (Revelation 21:1-8).

In Scripture death is not treated as natural to man. It is instead something foreign and hostile to human life, expressing divine anger (Psalms 90:7, 11), a judgment (Romans 1:32), a curse (Galatians 3:13). It produces a disturbing dread and fear in men's hearts as they anticipate it (Hebrews 2:15).

Because of the connection between sin and death, Christ's redemptive mission entailed his own death in our behalf (1 Corinthians 15:3; Romans 4:25; 1 Peter 3:18). He tasted death for every man (Hebrews 2:9), and provisionally abolished it for all. Although Christians must die as do others— except those alive at Christ's second coming (1 Thessalonians 4:13-18; 1 Corinthians 15:51-52)— death for them has lost its sting because of Jesus' victory over it (1 Corinthians 15:54-57).

Only gradually, however, is death to be abolished from God's universe. At the final consummation of history Death and Hades (the place to which the unrighteous dead have gone during human history) will be cast into the Lake of Fire, which is called "the second death." On the new earth "there shall be no more death" nor any of its age-old companions— pain, sorrow, and crying (Revelations 21:4). Because of the death Jesus died, Christians can now face that "last enemy" in victory and with positive gain (1 Corinthians 15:26, 54-57; Philippians 1:23), and say with the Psalmist, "Precious in the sight of the Lord is the death of his saints" (Psalms 116:15).

The Immortality of the Soul

Throughout history, in most if not all cultures, men have developed "symbols of transcendence" by which they connect their past in this world with their future in the next.

Unlike her neighbors, ancient Israel's religion and literature did not develop a cult of the dead. While the "beyond" is clearly presupposed in the Old Testament, only a limited number of explicit statements on immortality can be found there. For Israel, believing in "God as a living and life-giving God (Numbers 14:21; Psalms 42:2; 1 Samuel 2:6) was doubtless the main ground for the belief in a life beyond death."[13]

The accounts of God's creation of man (Genesis 1:26-28; 2:7; Job 33:4) of Enoch's and Elijah's translation (Genesis 5:24; 2 Kings 2:11), and of King Saul's attempt to communicate with the deceased Samuel, are a few of the evidences that the Israelites generally believed in survival after death (1 Samuel 28:4-25)

Sheol, the abode of the dead, while a place of obscurity (Job 10:20-22; Psalms 88:10-12), was not the end. It was a place from which men could be delivered (Psalms 16:10; 49:14ff; Job 19:25-27). Optimistically the Psalmist sings: "...God will redeem my soul from the power of *Sheol*; for he will receive me" (Psalms 49:15). Perceptive Israelites saw far more than merely the physical side of man's nature.

> Those passages in the OT that seem to speak of death as cessation, must be taken in the light of the entire context... Ecclesiastes is commonly thought to express unqualified pessimism about man's future state... nevertheless, before the book ends, we find one of the strongest and plainest statements about man's ultimate destiny: "and the dust will return to the earth as it was, and the spirit will return unto God who gave it" (12:7).[14]

The Old Testament hope is climaxed by such prophecies as Hosea 13:14; Ezekiel 37:1-14; and Daniel 12:2, where bodily resurrection is also clearly in view. "Thy dead men shall live," exclaimed Isaiah; "awake and sing, ye that dwell in the dust; for thy dew is as the dew of herbs, and the earth shall cast forth the dead" (Isaiah 26:19).

What Old Testament believers could only dimly perceive, about either the soul's existence between death and resurrection, or the resurrection body itself, Jesus brought to light through the Gospel (2 Timothy 1:10).

The biblical view is that eventually the whole man, body, soul and/or spirit, will be immortalized (that is, rendered indestructible) even though the body undergoes death, dissolution, and then resurrection in order to reach its immortality. Only as man's bodily and spiritual natures exist in harmonious union is man truly man (Genesis 1:26-27; 2:7).

The Intermediate State

Paul witnesses that those believers who die are, in their spirit-being present with the Lord, conscious of joys far better than those of earth (2 Corinthians 5:8; Philippians 1:23). Then at his Second Advent Christ will bring back the spirits of the departed saints and reunite them with their raised, glorified bodies (1 Thessalonians 4:13-17).

Oscar Cullmann has not so read the New Testament. He contends for two things: (1) That a soul is not immortal since Jesus stated in Matthew 10:28 that it can be killed. For him "soul" is more biblically expressed as the "inner man." (2) That the "inner man" experiences an interim state of sleep between physical death and resurrection.[15]

Dr. Robert H. Hoerber, chairman of the department of Greek and Latin at Westminster College in Fulton, Missouri, challenges Cullmann's position. In my judgment, Dr. Hoerber shows conclusively that Cullmann has overgeneralized the Greek view, especially Plato's, which he claims has influenced the historic Christian view of immortality of the soul. And, further, he has failed to grapple adequately with the New Testament evidence that at death the soul— in its self-conscious, disembodied state— goes to be with Christ, in the presence of God, and that only the body slumbers in the earth between physical death and resurrection.

Moving from Ecclesiastes 12:7 to Luke 23:46, to Acts 7:59, to 1 Peter 3:19, and on to Revelation 6:9—along with the account of the rich man and Lazarus—Hoerber shows that the two Testaments unite in affirming that the immortality of the soul is not an idea foreign to the Scriptures as Cullmann has claimed.[16]

As presented in the New Testament the soul of the dying righteous enters Christ's heavenly presence (2 Corinthians 5:8; Philippians 1:23; Luke 23:43)— a conscious state greatly preferable to life in this world (2 Corinthians 5:8; Psalms 16:11; Luke 16:19-21; John 17:24)— concerning which the heavenly voice declared: "Blessed are the dead who die in the Lord from henceforth: yea, saith the Spirit, that they may rest from their labors; for their works follow with them" (Revelation 14:13).

From Jesus' own words it seems amply clear that the unsaved soul enters a place of torment (Luke 16:23-24), and none of the New Testament writers gives witness contrary to this. Some have sought New Testament evidence, as in 1 Peter 3:18-20, for "a second chance," or a continued probation after death, leading to universal salvation; but evangelical scholarship, generally, has not been convinced by either the exegesis or the apologetics of these thinkers.[17]

The Roman Catholic Church sets out four distinct places in the intermediate state. The impenitent wicked go at once to hell; the fully righteous, such as martyrs, go immediately to heavenly blessedness; all other accountable ones are retained in Purgatory for a longer or shorter period, suffering the effects of purgatorial fire. While opinion varies, the prevailing view has been that baptized infants go directly to Heaven, but infants dying unbaptized (of both heathen and Christian parents) go to a place called *Limbus Infantum*, to spend eternity in a dreamlike state where they neither feel pain nor heavenly bliss.[18]

For Catholicism Purgatory is "a place and state of temporal penal purification," built directly upon the passage in 2 Maccabees 12:42-46 (an apocryphal book), and indirectly upon such Scriptures as Matthew 12:32, 1 Corinthians 3:12-15; and Matthew 5:26.[19] Generally speaking, evangelical Protestants have vigorously rejected this doctrine of Purgatory which has no clear basis in the Scriptures, and because of its abuse by the Church of Rome. Some non-Catholics, however, have been tolerant of the Purgatory doctrine.[20]

World or Cosmic Eschatology

The Kingdom of God

We turn now to World or Cosmic Eschatology and consider first its most comprehensive theme— the Kingdom of God. Some biblical scholars view the Kingdom as the central unifying concept of the Bible's sixty-six books. Dr. John Bright claims that "the bond that binds [the two Testaments] together is the dynamic concept of the rule of God."[21]

The Kingdom of God, according to George E. Ladd, is "the sovereign rule of God, manifested in the person and work of Christ, creating a people over whom he reigns, and issuing in a realm or realms in which the power of his reign is realized."[22] A person's Kingdom-view, needless to say, largely determines his eschatology.

While different stages of the Divine Kingdom appeared between the times of Eden and John the Baptist, it was in Christ's incarnation that God's rule became personally and perfectly embodied. Two bold claims of Jesus support this view: "For I am come down from heaven, not to do mine own will, but the will of him that sent me" (John 6:38, ASV); and "...he that sent me is with me... for I do always those things that are pleasing to him" (John 8:29, ASV). But his own people rejected God's rule through him. Therefore, claims Ladd, in the Second

Advent Jesus will bring his full messianic salvation to its proper consummation.[23]

The present Church Age, between the Advents, is another phase in God's Kingdom, under his larger cosmic rule. The Church is not co-extensive with the Kingdom, as some have claimed; neither is the Kingdom limited to the Church. For the time being— some would say "forever"— the Church supersedes Israel in God's plan for Kingdom extension (Matthew 21:43; Acts 1:6-8). That means God's Kingdom is *present now*— reigning "in righteousness, peace, and joy in the Holy Spirit" in the hearts of full-fledged believers (Romans 14:17). An adequate biblical view of the Kingdom includes its present and its future phases. The Kingdom has been "inaugurated" on earth but it is not yet fully "realized." In the age to come, beginning with Christ's Second Advent, what is now invisible, discernible only to the eyes of faith, will be made visible. In its future form the Kingdom will be both spiritual and literal, both heavenly and earthly, both a fulfillment within history (redeeming it) and the beginning of a transition to its eternal form beyond history.[24]

The visible kingdom era, often called the millennium, will be ushered in by Christ's descent from Heaven, coming as King of kings and Lord of lords (Revelation 11:15-18, and 19:11-20:6). That heavenly invasion will mark the overthrow of the Antichrist's kingdom which will have become universally visible and vicious. Its totalitarian control of the politics, economics, and religion(s) of mankind will be overthrown by Christ's coming with power (Revelation 13:1-18:24; 19:17-21).

The eternal Kingdom Stage begins after the millennium ends, when Christ shall have put down all hostile rule, authority, and power. He will then deliver up to God the Father the Cosmic Kingdom-rule which he will have retrieved through his vast redemptive mission. At that point in the future the Son will subject himself to the Father that the latter may be all and in all (1 Corinthians 15:23-28). The eternal Kingdom Stage seems to coincide with God's everlasting Kingdom in the New Heaven and the New Earth (Isaiah 65:17; 66:22; 2 Peter 3:13; Revelations 21:1ff). The sure message of Scripture is that God's beneficent, uncontested, sovereign rule will in the future extend over all the cosmic reaches of his universe (2 Corinthians 15:25-28; Ephesians 1:20-23).[25]

The Kingdom of Antichrist

"The final goal of Christianity is Jesus Christ," wrote Erich Sauer; but "the end of nominal Christendom is the Antichrist."[26] In his greatest of eschatological messages Jesus foretold the coming era of widespread lawlessness in the world and of apostasy in the Church (Matthew 24:10-14). Paul picked up the same theme in 2 Thessalonians 2:3, 4, 8, and emphasized the rise of "the Man of Sin" as a consequence of that apostasy. St. John's first two epistles warn of the Antichrist, another name for "the Man of Sin" (1 John 2:22; 2 John 7).

"The Antichrist is at once a person and a system... the leader and embodiment of a general human revolt" against God.[27] The Revelation, chapters 13-19, pictures his kingdom's rise to universal power and then its great collapse under judgment.

Having turned from God's true Messiah, humanity generally will look to Antichrist as "the messiah of the world, its cultural savior, its saving Head," and by him-- the pseudo-Christ— be deceived. The union of government, business, and religion under his rule will be "the summit of human revolt" against God and his Christ (Revelation 13:1-18; 17:1-18:24).

To gain this prestigious position Antichrist will doubtless be a leader, writes Erich Sauer, with "a surpassing personality, an inventive, unique organizer, 'a genius in statecraft, science, art, and social finesse...and endowed with the occult powers of the unseen world'" (2 Thessalonians 2:9).[28]

But the Lawless One and his kingdom will be utterly destroyed by the Lord Jesus at his coming (2 Thessalonians 1:7-10; 2:8; Revelation 19:15-21).

The Second Advent

The limitations on this paper preclude treating numerous other matters of prophetic importance. But the foregoing view rests squarely upon a premillennial understanding of history. It sees Christ demonstrating within this temporal, spatial, material world that he is truly Lord of all.

New Testament writers employed four important words to designate our Lord's return. First, the word *parousia*, which basically means "presence," is used by Paul in I Corinthians 15:23; I Thessalonians 2:19; 3:13; 4:15; 5:23. Second, the term *epiphaneia*, meaning "appearance," which stresses "a visible manifestation" of that which has been out of view (1 Timothy 6:14; 2 Timothy 4:1, 8; Titus 2:13). Third, *apokalupsis*, a term meaning the "revelation" of that which has been hidden. Peter uses this word (1 Peter 1:7, 13; 4:13) as well as Paul (2 Thessalonians 1:7). And, fourth, the word *erchomai*, meaning "to come" or "to arrive." While this term is used to refer to the coming of false christs (Matthew 24:5), it is especially used to point to Jesus' return (Matthew 24:30, 42, 44; 25:31).

The Second Advent (Hebrews 9:28), called by Paul "the blessed hope" for Christians (Titus 2:13), will inaugurate Christ's overthrow of the kingdom of evil and the establishment of the millennial stage of the Kingdom (Revelation 19:11-20:6).

The millennial glories of Christ's personal, visible reign from Jerusalem, the world capital of his government, include these marvels: a converted and restored Israel; a reconciled and converted gentilism (Isaiah 9:6-7; 2:1-4; 11:11-13; Micah 4:1-5; 5:2; Romans 11:1, 11-36); a world of nature freed from the bondage of the ancient curse (Genesis 3:13-19; Isaiah 11:6-10; Romans 8:15ff); and human life on this planet blessed with extraordinary measures of health, longevity, knowledge, material plenty, and tranquility (Isaiah 65:20; 30:23, 24; 41:18, 20; 43:20, 21; 55:13; Micah 4:1-4).[29]

Reigning with Christ over these earthly scenes will be the glorified Church, the Bridehood of Christ. In their glorified bodies, like unto his own, they will be free to function either in the temporal-spatial world or beyond it, just as the Lord Jesus was and is able after his resurrection (John 20:24-21:14). And these will reign with him a thousand years upon earth (1 Thessalonians 4:13-17; 1 Corinthians 15:51-53; Philippians 3:20-21; 2 Timothy 2:10-13; Revelation 20:4-6).

The foregoing interpretation cuts radically across the a-millennial position which rejects a literal, earthly, visible reign of Christ, holding that the thousand years of Revelation 20 are symbolical, having no literal fulfillment within history.

A post-millennial viewpoint holds that the Holy Spirit, working through the Church and its agencies, will usher in a reign of peace of considerable duration, possibly even a thousand years. After that "golden age" Christ appears to terminate time, arraign mankind for final judgment and bring in the eternal Kingdom of God. The post-millennial view negates the Bible's emphasis upon the immanency of Christ's Second Advent (Matt. 24:42-44).

Modern critical theologians, generally speaking, have not incorporated millennial or antichrist considerations in their respective eschatologies.[30] I can only list them here: the "idealist eschatology" of the older liberalism; the "consistent eschatology" of Albert Schweitzer; the "realized eschatology" of C. H. Dodd; the "realistic eschatology" (called by some *Heilsgeschichte* Eschatology) of Oscar Cullmann; the "symbolic eschatology" of Tillich and Reinhold Niebuhr; the "existential eschatology" of Rudolf Bultmann; the "dialectical eschatology" of Barthianism; and "the theology of hope" of J. Holtmann.[31]

The whole tenor of New Testament prophecy at this point is that Christ's appearance will be personal, sudden, visible, and glorious— just as was his ascension to Heaven (Acts 1:9-11; Matthew 24:27; 2 Thessalonians 1:7-10). The purpose of his coming is to carry forward his total redemptive mission, moving history and the human race forward to their final destiny and the full establishment of God's eternal reign.[32]

The *Parousia* itself will be an unannounced event— like a thief's appearance in the night (1 Thessalonians 5:2-4). The *time* of his coming again has been called "earth's best kept secret." Since no man knows the day, nor the hour, he is thereby forbidden to become a "date-setter"— a craze which has brought disrepute upon legitimate prophetic studies in almost every generation (Mark 13:32, 21-23).

"Again and again throughout the Scriptures," writes the noted British Methodist, A. Skevington Wood, "the approaching Return of...Christ is closely related to the message of sanctification...Nothing would do more to reinstate the doctrine of sanctifying grace amongst the churches of our day than a recovery of vital belief in the reality and significance of the Lord's Return in power and judgment."[33]

Each of the apostles linked in inseparable union, true hope, and holiness (Titus 2:11-14: 2 Peter 3:11-14; 1 John 3:3). "Blessed and holy is he that hath part in the first resurrection: over these the second death hath no power; but they... shall reign with him [Christ] a thousand years" (Revelation 20:6 ASV).

The Last Judgment

Emil Brunner rightly affirms that "the conception of judgment flows necessarily from a recognition of the holiness of God. God is He who takes His Will in absolute seriousness." And, Brunner continues, "If there is no last judgment it means that God does not take His own will seriously."[34]

This cosmic event has a threefold thrust. First, at that assemblage God's attributes and actions will come in majestic review before the "countless myriads of angels and men." All his moral creatures will then confess— either gladly or grudgingly— "Thou art righteous, O Lord, which art, and wast, and shalt be, because thou has judged thus... Even so, Lord God Almighty, true and righteous are thy judgments" (Revelation 16:5,7; 19:2; Acts 17:30-31).[35]

Secondly, the full glory of Christ's redemptive work will only then become manifest, when the redeemed fully see what they have been saved from as well as what they are being saved to! Thirdly, the Last Judgment will fulfill what both Christians and pagans have inwardly felt must be-- a final day of giving account for one's deeds. And whoever is "aware of his freedom as bound by responsibility," wrote Brunner, "is aware at the same time of the fact of the last judgment. Without the conception of judgment all talk of responsibility is idle chatter."[36]

At that day God's ways with each person will be vindicated, and due rewards and/or punishments justly distributed, as they could not be in this ambiguous world. John Wesley believed each person's tempers, desires, thoughts, and heart-intentions, as well as transgressions, would be placed in open view along with all of each one's circumstances in this life. Shocking as this sounds the redeemed will not see these things mentioned to their disadvantage; for all this will only magnify the grace of God which has delivered them from such depths of sin and misery. We cannot but believe that God in that Judgment will take into full account all the hereditary and environmental factors in each person's life.[37]

"The supreme purpose of the general judgment is," wrote H. Orton Wiley, "not so much the discovery of character, as it is its manifestation."[38] At that "moment of truth," each one will be known for what he or she truly is, and not for what one has appeared to be. There will be a once-for-all disclosure that resistance to God reaps ruin, and that obedience to his will means life and peace, "and that man cannot dwell partly in the one and partly in the other."[39]

Let it be remembered that men are saved by faith, but they are rewarded according to their works, and these works spring out of the true nature of faith. As we are justified now by faith without works in the sense of merit, but by a faith that is always evidenced in works; so will it be in the final judgment, when the righteousness which is by faith will be vindicated by the works which flow from it."[40]

"…it is appointed unto men once to die, but after this the judgment" (Hebrews 9:27), which affirms judgment is as certain as death itself. In fact, even more so, for some will not die, if alive when Jesus comes, but all will be judged. J. Jeremias reminds us, "The message of Jesus is not only the proclamation of salvation, but also the announcement of Judgment, a cry of warning, and a call to repentance... The number of parables in this category is nothing less than awe-inspiring."[41]

"This aspect of Jesus' teaching is unpalatable to modern man," writes Leon Morris. "So he simply rejects it. He has largely dismissed the thought of final judgment from his mind. He does not think of himself as accountable."[42]

While all must face judgment, genuine believers can do it with confidence and joy. "Who shall lay anything to the charge of God's elect?" asks Paul. "It is God that justifieth" (Romans 8:33). Hear the great affirmation from the Apostle John: "Herein is our love made perfect, that we may have boldness in the Day of Judgment: because as he is, so are we in this world" (1 John 4:17:18).

The perfect wisdom and goodness of God shine forth, as in few other places, in the selection of the final Judge of all. "...the Father judgeths no man, but hath committed all judgment unto the Son: that all men should honor the Son, even as they honor the Father" (John 5:22-23). The Divine-human Son who sees and feels from the standpoint of both Deity and humanity is "the most proper person to judge" (Acts 10:42; 17:30-31). This divine arrangement means, "the final judgment will be a judgment of love. But ...the self-sacrificing love we see on Calvary is in itself the most damning judgment imaginable on the self-seeking life."[43]

The Final State

The thought of eternal punishment for the unsaved is a terrifying one. Doubtless, for that reason, "there is no other doctrine that is clearly taught in Scripture which is so generally denied or ignored in our modern theological world."[44] Many have sided with the Norwegian bishop who publicly denied this teaching, declaring, "The doctrine of eternal punishment is not at home in a religion of love."[45]

However, four decades ago Nicolas Berdyaev, an exiled Russian philosopher, wrote, "It is remarkable how little people think about hell or trouble about it. This is the most striking evidence of human frivolity."[46]

A serious examination of the Old Testament convinces me that biblical theologian, A. B. Davidson, was correct when saying that "so far as the Old Testament is concerned, a veil is drawn over the destiny of the wicked in death; they descend into *Sheol*; ...[but] there is no indication that their personality in *Sheol* ceases, or that they are annihilated..."[47]

But in turning to the New Testament we are startled to find that "the loving Savior has more to say about hell than any other individual in the Bible." Consequently those who still believe in the eternal punishment for the wicked find their strongest support for it in the Gospels. Theologian W. T. G. Shedd claims "Jesus Christ is the Person who is responsible for the doctrine of Eternal Perdition."[48]

For Jesus to preach of people going into hell (*Gehenna*) where their worm dieth not, and the fire is not quenched" (Mark 9:44, 47-48), and to say to some, "Depart from me, ye cursed, into the eternal fire which is prepared for the devil and his angels," and closed his greatest judgment sermon with these words, "And they shall go away into eternal punishment: but the righteous into eternal life" (Matthew 25:41, 45) give ample basis for claiming that "the Christian doctrine of eternal punishment is Christ's doctrine."[49]

If Jesus knew better than he taught, then he is utterly unworthy to be our Savior; and, if he were only "a child of his times" and ignorantly taught an erroneous theology of "last things," then he is incompetent to be the world's Savior. But, supported by Peter, Paul, and John in their teachings, Jesus heads the line of biblical spokesmen, affirming that there are only two ultimate destinies for men: Hell (*Gehenna*) for the impenitent, and Heaven for the believing penitent.

The New Testament divides all of history into the present *aion* ["age"] and the *aion* which is to come. The Greek language contains no other word which better describes the concept of endlessness. *Aionios* is used in the New Testament sixty-six times... The strongest evidence that the word *aionios* [rendered "eternal," or "everlasting"] "is meant to teach the endlessness of the punishment of the wicked is in fact that the same word is used to describe the blessed life of the godly. In a number of passages they lie side by side... if *aionion* describes life which is endless, so must *aionion* describe endless punishment. Here the doctrine of heaven and hell stand or fall together.[50]

Wesley also used this same argument in his *Explanatory Notes Upon the New Testament* (Matthew 25:46).

It needs to be pointed out repeatedly that "the denial of hell has gone hand in hand with the denial of the infallibility of the Scriptures."[51]

In general, the modern evangelical pulpit and press have been all too silent on this biblical message. Billy Graham has set us an example. Says he, "I am conscious... the subject of hell... is very unpopular, controversial, and misunderstood. In my campaigns across the country, however, I usually devote one evening to the discussion of this subject."[52]

Arguments against everlasting punishment usually rest upon either or both of the following affirmations: God is too good, too merciful, for that teaching to be true; or, We are too good, too worthful, for that to happen to us. But neither of these claims has solid scriptural support, nor sound reasoning behind them as C. S. Lewis has effectively shown.[53]

Contemporary theologians usually settle for either (1) universalism—in which all will ultimately be saved, possibly even the devil—or (2) annihilation for the wicked, which amounts to "a conditional immortality." But both of these undermine the abiding moral seriousness of the Bible.[54]

In their denial of the doctrine of eternal punishment many lauded theologians have strengthened the popular public appeal of some of the fastest growing heretical cults of our time— who likewise reject the doctrine of hell (*Gehenna*). These include Christian Science, Jehovah's Witnesses, Mormonism, Spiritualism, Theosophy, and Unity.

Since the Bible and spiritual reality must be interpreted by men, and no one person or group of people is infallible, would it not be supremely wise always to hold that interpretation (or theological position) which, if it should be seriously wrong in the End, we would be on the "eternally safe side" of things?

To illustrate: It would be far wiser to believe in an "eternal hell" for the wicked and tell men so— warning them to flee from the wrath to come— and then at the End learn there is no such place, than it would be to deny eternal punishment (thereby giving a deceptive comfort to the sinful and careless) and then be rudely awakened at the End— when it is too late to reverse one's decision and influence— and find there is a "lake of fire" awaiting the rebels against God (Revelation 19:20; 20:10,14-15).

True Christianity is that pure religion which holds out hope for all men during Time, but which furnishes and feeds hope only for the redeemed after Time.

While Heaven is above and beyond us during Time, the Book of Revelation shows that in the New Creation of the future, Heaven's glories will be transferred to the New Earth.[55] In that Eternal Age the redeemed of all generations, in their glorified bodies, will engage in activities as congenial to their redeemed natures as the unfallen Adam and Eve ever knew in their earthly Eden. Then, all that sin has brought into the old creation will have been eliminated. In the Holy City-come-to-earth will be the Throne of God and of the Lamb— and his servants will serve him. "They will see his face, and his name will be on their foreheads. There will be no night there ["No more death or mourning or crying or pain, for the old order of things has passed away"]. They will not need the light of a lamp or the light of the sun, for the Lord God will give them light. And they will reign for ever and ever" (Revelation 22:3-5; 21:4).

Within that holy, happy, harmonious City of God will be myriads of serving angels; and the redeemed from every race and nation and tribe and people will be fully devoted to the worship of the Triune God and to the well-being of each and every eternal inhabitant.

Language and thought both fail to capture the glories and joys of that Eternal Paradise.[56]

Note

[1] Emil Brunner, *Eternal Hope*, trans. Harold Knight (Philadelphia: The Westminster Press, 1954), p. 28.

[2] *Ibid.*

[3] Today's revived interest in prophecy can be found at all levels, from radio "Talk Shows" to the scholar's study, from the best sellers on book lists—such as Hal Lindsay's *The Late Great Planet Earth*—to the free literature distributed on street corners, from door to door, and by mail (usually offered in response to a religious program over TV or radio).

[4] J. Barton Payne, "The Bible Looks Ahead," *The Presbyterian Journal*, January 30, 1974, p. 9.

[5] *Ibid.*, p. 10.

[6] Paul Tillich, *Biblical Religion and the Search for Ultimate Reality* (Chicago: University of Chicago Press, 1955), p. 41.

[7] George Eldon Ladd, *Crucial Questions About the Kingdom of God* (Grand Rapids: Eerdmans, 1952), p. 141.

[8] In this procedure I am following the suggestion of our Dean, Dr. Robert A. Traina.

[9] "University Offers Course in Death," *The Lexington Leader* [Kentucky], October 1, 1973; Kenneth L. Woodward, "How America Lives With Death," *Newsweek*, April 6, 1970, p. 81.

[10] *Newsweek, Ibid.*; Elizabeth Kubler-Ross, *On Death and Dying* (New York: Macmillian, 1969), *passim*.

[11] *Newsweek, op. cit.*, p. 81.

[12] Everett F. Harrison, "Death," *Baker's Dictionary of Theology* (Grand Rapids: Baker, 1960), p. 158; Karl Rahner, *On the Theology of Death* (New York: Herder and Herder, 1962), pp. 21-63.

[13] William J. Martin, "Immortality," *Baker's Dictionary of Christian Ethics* (Grand Rapids: Baker, 1973) p. 316.

[14] *Ibid.*, p. 317.

[15] Oscar Cullmann, *Immortality of the Soul or Resurrection of the Dead?* (New York: Macmillan, 1958), *passim*.

[16] Robert H. Hoerber, "Immortality and Resurrection—A Reply to Oscar Cullmann," *The Christian News*, August 6, 1973, pp. 5-8; Harold B. Kuhn, "Immortality, Resurrection: Antithetical?" *Christianity Today*, June 22, 1973, p. 42.

[17] Arthur M. Climenhaga, "Universalism in Present Day Theology," unpublished lecture by a former Executive Director of the National Association of Evangelicals, Wheaton, Illinois.

[18] Ludwig Ott, *Fundamentals of Catholic Dogma* (St. Louis: B. Herder Book Co., 1964), pp. 482-485; L. Berkhof, *Systematic Theology* (Grand Rapids: Eerdmans, 1946), pp. 686-688.

[19] Ott, *Op. cit.*, pp. 482-485.

[20] H. Orton Wiley, *Christian Theology* (Kansas City, Mo.: Beacon Hill Press, 1965), III, 240-242; James Oliver Buswell, *A Systematic Theology of the Christian Religion* (Grand Rapids: Zondervan, 1962), II, 321-322.

[21] Quoted in George Eldon Ladd, *The Presence of the Future* (Grand Rapids: Eerdmans, 1974), xi.

[22] Ladd, *Crucial Questions About the Kingdom of God*, op. cit., p. 80.

[23] Ladd, *The Presence of the Future*, p. 307.

[24] *Ibid.*, *passim;* Wiley, *op. cit.*, pp. 298-300.

[25] Erich Sauer, *The Triumph of the Crucified* (Grand Rapids: Eerdmans, 1953), pp. 178-185; J. Barton Payne, *Encyclopedia of Biblical Prophecy* (New York: Harper & Row, 1973), pp. 547-548.

[26] Sauer, *op. cit.*, p. 117.

[27] *Ibid.,* p. 119.

[28] *Ibid.,* p. 129.

[29] *Ibid.,* pp. 144-169; Erich Sauer, *From Eternity to Eternity* (Grand Rapids: Eerdmans, 1954), pp. 140-194.

[30] Alan Richardson, ed., *A Dictionary of Christian Theology* (Philadelphia: The Westminster Press, 1969), p. 115. However, modern critical theologians occasionally attempt a reinterpretation of "Antichrist." A. L. Moore, *The Parousia in the New Testament* (Leiden: E. J. Brill, 1966), pp. 1-79.

[31] Moore, *ibid., passim*; Ladd, *The Presence of the Future, passim*; Rev. Fr. Gerald O'Collins, "The Principle and Theology of Hope," Scottish *Journal of Theology.* Vol. 21, No. 2 (June, 1968), 129-144.

[32] Wiley, *ibid.,* pp. 259-262.

[33] Stanley Banks, ed., *The Right Way* (Fort Washington, Pa.: Christian Literature Crusade, 1964), p. 75.

[34] Brunner, *op. cit.,* pp. 173, 179.

[35] While these Scriptures— Revelation 16:5, 7; 19:2— are not immediately connected with the Last Judgment, they are reflective of the responses of holy angels and the redeemed as they behold God's judgments upon the wicked.

[36] Brunner, *op. cit.,* p. 179.

[37] John Wesley, *Sermons on Several Occasions* (New York: Phillips & Hunt, n.d.), Vol. I, pp. 126-135; Wiley, *op. cit.,* pp. 345-354.

[38] Wiley, *ibid.,* pp. 350-351.

[39] Brunner, *op. cit.,* p. 175.

[40] Wiley, *op. cit.,* p. 351.

[41] Quoted in Leon Morris, *The Biblical Doctrine of Judgment* (Grand Rapids: Eerdmans, 1960), p. 65.

[42] Morris, *ibid.,* p. 65.

[43] *Ibid.,* pp. 61-62.

[44] Harry Buis, *The Doctrine of Eternal Punishment* (Philadelphia: Presbyterian and Reformed Publishing Company. 1957), p. ix.

[45] *Ibid.*

[46] Nicolas Berdyaev, *The Destiny of Man* (New York: Scribner's, 1937), p. 338.

[47] A. B. Davidson, *The Theology of the Old Testament* (New York: Scribner's, 1904), p. 531.

[48] W. G. T. Shedd, *Dogmatic Theology* (New York: Scribner's, 1888), pp. 675ff.

[49] Buis, *op. cit.,* p. 34.

[50] *Ibid.,* p. 49.

[51] *Ibid.,* p. 127.

[52] Billy Graham, *Peace With God.* (Garden City, New York: Doubleday, 1955), p. 73; Lon Woodrum, "The Great Anger," *United Evangelical Action*, Vol. 23, No. 11, January 1965, p. 14.

[53] C. S. Lewis, *The Problem of Pain* (New York: 11acmi11an, 1943), pp. 106-116.

[54] Buis, *op. cit.,* pp. 112-126.

[55] George Eldon Ladd, *The Pattern of New Testament Truth* (Grand Rapids: Eerdmans, 1968), pp. 108-110.

[56] Sauer, *op. cit.,* pp. 186-195; Bernard Ramm, *Them He Glorified* (Grand Rapids: Eerdmans, 1963), pp. 62-136.

Works Cited

Boettner, Loraine. *Immortality*. Philadelphia: Presbyterian and Reformed Publishing Company. 1956.

Brunner, Emil. *Eternal Hope*, trans. Harold Knight. Philadelphia: Westminster Press, 1954.

Buis, Harry. *The Doctrine of Eternal Punishment.* Philadelphia: Presbyterian and Reformed Publishing-Company, 1957.

Girdlestone, R. B. *The Grammar of Prophecy.* Grand Rapids: Kregel Publications, 1955.

Henry, Carl F. H. (ed). *Prophecy in the Making*. Carol Stream, Ill.: Creation House, 1971.

Kac, Arthur W. *The Rebirth of the State of Israel: Is it of God or of Man?* Chicago: Moody Press, 1958.

Ladd, George Eldon. *Crucial Questions About the Kingdom of God.* Grand Rapids: Eerdmans, 1952.

_____. *The Pattern of New Testament Truth*. Grand Rapids: Eerdmans, 1968.

_____. *The Presence of the Future.* Grand Rapids: Eerdmans, 197.

Lewis, C. S. *The Problem of Pain*. New York: Macmillan, 1943. Pp. 106-116, 132-142.

Moore, A. L. *The Parousia in the New Testament*. Leiden: E. J. Brill, 1966.

Morris, Leon. *The Biblical Doctrine of Judgment.* Grand Rapids: Eerdmans, c1960.

Payne, J. Barton. *Encyclopedia of Biblical Prophecy.* New York: Harper &Row, 1973.

_____. *The Imminent Appearing of Christ.* Grand Rapids: Eerdmans, 1962.

Ramm, Bernard. *Them He Glorified*. Grand Rapids: Eerdmans, 1963.

Sauer, Erich. *From Eternity to Eternity*. Grand Rapids: Eerdmans, 1954.

_____. *The Triumph of the Crucified*. Grand Rapids: Eerdmans, 1953.

Tenney, Merrill C. *Interpreting Revelation*. Grand Rapids: Eerdmans, 1957.

Wiley, H. Orton. *Christian Theology, Vol. III.* Kansas City, Mo.: Beacon Hill Press, 1965.

Wood, A. Skevington. *Prophecy in the Space.* Age. London: Marshall, Morgan & Scott, 1963.

Wesley, John. *Sermons on Several Occasions*. New York: Phillips & Hunt, n.d. Vol.: Sermon XV—The Great Assize"; Vol. II: "Sermon LIX—On Eternity"; "Sermon LXXVIII—On Hell"; and "Sermon CXVII—The Rich Man and Lazarus."

www.ingramcontent.com/pod-product-compliance
Lightning Source LLC
Chambersburg PA
CBHW061426040426
42450CB00007B/924